A JOURNAL OF THE

Florentia Sale (1787–1853) was a Dubbed as the 'Soldier's wife *par exce* dier in Petticoats' by her husband's fellow officers, she was a force to be reckoned with. Born in 1787, she married 'Fighting Bob Sale' in 1808 and travelled with him to Mauritius, Burma, and back to India with her five children in 1823.

Patrick Macrory (1911–1993) was a barrister, businessman, and military historian. His first book, *Borderline* (1937), was a Buchanist thriller, thereafter publishing best-selling military histories such as *Signal Catastrophe* (1966), telling the story of the Indian Army retreat from Kabul and its massacre by Afghans. Other books include *The Siege of Derry* (1980) and *Days that Are Gone* (1983), fond reminiscences of his Ulster childhood. He was knighted in 1972 for his services to Northern Ireland.

Jane Robinson's abiding love of book-collecting was forced upon her at the age of seven when the local library banned her from using a jam tart as a bookmark. Her first book, *Wayward Women*, was published in 1990. Her other books include *Parrot Pie for Breakfast: an anthology of women pioneers, Angels of Albion, Wayward Women: A Guide to Women Travellers*, and editor of *Unsuitable for Ladies: An Anthology of Women Travellers*, a collection of writings from women during the Indian mutiny.

Lady Sale

LADY FLORENTIA SALE

A Journal of
The First Afghan War

EDITED BY
Patrick Macrory

OXFORD
UNIVERSITY PRESS

OXFORD
UNIVERSITY PRESS

Great Clarendon Street, Oxford OX2 6DP

Oxford University Press is a department of the University of Oxford.
It furthers the University's objective of excellence in research, scholarship,
and education by publishing worldwide in

Oxford New York

Auckland Bangkok Buenos Aires Cape Town Chennai
Dar es Salaam Delhi Hong Kong Istanbul Karachi Kolkata
Kuala Lumpur Madrid Melbourne Mexico City Mumbai Nairobi
São Paulo Shanghai Singapore Taipei Tokyo Toronto

Oxford is a registered trade mark of Oxford University Press
in the UK and in certain other countries

Published in the United States
by Oxford University Press Inc., New York

First published in 1969 by Longmans, Green and Co Ltd
First issued as an Oxford University Press paperback 2002

British Library Cataloguing in Publication Data

Data available

Library of Congress Cataloging in Publication Data

Data available

ISBN 0–19–280390–5

1 3 5 7 9 10 8 6 4 2

Printed in Great Britain by
Clays Ltd., St. Ives plc

Contents

Foreword

There can be precious few corners left in this world, I sometimes think, that have not been swept out in their time by a British lady traveller. A Victorian British lady traveller, probably: the age of empire lent women the assurance and opportunity necessary to begin venturing abroad, and hundreds took advantage.

In retrospect, it is possible to categorize many of these travellers into four fairly distinct types, of which the best known must be the lone and intrepid 'globe-trotteress'. She bustled ingenuously about the world marvelling at how different everything and everyone was, and writing her impressions in a series of sprightly books. She tended to justify the recklessness of leaving home unchaperoned, by declaring an initial purpose to her travels. With Isabella Bird (1831–1904) it was the search for better health; for Marianne North (1830–90), the fulfilment of a self-appointed mission to paint every known (and a few unknown) species of tropical plant in its own natural habitat. To Mary Kingsley (1862–1900), travel was a matter of science, and she went to West Africa to further her late father's work on ichthyology and anthropology—or 'fish and fetish', as she put it. And there were sportswomen and mountaineers, explorers and butterfly-hunters, artists, botanists, even a diamond-hunter, and a woman who collected human skulls in Mongolia. Globe-trotteresses got everywhere, and were indomitable.

Then, by contrast, come the self-confessed tourists, usually following in the wake of a husband, brother, or father, and whose dainty kid-booted expeditions across the Mer de Glace, or exhaustive investigations of the galleries of Rome, blossomed into print in fussily illustrated volumes of reminiscence. These were among the first women chroniclers of the traditional Grand Tour, and usually their careers as travellers (and writers) began and ended with the one big trip.

The third category—and I dislike over-generalizing like this, but when talking of 'women travellers' as a species, it is inevitable—is the vocational traveller. The indigent gentlewoman forced to seek employment as a governess in Russia or Hungary or somewhere; the missionary gladly embracing the utter unfamiliarity of China or Africa; even the odd enterprising emigrant finding a career in Australia or Canada in domestic service, in business, or perhaps in gold. Some were luckier than others.

Lastly, there is the sort of woman I call an Ornament of Empire, who travelled out of duty. 'It ought to be part of our patriotic feeling', one of them rather dauntingly maintained, 'to endeavour to convey as agreeable an idea as possible of ourselves to those countries which we honour with our distinguished presence . . .'. As adjuncts of diplomats, civil servants, or army officers, such women—ladies, rather—were posted all over the British Empire, stout-hearted champions of morality and good character. They were 'God's police', as the writer Caroline Chisholm put it, expected to teach by example a benighted and naughty world to behave properly.

All these women travellers had certain things in common, of course. Stays, for example. Constance Larymore, a traveller in Africa, once wrote that for anyone 'to leave off wearing [stays] at any time for the sake of coolness is a huge mistake: there is nothing so fatiguing as to lose one's ordinary support'. She meant moral as well as physical support. No self-respecting Victorian woman would be seen in public (probably rarely in private, either) without her stiffening whalebone corset and all the requisite layers of clothing above and below. 'Dr Jaeger's woollen underwear' was recommended for travelling in particularly humid climates, since it required so seldom to be washed. And two pairs of stockings were better than one, to foil the mosquitoes. How these poor people must have sweated and itched and stank.

Something else most would have shared is their social class. To travel successfully, especially alone, a woman would not only need money but also letters of introduction to influential Britons—or foreigners—abroad; she would need the stamina and tact born of good breeding, and most importantly of all, she would need self-confidence.

Which brings us to Florentia, Lady Sale.

Patrick Macrory's excellent introduction to Lady Sale's *Journal*, which follows this foreword, will explain the author's background and the circumstances in which, and of which, she was writing. What I want to do here is briefly to put her into context as a traveller, and as a woman of her time.

Florentia Sale belonged, of course, among the Ornaments of Empire, being a particularly doughty, dutiful, and self-assured individual. Her role was to support her army officer husband on his posting to Afghanistan in 1840, and to exemplify the best of British womanhood to all those around her. The public lives of ladies like Florentia were rigidly structured, swathed in a highly patterned fabric of social rigmarole and the exigencies of etiquette. Everything depended on the rank of one's husband (Lady Sale was second in command of the drawing and dining-rooms of Kabul). And everything was circumscribed by tradition and hierarchy: what one wore at specific times of the day or season, to whom one spoke (before or after being spoken to oneself), the arcane lore of making and returning visits, the number and duties of one's servants, the order in which one was expected to sit and rise at dinner-parties: everything.

To some ladies more impulsive than Florentia, this circumscription was too much to bear. Emily Eden, sister of India's Governor-General from 1837 to 1840, used to long for a bit of spontaneity and excitement, writing wearily after one society 'fête' too many, 'I am in that mood that I should be almost glad if the Sikhs, or the Russians, or anybody, would come and take us all. It would be one way out . . .' But Lady Sale was made of sterner stuff. She relished her position in Kabul as the wife of the famously brave 'Fighting Bob', and found both propriety and satisfaction in the tending of her garden, and in the comfortable, predictable confines of the British cantonments. All over the world women like her were tending pallid-looking cauliflowers and tight-lipped roses, ordering interminable menus, sending their sons and daughters thousands of miles home to be educated or groomed for the imperial marriage market, and generally doing their bit in an alien but strangely uniform and tranquil home from home.

Except that in so many cases, beneath the veneer (where ladies did not venture) it was not tranquil at all. And occasionally, wars broke out, catching the naïve unawares, and shaking the foundations of British society abroad.

It is interesting to read parallel accounts—men's and women's—of the various conflicts that punctuated the progress of imperial Britain during the nineteenth century. Women travellers have been involved in warfare, and have either written about it or themselves been written about since before Queen Artemisia of Halicarnassus set out with her fleet to fight the Persian Wars in 480 BC. In a comparatively modern age women combatants operated in disguise, like Dragoon Kit Cavanagh, distinguishing herself in Flanders in 1702, or the Royal Marine Hannah Snell, fighting in the East Indies some 40 years later.

It is not until the Napoleonic Wars, however, that it is easily possible to compare the war experiences of men and women involved in the same campaign. In Charlotte Eaton's *Narrative of a Residence in Belgium . . . and of a Visit to the Field of Waterloo* (1817) she does not dwell on the strategic or political aspects of the battle, nor even—as William Thackeray does in

Vanity Fair—on the many thrilled and twittery wives, sisters, and daughters who put up in Brussels while the battle was going on. She concentrates instead on the messy reality behind cosmetic glory: on the squalor of the sick, the grief of the bereft, and the despair of refugees. Charlotte sets an important precedent in consciously highlighting the social history of the battle, rather than its military significance.

Many women followed. When Mrs Harriet Ward wrote of her part in the Kaffir Wars in South Africa in the early 1840s, she recalled the domestic implications of coping with a sick child while accompanying her husband's troops on a cattle-waggon trek, and enduring the anxiety, physical discomfort, and sheer boredom of army life at one remove from the battlefield. The Crimean War had its female chroniclers, too. Think of Florence Nightingale and Mary Seacole stressing in their work and their writing the individual suffering of those men involved. Other women present—more nurses, and the odd officer's wife—recorded what was going on beyond the fighting, in the hospitals, camps, and kitchens: such accounts fatten out the military histories, and illuminate them.

It is the same with the so-called Indian Mutiny of 1857, which shocked the British nation not just because of its perceived suddenness and ferocity, but for the first-hand involvement in it of British women and children, scores of whom were killed. And that shock turned to (rather mawkish) horror when the letters, journals, and accounts of the Mutiny written by those women began to be published. They gave war a human, subjective, and personal aspect lacking in the stiff and official writings of fighting soldiers and posturing politicians. They brought war *home*. This quality of immediacy and personal response hallmarks Lady Sale's chronicle, and together with her political and military commentary, is what made it such a success on its publication and such a good read now.

An important concept throughout the nineteenth century was that none of the empire's overseas enemies could ever be so powerful as to rid Britain's women of their inherent spirit and dignity. The implication was that a true lady could never be a true victim. Certain characters strengthen the image: Lady Durand in Indore, for example, who took the whole of the Indian Mutiny as a personal insult and remained outraged (and unmolested) throughout. Lady Hodgson described the inconveniences of trying to avoid attackers during an uprising in what is now Ghana in the 1890s by noting laconically that 'skirts are an impediment when fleeing for your life in Ashanti-land'. Lady Sale is equally unassailable.

Florentia copes with the loss of life's tranquillity admirably. She refuses to blame exclusively the 'fine, manly-looking set' of Afghans for what she calls the 'disasters' of 1841–2, noting with asperity that the war was just as much the fault of certain insular British 'Big-wigs' and a pitifully inferior sort of officer with which Kabul was, at the time, afflicted. 'There is much reprehensible croaking going on', she complains, among those indecisive cowards within the British establishment in Kabul who lack the moral fibre of her own husband. But she assures us that she has 'been a soldier's wife too long to sit down tamely, whilst our honour is tarnished in the sight of our enemies'. While the siege of Kabul is in progress she spends the nights behind chimneys on the roofs of the cantonments, dodging bullets while helping to keep watch. And when the infamous retreat begins, even though she does not expect to survive, she ties up her journal in a bag about her waist, puts on a 'poshteen', or thick sheepskin waistcoat against the wind and snow, swigs a shot of sherry to fortify herself ('which at any other time would have made me very unlady-like'), and sets out with her pregnant daughter to face whatever will be.

I must not spoil the extraordinary story of Florentia's Afghan adventure here. Her own words are by far the best. Suffice it to say that even though she mentions *en passant* the desperate hardships of the retreat from Kabul—including picking her way through the bodies of those companions who had starved or frozen during the nights; witnessing her son-in-law's death; gouging out bullets from her arm, and finally being captured by the enemy—she never deigns to complain about personal discomfort. She was proud of her fortitude, and rather despised those who could not share it. Lady Sale was not a croaker. Indeed, to her adoring public at home, once the war was over and the *Journal* out in print, she was a heroine.

Fashions come and go, however, and until very recently, Lady Sale and her ilk have rather been forgotten, their attitudes and responses embarrassing modern audiences a little in their trenchancy and imperial arrogance. Florentia deserves better.

She did have a memorial of sorts, besides her grave and this *Journal*. It was in Afghanistan. Somewhere in that unquiet land, at the gutter of a defile leading to the Khoord Kabul pass south-east of the capital, there once stood an impressive-looking slab of rock. Three members of Florentia's family were wounded close to this rock: her husband, whose ankle was shivered by enemy fire; her son-in-law, who subsequently died; and Florentia herself, shot in the wrist. In their honour, the rock was christened by the British 'Sales' Stone'.

I expect it stands there still, a silent witness to the violence, bravery, and turmoil not only of Florentia's age but, sadly, of our own.

Introduction

The First Afghan War began in the autumn of 1838, when Lord Auckland, the Governor-General of India, launched the 'Army of the Indus' (as it was grandly called) upon an invasion of Afghanistan. The campaign ended four years later when General Pollock's 'Army of Retribution' withdrew to India, 'leaving to the Afghans the unmolested possession of the liberty they had acquired, and not attempting to place upon their necks the yoke they so roughly shook off' (Charles Greville). In between it had witnessed one of the greatest defeats ever inflicted upon the British by an Asian enemy, an ugly massacre and a blow to Britain's prestige unequalled until, one hundred years later almost to the month, Singapore fell to the Japanese.

Compared to the casualties of later wars, the numbers lost in General Elphinstone's disastrous attempt to retreat from Kabul to Jellalabad were no doubt trivial—but consider the scale. Here was a force that, with its camp-followers, women and children, had numbered some 16,000 souls on the day it marched from Kabul under a shameful capitulation and an illusory safe-conduct; one week later, on 13 January 1842, Surgeon William Brydon rode alone into Jellalabad, the only British survivor. In the nights that followed a great light would be kept burning over the Kabul gate at Jellalabad and every fifteen minutes four buglers would sound 'Advance'. But there were no other stragglers to respond to beacon or bugle. The Kabul force had been annihilated with a finality that would wring from Sir John Kaye, the war's first historian, the cry that 'there is nothing more remarkable in the history of the world than the awful completeness, the sublime unity of this Caubul tragedy!' Small wonder that back in England the old Duke of Wellington was writing to a friend that 'I could almost eat my fists from vexation; and with not a little feeling that I am too old to go to the Spot and set it all right; or that I shall even live to see this disaster remedied'.

This disaster forms the core of the Journal that follows. It must be remembered that Lady Sale was writing for a public who could be assumed to possess much background knowledge that cannot now be taken for granted. Her readers would know, for example, of that curious dyarchy under which British India was governed by the

Honourable East India Company, yet subject to the overriding authority of the British Cabinet through the President of the Board of Control. They would be aware that the troops at the Governor-General's disposal consisted partly of units of the British regular army, partly of the much larger Company's army, and that the latter was composed mainly of native regiments officered by British who held the Company's, not the Queen's, commission. Very likely they would know something of the jealousy that prevailed between 'Queen's officers' and 'Company officers'. Certainly they would understand, at least in outline, the chain of events that had led the British to undertake the invasion of Afghanistan.

In the eighteen-thirties, as the armies of the Tsar continued their incessant probe into Central Asia, British statesmen had become increasingly alarmed by the Russian threat to India, and none more so than Lord Palmerston. It was Palmerston who took the lead in planning a counter-stroke. The Russians had defeated Turkey; they had defeated Persia; and now they were moving against the independent Khanates of Central Asia and egging on the Persians to seek compensation for their own defeat by an attack on Afghanistan. Palmerston's projected riposte was to balance a pro-Russian ruler in Persia by a pro-British ruler in Afghanistan, one who could be relied upon to keep Persia in her place and to bar the door to any further Russian aggression. This role was assigned by Lord Auckland to Shah Soojah-ool-Moolk, a scion of the original royal house of Afghanistan who had been driven from the throne of Kabul many years before by tribal strife and who for nearly a quarter of a century had been sustained in his exile in India by a generous pension from the East India Company.

There was an alternative. Instead of the somewhat discredited Soojah, Auckland could have backed the existing ruler of Afghanistan, the able and popular Dost Mahomed. Indeed, this course had been urged by Alexander Burnes, a talented young Political officer who had been sent to Kabul to spy out the land on the pretext of a 'commercial' mission. The Dost (the word means 'Friend') was deeply suspicious of Russian ambitions and would have welcomed a British alliance. Unfortunately he was in a state of almost perpetual feud with his eastern neighbour, Runjeet Singh, ruler of the still independent Sikh state of the Punjab. In 1834 Runjeet had seized Peshawar, one of the greatest of Afghan cities, and had thereby exacerbated the quarrel beyond reconciliation. The British had been in treaty with Runjeet for nearly thirty years and had no mind to jeopardize the well-tried Sikh friendship for Dost Mahomed's more problematical support. They therefore decided to replace the Dost by the more amenable Soojah, and Runjeet Singh obligingly agreed to participate in the plan for his restoration. The British were thus able to advance upon Afghanistan not only with Sikh allies but in a loudly proclaimed support of the principle of legitimacy.

The Army of the Indus, the usual mixture of British regiments and Company troops, under the command of Sir John Keane, a rough-tongued fighting soldier from County Waterford, duly accomplished its task. The leisurely pace at which it did so was made inevitable by the vast quantity of baggage and hordes of servants that accompanied the army. One brigadier required sixty camels to carry his personal kit and junior subalterns went to war with anything up to forty servants apiece. The 16th Lancers took their pack of foxhounds and many young officers 'would as soon have thought of leaving behind them their swords and double-barrelled pistols as march without their dressing-cases, their perfumes, Windsor soap and eau-de-Cologne' (J. H. Stocqueler). Administrative incompetence and the inefficiency of the Commissariat—'no language can describe it nor give any idea of the rascality of its native agents' (General Nott)—brought the Army of the Indus more than once to the brink of starvation and the wretched camp followers were reduced to eating sheepskin fried in dry blood. Nevertheless, after the reputedly impregnable fortress of Ghuznee had been stormed at a cost of seventeen killed and one hundred and sixty-five wounded (a feat presently described by Sir Robert Peel with some exaggeration as 'the most brilliant achievement of our arms in Asia'), Kabul was entered on 7 August 1839, and Shah Soojah was restored to his throne. Dost Mahomed fled into the interior, where for some fifteen months he carried on a desultory guerrilla warfare. He then made his surrender to the British Envoy at Kabul and was sent off to an honourable exile in India. There he was presently joined by all his family, with the significant exception of his favourite son, Akbar Khan. Akbar preferred to live an outlaw's life somewhere out beyond the Hindu Kush and implacably bided his time.

The famous Simla Manifesto, the proclamation with which Auckland had attempted to justify to public opinion his attack on Afghanistan, had concluded with a promise that when once Soojah had been secured in power, and the independence and integrity of Afghanistan established, 'the British army will be withdrawn'. The promise was genuinely meant, for Auckland had no wish to saddle the revenues of India with the cost of a permanent occupation. But it soon became clear that withdrawal was easier said than done, and that if Soojah were deprived of the support of British bayonets his chances of survival would be slim. It was, in fact, a dilemma. No one saw more clearly than Soojah that, so long as the British troops remained in the land, he would be despised and hated by his fiercely independent countrymen as the puppet of foreigners—and infidel foreigners at that; yet if the British left him, he was lost.

It was true that the British had provided him with a small army of his own, mercenaries who had been recruited in the Upper Provinces of India prior to the invasion of Afghanistan and who were presently supplemented by local enlistment. These are the regiments to whom Lady Sale refers by such titles as 'the Shah's 6th', 'Anderson's Horse' and so on, and they were often designated collectively as 'Shah Soojah's levies'. They were trained and led by British officers seconded from the Company's army, one of their first commanders being Brigadier Abraham Roberts, father of the future Lord Roberts of Kandahar. When it came to the crunch of the Afghan rebellion some of these levies fought with spirit against their fellow countrymen and showed a splendid courage and loyalty to their British paymasters. The majority, however, were inefficient and unreliable. General Nott's report on his inspection of the Shah's 2nd Cavalry is a fair sample: 'I think it my duty to acquaint you that the regiment is quite inefficient. The majority of the men are of that description which assures me they never can be brought to any serviceable state.' One complete regiment of Soojah's infantry deserted *en masse*, in disgust, so they said, at the behaviour of their British N.C.O.s.

Reluctantly, in the face of such evidence, the British decided that some of their own troops must remain in Afghanistan for Soojah's protection. So, when General Keane and the greater part of the original Army of the Indus marched back to India at the end of 1839, a division was left at Kandahar under General Nott and a force of two brigades at Kabul itself. At once a wrangle broke out as to where this Kabul force was to be quartered. Soojah, for reasons of prestige, opposed the sensible suggestion that they should be housed in the Bala Hissar, the great citadel of Kabul that contained his own palace, and it was eventually decided to build cantonments on the plain a mile or so outside the city. The cantonments were as badly designed as they were badly sited. Lieutenant Vincent Eyre[1], who was there, commented that 'our cantonment at Caubul, whether we look to its situation or its construction, must ever be spoken of as a disgrace to our military skill and judgement'. He added that 'it must always remain a wonder that any government, or any officer or set of officers, who had either science or experience in the field, should in a half-conquered country fix their forces in so extraordinary and injudicious a military position'. Brigadier John Shelton, who was second-in-command of the Kabul force at the time of the rebellion, found the cantonments to be 'of frightful extent—with a rampart and ditch an Afghan could run over with the facility of a cat, with many other serious defects'. Not the least of these was that the garrison's main supplies were stored in a small fort—'an old crazy one, undermined with rats', says Lady Sale—a quarter of a mile away from the main camp.

At one end of the cantonments was an enclosure called 'the Mission Compound', which, according to Eyre, 'rendered the whole face of the cantonment to which it was annexed nugatory for the purposes of defence'. This compound housed the Political Mission attached to the army of occupation, its main feature being the residence of the Mission head, William Macnaghten. As Chief Secretary to the Calcutta Government, Macnaghten had reputedly been one of the chief authors of the forward policy for Afghanistan, and in due course had accompanied the Army of the Indus as 'Envoy and Minister on the part of the Government at the Court of Shah Soojah-ool-Moolk'. In the honours that were freely bestowed to mark the initial success of the campaign he had received a baronetcy, and now he was undisputedly the leader of British society in Kabul as well as the dominant personality. Elphinstone was presently to complain that he had been 'tormented by Macnaghten from the start' and had been reduced from a general to being the Lord Lieutenant's head constable.

Before the year 1839 was out Macnaghten, realizing that the occupation was going to be indefinitely prolonged, sent for his wife to join him at Kabul, and the officers of the army followed his example. (The sepoys, too, were encouraged to bring up their families, the better to reconcile them to exile in Afghanistan; the British other ranks were forbidden to do so and, disgruntled, sought consolation in the

[1] Lieutenant Vincent Eyre, Bengal Artillery was 'Deputy Commissary of Ordnance'. Eyre wrote a very readable account of *The Military Operations at Cabul* (John Murrary, 1843) and later became General Sir Vincent Eyre.

brothels of Kabul.) And presently, probably some time in 1840, there arrived upon the scene, together with her twenty-year-old daughter, Alexandrina, that formidable General's Lady, Florentia, Lady Sale.

Florentia Wynch had been born on 13 August 1787, probably at Madras and certainly the daughter and granddaughter of Civil Servants of the East India Company. In May 1808 she married Robert Sale, a twenty-seven-year-old captain of the 12th Foot (Suffolk Regiment). Thirteen years later he transferred by purchase into the 13th Foot (the Somerset Light Infantry) and the Sales, who had already spent some years of married life in Mauritius, in England and in Ireland, returned to India with a family of five children between the ages of eleven and one. (Florentia bore her husband twelve children in all, of whom four died in infancy and one, George, the eldest son, at the age of ten.) Florentia and the children remained in Calcutta when Sale went off to fight in the first Burmese War, which broke out in 1823 and in which he earned his nickname of Fighting Bob. He returned to India to command the 13th, an assignment that turned out to be far from a sinecure. The battalion had been decimated by disease in Burma and had been brought up to strength by drafts from England who were described as the sweepings of the London jails. As a result, it was, said Colin Mackenzie,[1] 'in a frightful state of insubordination', and several N.C.O.s and at least one officer were murdered by malcontents. The Commanding Officer himself received several anonymous threats of death. On each such occasion Sale would ride on to the parade ground with the letter in his pocket and order a volley to be fired with blank. As the roar of the muskets died harmlessly away the voice of Fighting Bob would be heard shouting triumphantly, 'Ah, its not my fault if you don't shoot me!'

This jovial challenge, combined with savage floggings at the triangles, presently brought the 13th back to a proper state of discipline, and the men, said one of their officers, became 'mere babies, you could do anything with them'. Moreover, they felt a genuine affection for their Colonel, largely because, as was said of him when he had risen to a higher rank, 'nothing could induce him to behave himself as a General should do. Despite his staff's protests, he used to ride about two miles ahead of his troops, and in action would fight like a private'. The fact that he almost invariably succeeded in getting wounded enhanced his popularity.

From 1826, for four years, Sale commanded the Agra station,

[1] *Storms and Sunshine of a Soldier's Life* (1886).

where he was allotted a large house 'standing in ample grounds and possessing the luxury of a swimming pool 60 ft by 30 ft', and where he occupied his leisure in chess and in gardening, for which, as his wife's journal tells us, he had a *shoke* or 'mania'. As for Florentia, 'she was a clever woman, had been brought up a great deal with her uncles, from whom she had early acquired literary tastes, which enabled her to instruct while amusing her children'. Her great-granddaughter reminds us, more pithily, that she was known as 'the Grenadier in petticoats'. At all events, 'with these advantages, household occupations, daily rides and drives, and swimming lessons in the bath, together with the society of the station, where the Sales were popular, their sojourn at Agra passed pleasantly by'.[1]

And then came the Afghan War, a campaign that in prospect seemed 'fraught with so much promise of distinction and advancement that not a soldier in the whole length and breadth of India could for a moment tolerate the idea of being left behind (J. H. Stocqueler). Sale was not left behind'. The 13th was mobilized as part of the 1st Brigade of the Infantry Division of the Bengal Column, and he was given command of the brigade. His great chance came at Ghuznee, where Keane gave him command of the main storming column. Sale was distinguished more for personal courage than intellectual capacity (although we are told that at Agra he 'amused himself by studying military situations and problems, and working them out with blocks of wood to represent the contending forces'), and he nearly muffed the whole operation. Inevitably he managed to get wounded, in furious hand-to-hand combat with an Afghan whom he eventually dispatched with a sabre blow that split his enemy's skull from crown to eyebrows. But Ghuznee was captured, and when the spate of honours and awards began to flow in the general euphoria after Soojah's restoration, Sale was gazetted a Knight Commander of the Bath and at the same time, or shortly afterwards, promoted major-general.

When Florentia joined him in Kabul she was therefore one of the biggest fish in this not very large pond. As the wife of Sir Robert Sale, K.C.B., she ranked second only to Lady Macnaghten in British society. Her husband was now second-in-command at Kabul and, as such, entitled to a married quarter in the cantonments, a house which was, she says, 'the best and most commodious' in the camp. It had a

[1] R. Sale-Hill, 'Major-General Sir Robt. Henry Sale, G.C.B.', *Illustrated Naval and Military Magazine*, January 1890.

garden, in which Sale was able to indulge his *shoke*, and seems to have been built after her arrival in Kabul to plans supplied by herself and her husband. It was, no doubt, from this house that in August 1841 Alexandrina was married to Lieutenant John Sturt of the Royal Engineers, who was in charge of the Public Works Department. The sad outcome of this brief marriage will appear from the Journal.

Life in the cantonments was a gay butterfly existence. There were horse-racing, hunting and amateur theatricals. When winter gripped the land the British had skates made by the farriers and skimmed over the frozen lakes to the admiration and astonishment of the Afghans, who had never seen the like. The same could be said, in summer, of cricket, and the Reverend G. R. Gleig, an Army chaplain, records that the Afghans 'looked on with astonishment at the bowling, batting and fagging out of the English players; but it does not appear that they were ever tempted to lay aside their flowing robes and huge turbans and enter the field as competitors'. In the plan of the cantonments published with her Journal—it was drawn for her from memory by Captain Souter while they were both in captivity—Lady Sale has marked 'the Spot where the Band used to play and where the reserve was posted', and one feels that the order of her words unconsciously reveals the British notion of priorities at the time. Nor was there any lack of creature comforts, and Alexander Burnes, now Sir Alexander, living as 'British Resident' in a courtyarded mansion in the heart of Kabul, was writing to a friend that at his weekly dinner parties he could lay before his guests 'champagne, hock, madeira, sherry, port, claret, sauterne, not forgetting a glass of curaçoa and maraschino, and the hermetically sealed salmon and hotchpotch (veritable hotch-potch, all the way frae' Aberdeen), for deuced good it is, the peas as big as if they had been soaked for *bristling*'.

The whole merry way of life was underpinned by the vast horde of servants whom the British had brought with them from India and who, when the retreat began, would prove to be, in the words of Eyre, 'a serious clog upon our movements and . . . indeed the main cause of our subsequent misfortunes'. We learn from Lady Sale that about 5,000 registered camp-followers to a battalion was a normal quota, and she sees nothing remarkable in the fact that she, Sturt and a Lieutenant Mein who had joined her household mustered forty servants between the three of them. But she does make the perceptive comment that in Afghanistan 'the English act as they do in all countries they visit,—keep to themselves, and even (generally) employ only servants brought with them'. In so doing they deprived themselves of a useful source of intelligence, and though Sturt to some extent remedied the deficiency through his Afghan workmen in the Public Works Department, his warnings of impending trouble were ignored.

Yet, in truth, the position of the British in Afghanistan was potentially one of the utmost peril. Their forces, never all that strong, were about to be reduced still further, in response to Calcutta's insistent calls for economy. They were separated from their base by several hundred miles of unguarded lines of communication, passing through a series of formidable defiles which in winter were often blocked by snow. Their two main garrisons, Kabul and Kandahar, were over three hundred miles apart. And, to crown all, they had the misfortune at the moment of crisis to find themselves commanded by the elderly, gout-ridden and indecisive Major-General Elphinstone, who must surely rank as one of the most incompetent generals ever to have been given command of a British army; a general who allows his second-in-command—Brigadier Shelton—to attend conferences lying on the floor rolled up in his sleeping-bag, in real or pretended slumber; who, when a subaltern reports a threatened attack on the cantonments, throws all the responsibility back on the subaltern—'gave him *carte blanche* and desired that all his instructions should be obeyed'; and who, after a futile attempt to rally his demoralized troops, is heard by an amused Lady Sale pathetically complaining to Macnaghten, 'Why, Lord, sir, when I said to them "Eyes right", they all looked the other way!'

In September 1841, when the Journal begins, the Kabul garrison was about to be rid of this disastrous commander. Elphinstone's urgent and genuine pleas of ill health had at last been heard in Calcutta and the competent and irascible Nott had been ordered up from Kandahar to relieve him. It only wanted Nott to arrive and take over and then Elphinstone planned to depart for India. So, too, did the Macnaghtens, for the Envoy's long exile was now to be rewarded by one of the sweetest plums in the Company's gift, the Governorship of the Bombay Presidency. In the Residency in Kabul, Alexander Burnes ('a highly paid idler', in his own words, and 'in the most nondescript of situations') waited expectantly to step into the Envoy's shoes. But Macnaghten decided that, before he went, he would make one more attempt to placate Calcutta's constant demand to cut the costs of the occupation, and with his fatal readiness to see only what he wished to see, he now took two rash decisions. One was to allow

Sale's brigade to return to India before the relieving troops had arrived; the other, to reduce the subsidies paid to the Afghan tribes (the Eastern Ghilzyes) to secure safe passage through the mountain passes on the road that led back through Jellalabad to India. The Ghilzyes had scrupulously kept their side of the bargain and 'had prevented even a finger from being raised against our posts, couriers and weak detachments. Convoys of all descriptions had passed through these terrific defiles, the strongest barriers of mountains in the world, with little or no interruption from these predatory tribes' (Henry Havelock). The chiefs, incensed at what they understandably regarded as a flagrant breach of faith by Macnaghten, retaliated in the most effective way they knew; they rose in rebellion and blocked the passes. In so doing, they had lit a torch that would soon set all Afghanistan ablaze, and Akbar Khan, expectant in the wings, made ready to return to the stage.

Macnaghten found the Ghilzyes' impudence 'very provoking to me at this juncture', but nevertheless made light of the affair. He described the Ghilzyes as 'kicking up a row about some deductions which have been made from their pay' and added that 'the rascals will be well trounced for their pains'. Sale's brigade would return to India as planned and would take the contumacious tribesmen in their stride. The Macnaghtens, with General Elphinstone and Lady Sale, would follow down a day's march or so behind the brigade; and the country, the Envoy hoped, 'will be left in a state of tranquillity, with the exception of the Ghilzyes between this [Kabul] and Jellalabad, and I hope to settle *their* hash on the road down, if not before'. The utter wreck of this optimistic forecast will appear from the narrative that follows.

The Journal begins, then, in September 1841. It ends a year later with the romantically appropriate rescue of Florentia by her own husband from nine months of captivity in Afghan hands. In the intervening period she had witnessed battle, murder and sudden death, had been exposed to freezing cold and burning heat, had endured the discomfort of vermin-infested lodgings and the terror of incessant earthquakes. All that man and nature could do to molest her was recorded with a laconic imperturbability and an occasional flash of sardonic humour that gives us some notion of the tough fortitude of those early Victorian *mem-sahibs*. It is clear that from an early stage, perhaps from the start, she was writing with an eye to publication. (Her forethought was well rewarded; the Journal was published in 1843 by John Murray and in that year and the next was reprinted four times, a total printing of 7,500 copies). The thoughts that she sets down are therefore not always entirely spontaneous and it can safely be inferred that at times her comments are coloured with the wisdom of hindsight. She was helped, too, by having access to the unpublished journals of Captain Johnson and, according to Sir John Kaye, has 'used them freely without acknowledgment'. Yet, when this is said, her Journal remains a vivid and readable account of old unhappy far-off things and battles long ago.

'No one can read of the retreat from Kabul', it was recently written,[1] 'without being moved, yet again, by the sufferings we human beings inflict on ourselves, nor deny the dignity with which they can be borne —by a few. No one can read of the fatuity in Kabul without being pained by our own foolishness. They played cricket at Kabul. They ran their own horse-races. They set up their own zenanas. And later they died, cursing the sepoys and Indian followers who, in their eyes, clogged the pass to safety.'

None of the participants has told the whole sad story better than Florentia Sale.

PATRICK MACRORY

[1] By Mr Gordon Lee.

Acknowledgements

Miss Ethel Mainwaring and her sister, Mrs Violet Stagg, have given me much interesting information about their great-grandmother, Lady Sale. I am also indebted to Miss Mainwaring for the cutting from the *Pictorial Times* quoted on p. 158. When General Elphinstone's army attempted its ill-fated retreat from Kabul the Brown Bess musket was still the standard weapon of the British infantry, the gunners were touching off their muzzle-loading cannon with port-fires, and the Duke of Wellington was still Sir Oracle on all matters military. It is therefore noteworthy that there should be two ladies living in 1968 whose *own father* took part in this retreat. The reader who thinks this a chronological impossibility will find the explanation in the footnote on p. 153.

Sir Robert Sale is one of the heroes of the 13th Foot (the Somerset Light Infantry) and I am grateful to Lieut.-Colonel A. T. M. Urwick of the 13th's Regimental Depot—appropriately named 'Jellalabad House'—for giving me access to the relevant issues of the regimental magazine, *The Light Bob Gazette*. These provide details of the Sales' married life together, particularly in the earlier years.

Mrs Heather Cocks, whose great-grandfather, Captain Bott of the 5th Light Cavalry, was killed at Jugdulluk Pass in January 1842, drew my attention to Dr Bydon's own account of his famous ride to Jellalabad, and kindly sent me a copy of the manuscript in her possession. So far as I know, Brydon's account has never been published, except in an appendix to Sir George Lawrence's *Forty-three Years in India*, which itself appeared as long ago as 1874. Brydon's account of the final days of the retreat, of which Lady Sale could only write from hearsay, forms a fitting supplement to her story.

Finally, I must thank my wife both for her encouragement and for much patient work at the typewriter.

P.A.M.

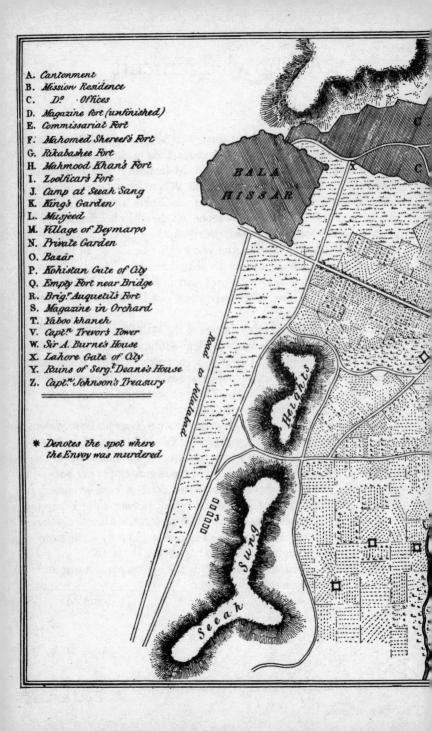

A. Cantonment
B. Mission Residence
C. D°. Offices
D. Magazine fort (unfinished)
E. Commissariat Fort
F. Mahomed Shereef's Fort
G. Rikabashee Fort
H. Mahmood Khan's Fort
I. Zoolficar's Fort
J. Camp at Seeah Sang
K. King's Garden
L. Musjeed
M. Village of Beymaroo
N. Private Garden
O. Bazar
P. Kohistan Gate of City
Q. Empty Fort near Bridge
R. Brig.r Auquetil's Fort
S. Magazine in Orchard
T. Yaboo khaneh
V. Capt.n Trevor's Tower
W. Sir A. Burne's House
X. Lahore Gate of City
Y. Ruins of Serg.t Deane's House
Z. Capt.n Johnson's Treasury

* Denotes the spot where
the Envoy was murdered

BALA HISSAR

Road to Jellalabad

Heights

Seeah Sung

PLAN
of the
CANTONMENT
and the
Surrounding
COUNTRY

SCALE.
150 300   600   1200 Yds

Vincent Eyre, Rec.ᵗ

KUZEILBASH QUARTER

DEH AFTCHAN

Heights

Beymaroo

J & C. Walker. lith: 9 Castle St

Lady Sale

A Journal of the Disasters in
Affghanistan, 1841-42

and

William Brydon

Account . . . of the Retreat from Cabool
in 1842

Introduction

. . . I have not only daily noted down events as they occurred, but often have done so hourly. I have also given the reports of the day, the only information we possessed; also such news as was telegraphed from the Bala Hissar,[1] or sent in by the King or by Capt. Conolly to the Envoy;[2] and many other reports brought by Affghan gentlemen of Capt. Sturt's[3] acquaintance, and by others of lower degree, who having had dealings with him in the engineer department and public works, and having received kindness from him, gave him such intelligence and warning as was in their power; all of which he communicated (to his superior officers) at different times; but the warnings were not attended to; and as when he gave his advice it was seldom adhered to, he became disgusted, and contented himself with zealously performing his duties and making himself generally useful, acting the part of an artillery officer as well as that of an engineer.

Had poor Sturt's life been spared, it was his intention to have worked up my Rough Notes, and to have added much valuable information: he was too much overworked to afford leisure to give me assistance at the time. . . . I believe several people kept an account of these proceedings, but all except myself lost all they had written; and had recourse to memory afterwards. I lost everything except the clothes I wore; and therefore it may appear strange that I should have saved these papers. The mystery is, however, easily solved. After everything was packed on the night before we left Cabul, I sat up to add a few lines to the events of the day, and the next morning I put them in a small bag and tied them round my waist. I am indebted to Capt. Souter, of H.M. 44th Regiment, for a plan, from recollection,

[1] Translation of this and other oriental words and phrases will be found in Lady Sale's 'Vocabulary', p. 169.

[2] The telegraph was, presumably, semaphore or heliograph; the King is Shah Soojah; and Captain John Conolly was a young Officer of the Political Branch, a cousin of Macnaghten's, who remained in the Bala Hissar throughout.

[3] Lady Sale's son-in-law. [F.S.]

of the cantonments and forts. The inaccuracies, if any, are but trifling; and it is sufficiently clear to indicate the positions of the principal places alluded to.[1] . . .

It is easy to argue on the wisdom or folly of conduct after the catastrophe has taken place. With regard therefore to our chiefs, I shall only say that the Envoy has deeply paid for his attempt to out diplomatize the Affghans. Gen. Elphinstone, conscious that his powers of mind had become enfeebled with those of his body, finding there was no hope of Gen. Nott's arrival to assume the command, called in another officer to his aid, who had but one object in view (to get back, at all hazards, to Hindostan).[2] He averred that a retreat to the Bala Hissar was impossible, as we should have to fight our way (for one mile and a half)! If we could not accomplish that, how were we to get through a week's march to Jellalabad? Once in the Bala Hissar, which would have been easily defended by one thousand men, we should have had plenty of troops for foraging purposes; and the village of Ben-i-shehr, just under the Bala Hissar, would have given us a twelvemonths' provisions if we had only made the demonstration of a night march, to have the appearance of taking them by force.

Independent of ——'s determination to return to India, he often refused to give any opinion when asked for it by the General, a cautious measure whereby he probably hoped to escape the obloquy that he expected would attach to the council of war, composed of Gen. Elphinstone, Brig. Shelton, Brig. Anquetil,[3] and Col. Chambers.[4] I might say nominally composed; numerically it was much more

[1] But the plan drawn by Lieutenant Vincent Eyre for his rival volume 'The Military Operations at Cabul (also published by John Murray in 1843) is even clearer and has therefore been preferred. Captain Souter fought right through the retreat up to the final stand of the 44th at Gandamack, where the Afghans spared his life because he had wrapped the colours round his body and they therefore supposed him to be a great lord and worth a princely ransom.

[2] 'Another officer' is unmistakably Brigadier Shelton; he was still alive when Lady Sale's Journal was published and Lady Sale's caution in referring to him may have been for fear of a libel action. But in view of what she says of him by name, it is hard to see why she bothered on occasions to take refuge in ——.

[3] Seconded from the Company's army to command Shah Soojah's forces; killed in the retreat.

[4] Commanding Officer of the 5th Light Cavalry (Company's army) and commander of the cavalry in the retreat, in which he was killed.

extended. Capt. Grant,[1] with cold caution, obstructed every enterprise, and threw all possible difficulties in the way; Capt. Bellew[1] was full of doubts and suggestions, all tending to hamper and retard operations; and numbers of young men gave much gratuitious advice; in fact, the greater part of the night was spent in confusing the General's ideas, instead of allowing a sick man time by rest to invigorate his powers. Brig. Shelton was in the habit of taking his rezai with him, and lying on the floor during these discussions, when sleep, whether real or feigned, was a resource against replying to disagreeable questions. Major Thain,[2] a sincere friend and good adviser of the General's, withdrew in disgust from the council: and Sturt, who was ever ready to do any thing or give his opinion when asked, from the same feeling no longer proferred it.

[1] Grant and Bellew were respectively Assistant Adjutant-General and Deputy Assistant Quartermaster-General of the Kabul Force; both were killed in the retreat. In later impressions Lady Sale apologized to Grant's brother for this criticism, which nevertheless seems amply justified.

[2] General Elphinstone's A.D.C.; killed in the retreat.

I

Cabul

Afghanistan, though the British had not realized it, was very close to general insurrection. The Eastern Ghilzye tribes had risen and blocked the passes on the road to India; but it was confidently supposed that Sale's brigade would sweep them aside. Sir William and Lady Macnaghten, General Elphinstone and Lady Sale would then follow the brigade down the road to Hindostan.

1841

9th October: The 35th Native Infantry, commanded by Col. Monteath C.B., with two six-pounder guns under Lieut. Dawes, were suddenly sent forward at a day's notice to Bhoodkhak, partly as being the first march towards the provinces (they forming a part of Sale's, or the 1st brigade), and partly in consequence of the disturbances.

11th October: The 13th light infantry, commanded by Lieut. Col. Dennie, C.B., were also sent at a few hours' notice to Bhoodkhak; but as they were not to proceed on their march until the arrival of Capt. Abbott with his guns, I remained at Cabul with my daughter, Mrs. Sturt, who had been staying with us during her husband's absence with Col. Oliver's force;[1] and Sale took his departure from Cabul, fully expecting me to follow him in three days at the latest.

12th October: The 13th and 35th, with the two guns under Dawes, moved forward, the whole under Sale, their object being to go through the Khoord Cabul pass, and place the 35th N.I. in an advanced position at Khoord Cabul, after which the 13th were to fall back again on Bhoodkhak. This movement was effected, but with considerable loss. The Khoord Cabul is a narrow defile, enclosed by high and rugged rocks; it is said that the number of the enemy did not exceed 60 men, but they possessed considerable advantage over our troops in their knowledge of the country and in the positions they took up;

[1] Oliver, who commanded the 5th Native Infantry, had been sent out with a large column of almost brigade strength on a punitive expedition at the end of September.

for until they commenced firing, not a man was known to be there. They were concealed behind rocks and stones, and by a stone breast-work that they had hastily thrown up, behind which, on our troops entering the pass, they laid in wait, and appeared to pick off the officers in particular. . . . Gen. Sale was wounded in the left leg; the ball entered near the ankle, shivered the small bone, and was taken out from the skin on the other side where it had lodged. . . .[1] It rained very heavily that night, and the 13th had the full benefit of it, for they were out all night, having two alertes; one of the sentries was mortally wounded, being shot on his post. Exertions were made to discover the persons who fired on our sentries: three men were seized who had in their possession the soldier's belt, which was a tolerable evidence of criminality; but the Envoy (*Macnaghten*) wrote to say, that the people about the King said that those men were good men and true, and they were to be released without any punishment!

13th October: Two companies of the 37th N.I. and two guns under Mr Waller, were sent to reinforce the 13th at Bhoodkhak, leaving only the remainder of the 37th in cantonments, and no guns. Should there be a rising in Cabul, we should be entirely without the means of defence.

18th October: The enemy came down (a chupao or night attack), 400 strong, on Khoord Cabul, where an action was fought with great loss on both sides; Lieut. Jenkins of the 35th was mortally wounded, and lingered on in great agony, having been shot through the spine. Col. Monteath sent to Sale for reinforcements, who despatched to him the two companies of the 37th that had lately arrived at Bhood-khak.

19th October: Sale and Sturt have agreed that I am to remain with him and my daughter at Cabul, and to come on with the Envoy, who is anxious to go to his government at Bombay, and Gen. Elphinstone, who returns to the provinces in consequence of ill health. . . . It appears that the Hazir Bash ('the king's bodyguard; the words imply

---

[1] 'I could not help admiring old Sale's coolness', wrote his Brigade Major, Hamlet Wade, describing the incident. 'He turned to me and said "Wade, I have got it," and then remained on horse-back directing the skirmishers, untill compelled from loss of blood to make over command to Dennie.'

"Ever ready"') the escort sent by the King with Capt. Trevor to Capt. Macgregor (political agent), were the people who let the Ghilzyes into the 35th's camp; they were partly of the same tribe, and whilst the rest were fighting, these every-ready gentlemen did a little work of their own, cutting down surwans and hamstringing camels. . . . Col. Monteath turned these people out of his camp as unsafe to be trusted; the Envoy has ordered them to be sent back to Cabul, and to be kindly treated, and will not believe them to be in fault. The Hazir Bash, as their name imports, are 'aye ready for the field', but I fear that just now—

'At a word it may be understood,
They are ready for evil and not for good,'

like Walter Scott's goblin page.

23rd October: Much firing has been heard, and great anxiety prevails. All the forts about Cabul are empty, and the Juwans have gone (it is said) to aid in the fight against us at Tezeen: Sale writes that the report is, that the people at Tezeen say they are unable to cope with us in battle, but that they intend to plunder and annoy the force on its way down.

24th October: Gen. Elphinstone told me that Sale had been very imprudent in using his leg, and had consequently been suffering a great deal of pain, but that the remedies applied had given him relief; he expressed great regret that he had not communicated any information to me, taking it for granted that the Envoy had done so, if I had not a letter from Sale himself; but he was wounded, and with plenty of military occupation, could not always find time to write me many particulars, as he had to send his despatches off as quickly as possible to the General.

25th October: I received a letter from Sale, in which he informs me, that the conduct of the troops employed in the affair at Tezeen was good beyond all praise. . . . He was to halt that day (the 24th), as Macgregor was in treaty with the chiefs, who he says are willing to refrain from all further opposition, and say they are convinced they have no chance against us. . . . Lady Macnaghten called on me, and told me that Capt. Macgregor, Political Agent, wrote that the chiefs

8

received him with great politeness, and were pleased at the confidence reposed in them by his going to meet them attended by only one suwar. . . . The Envoy was some time since warned by three Affghans not to ride so early in the morning or so late in the evening as was his wont; but, whether from policy or natural fearlessness, he has not attended to their advice.

26th October: Major Thain called: he owned he was puzzled as to what was going on, but hoped that affairs would remain quiet until we got out of the country. He said it was the present intention that the sick should move out on Saturday next, and the Envoy and the General should leave Cabul on Monday the 1st. . . . Capt. Paton writes mysteriously that he has much to communicate, 'better spoken than written'. He adds that a force to be of any use in that country must not be hampered with camels, tents, or baggage, and that the ammunition should be carried only on mules or yaboos. . . . Last year, when Sir Willoughby Cotton commanded, and during the disturbances in the Kohistan, every dispatch from Sale, who commanded the troops there, was promulgated in orders, and the present system of keeping information close is disgusting; there can be no secrets regarding what passes in action in the field. The general impression is that the Envoy is trying to deceive himself into an assurance that the country is in a quiescent state. He has a difficult part to play, without sufficient moral courage to stem the current singly. About two months since Sir William wrote to Lord Auckland, explaining to him the present state of Affghanistan, and requesting that five additional regiments should be sent to this country, two of them to be European. To these statements a written war succeeded between the Envoy and the Supreme Government of Bengal. Letter after letter came calling for retrenchment. Sir William had been appointed from home Governor of Bombay, and was particularly chosen for the office from his being a moderator and a man unlikely to push any violent measures; he hoped affairs might take a turn for the better and was evidently anxious to leave Cabul and assume his new appointment. In an evil hour he acceded to the entreaties of Sir Alexander Burnes (who appears to have been blinded on the subject) and wrote to Lord Auckland to nullify his former request for additional troops, and to say that part of those now in the country might be withdrawn. The 1st brigade under Sale was accordingly ordered to be in readiness to move down; and it was generally understood that all would be withdrawn as soon as the Shah had raised five more regiments of his own. The letter of recal [*sic*], as we may term Sir William's, was sent off only two days before the breaking out of the Zoormut affair.

Great stress had been laid upon the chiefs having given us hostages, but this is no certain proof of their sincerity; we have been long enough amongst them for them to know the British character; they also know that the Dost's[1] family were safely and honourably treated under our protection, whilst he and his son were in arms against us, and they naturally consider their safety as a proof of that of any hostages they leave with us.

27th October: I hear that Macgregor writes to the Envoy that the country about Tezeen never was in so tranquil a state as it is at present! Now, with a little variation in the wording, he might have cautiously written to the Envoy, so as to be understood by him alone, and have intimated that the country was now as quiet as it ever was; which, to those who know the wild tribes thereabouts located, indicated any thing but a state of pacification.

The sick are again ordered to be off to-morrow, with a wing of the 54th, to Tezeen, where the 37th awaits their arrival; and, at present, it is supposed that the Envoy and General will follow on the 1st.

Sale's brigade continued to march steadily on towards Gandamak, Jellalabad and India. Behind them, in Cabul, the signs of an incipient rebellion against the British were increasing daily.

30th October: Last night as the cavalry videttes went their rounds at Siah Sung, a party of men rushed out of a cave and fired at them; some were taken prisoners; part of them were Affghans, but four were Hindostanees, and one of them was a Chuprassy of Capt. Bygrave, who endeavoured to excuse himself by saying, he fired at the party supposing them to be Affghans, but could give no reason for being there himself.

Mr. Melville was attacked last evening, but set spurs to his horse and galloped off, on which the Affghans set up a shout; this is the fourth attempt on the part of the Affghans to assassinate British officers within a short time. I before mentioned Mr. Mayne's escape; Dr. Metcalfe was also nearly cut down; and Lieut. Waller, of the

[1] i.e. Dost Mahomed, former ruler of Afghanistan, whom the British had replaced by Shah Soojah. The Dost was now in honourable exile in British India, at Ludhiana.

Artillery, was wounded on the head whilst riding close to the Siah
Sung camp.[1]

October 31st The invalids, whose march had been countermanded, are
again under Orders to go out to Siah Sung on Tuesday, to be in
readiness to march on Wednesday the 3rd of next month. When the
barracks for the men and the officers' quarters were erected in the
Cabul cantonment, a committee assembled to value them and fix
the house rent, both for them and for the two houses to be occupied
by the Commander of the forces and the second in command. It was
fixed at ten per cent. on the actual outlay as specified by the engineer's
department. We paid ours monthly, as did the 13th, through the
regimental paymaster. The 35th also paid their rent monthly. There
was some dispute regarding it with some others, in consequence of
the rooms not being all quite finished, but as Capt. Sturt was not
ordered to collect the money, but only to pay over whatever he received, the business remained in abeyance. An inquiry is now making
about the house rent that has not been paid by the officers who have
gone away, so I feel quite delighted that Sale and I are out of the
scrape. Brig. Shelton[2] has written officially to the General to say that
it is very hard that he is kept at Siah Sung, when there is a good house
in cantonments to which he has a right, and applies officially to the
General to give him up either his own house or ours. Now, as long
as Brig. Shelton's duty keeps him at Siah Sing, he has no business in
cantonments. This is Sunday; both the General and I expect to march
on Wednesday, so, *par complaisance,* we neither of us expected to be
turned out; however, if we do not go, we both intend vacating our
habitations, when our house will be made over to Capt. Sturt, to
undergo repairs, so as to be ready for the reception of the next
Commander of the forces. Gen. Nott has been written to, to come up
immediately, and Gen. Elphinstone is to give up the command to him
from the 1st of November. The reason that our house is in future to
be appropriated by the chief arises from its being the best and most
commodious. Sir Willoughby Cotton gave his plan, and Sale his,
when the houses were built; and Sir Willoughby living *en garçon* had

[1] A detachment of the Kabul garrison, commanded by Brigadier Shelton, was in camp
in the lee of the Siah Sung hills, a mile or so both from the main cantonment and from
the city.

[2] Brigadier John Shelton, 44th Foot (the Essex Regiment), had become second-in-
command of the Cabul force on Sale's departure.

omitted many little comforts that we had considered indispensable. Added to which, Sale had a *shoke* for gardening, and had an excellent kitchen garden; whilst I cultivated flowers that were the admiration of the Affghan gentlemen who came to see us. My sweet peas and geraniums were much admired, but they were all eager to obtain the seed of the edible pea, which flourished well; and by being sown as soon as the frost was over we had plenty of succession crops, and we still have peas growing which we hope, if not cut off by frost, will give a crop next month.

The potatoes thrive well, and will be a very valuable addition to the *cuisine*. The cauliflowers, artichokes, and turnip radishes are very fine, and peculiarly mild in their flavour; they are all from seed we brought with us from our garden at Kurnaul. The Cabul lettuces are hairy and inferior to those cultivated by us; but the Cabul cabbages are superior, being milder, and the red cabbage from English seeds grows well.

Regarding the fruits of Affghanistan, I should not be believed were I to state the truth. Selected grapes off a bunch of those in the Kohistan have been known to weigh 200 grains; the largest I have ever weighed myself was 127 grains. It was the kind denominated the Bull's Eye by the English; I believe the natives call it Hoosseinee-Angoor; its form is nearly round, and the taste very luscious; it is of a kind not generally purchaseable. At Kardunah they grow in great perfection. Those I ate were sent as a present from a native gentleman to Captain Sturt, as also were some very delicious pears from Turkistan. The largest peaches I have myself weighed turned the scale at 15 rupees, and were fully equal in juiciness and flavour to those of the English hothouse. The finest sort are in the Kohistan but are so delicate they will not bear carriage to Cabul. I have been assured by my friends who have been there in the peach season that the best fruit of the kind at my table was quite inferior to those above mentioned. The Orleans blue plum is excellent. There is a green one resembling in appearance a greengage, but very tasteless. There are also many other kinds, with a great variety of melons, Water, Mush and Surda, which is accounted best.

While Lady Sale was thus busily recording squabbles over the rent for the officers' quarters and enthusing over the fruit and vegetables of Affghanistan, events in Cabul were hurrying to their climax. The first target of Afghan hatred was the British Resident, Sir Alexander Burnes, who was living in the heart of the city. Friendly Afghans, who knew what was coming, had urged him to leave his Residency for the safety of the cantonments. Burnes had scorned their advice. Now, as dawn broke on 2 November, he found himself trapped, besieged by a howling mob with murder in its heart.

Down in the cantonments, the noise of the tumult was plainly audible, with Shah Soojah's artillery booming out from the Bala Hissar in a vain but valiant attempt to crush the rising at its outset. With rumour, full of tongues, furiously at work, the British had little idea what was happening. They could certainly have no conception that the storm that had now broken was to swell into a tempest that would utterly overwhelm them.

November 2nd: Last night, a party of Kohistanees entered the city; a large body of horsemen were also seen proceeding towards the city from the road that leads by the Shah's camp behind Siah Sung.

This morning, early, all was in commotion in Cabul; the shops were plundered, and the people were all fighting.

Our Affghan servant, Mahomed Ali, who used to sleep in the city, when he passed out to come to my house in the morning was threatened, and reviled as the chuprassy of the Feringhee General, who, they asserted, had been beaten at Tezeen, and all his troops had run away, and he with them!

The Shah resides in the Bala Hissar, and his guns from that fortress were constantly firing; the Affghans in the city were doing the same from six in the morning. Capt. Sturt hearing that Capt. Johnson's (paymaster to the Shah's force) house and treasury in the city were attacked, as also Sir Alexander Burnes's, went to General Elphinstone, who sent him with an important message, first to Brig. Shelton at Siah Sung, and afterwards to the King to concert with him measures for the defence of that fortress. Just as he entered the precincts of the palace, he was stabbed in three places by a young man well dressed, who escaped into a building close by, where he was protected by the gates being shut. Fortunately for my son-in-law, Capt. Lawrence[1] had been sent to the King by the Envoy, and he kindly procured a Palkee, and sent Sturt home with a strong guard of fifty lancers, but they were obliged to make a long detour by Siah Sung. In the meantime, Lawrence came to tell me all that had passed and to break the bad news to my daughter, Mrs. Sturt.

[1] Captain George Lawrence, older brother of the famous Sir Henry and Sir John Lawrence. He was serving in Cabul as assistant to Macnaghten—'the man I loved and revered as a father' (Sir George Lawrence, *Forty-Three Years in India*).

Lawrence, (military secretary to the Envoy) had had a very narrow escape himself. An Affghan, grinding his teeth, and grinning with rage and hatred of the Feringhees, aimed a blow at him with a sword, which Lawrence parried, and putting spurs to his horse he escaped: one of his suwars received a cut in the leg, which was revenged by another horseman shooting the fellow.

It was Lawrence who came to tell me of Sale's wound; he is always kind and friendly, though he has now been twice the herald of ill news! It struck me as probable that the suwars would take Sturt to his own house; and as he and my daughter were staying with me, there would not even be a bed to place him on there. I, therefore, determined not to lose time by waiting till the bearers could get my palkee ready, but took my chuttah and walked off as fast as I could towards Sturt's house. I fortunately met Major Thain (aide-de-camp to General Elphinstone), for I soon saw a crowd of about fifty suwars in his compound. Thain ran on and told the bearers to bring him on to my house. I cannot describe how shocked I felt when I saw poor Sturt; for Lawrence, fearing to alarm us, had said he was only slightly wounded. He had been stabbed deeply in the shoulder and side, and on the face (the latter wound striking on the bone just missed the temple); he was covered with blood issuing from his mouth, and was unable to articulate. From the wounds in the face and shoulder, the nerves were affected; the mouth would not open, the tongue was swollen and paralysed, and he was ghastly and faint from loss of blood. He could not lie down, from the blood choking him; and had to sit up in the palkee as best he might, without a pillow to lean against. With some difficulty and great pain he was supported up stairs, and laid on his bed, when Dr. Harcourt dressed his wounds, which having been inflicted about ten o'clock, now at one were cold and stiff with clotted blood. The tongue was paralysed, and the nerves of the throat affected, so that he could neither swallow nor articulate; and the choking sensation of the blood in his throat was most painful to witness. He was better towards the evening; and by his wife's un-remitting attention in assisting him to get rid of the clotted blood from his mouth by incessant applications of warm wet cloths, he was by eleven at night able to utter a tolerably articulate sound. With what joy did we hear him faintly utter 'bet-ter'; and he really seemed to enjoy a tea-spoonful of water, which we got into his mouth by a drop or two at a time, painful as it was to him to swallow it.

It was most gratifying to see the attention and kind feeling manifested on the occasion by the sergeants of the engineer department, and their anxiety (particularly Sergeant Deane's) to make themselves useful to Sturt.

Capt. Warburton,[1] Capt. Johnson and Capt. Troup were all fortunately in cantonments; for their houses in the city were plundered and burnt. At Johnson's (the King's treasury) the guard of 40 men were massacred, as also all the servants but one, who luckily was not at home. The insurgents looted a lakh and 70,000 rupees of public property, and Johnson lost above 10,000 rupees of his own property.[2]

There were of course various reports. We first heard that, on the affair breaking out, Sir A. Burnes went over to the Wuzeer's to ascertain what could be done; and that he was safe there, except having been shot in the leg. The King, from the Bala Hissar, sent intelligence to the Envoy 'that Burnes was all right'; but a few hours afterwards the King acknowledged that he did not know anything of him, neither did the Envoy at seven in the evening, when Captain Lawrence and Captain John Conolly came to inquire after Sturt's health. Our only hope of Burnes's safety rests on the possibility of his having obtained refuge in some harem. His brother's fate is as yet unknown. Capt. Broadfoot was shot in the breast, and killed; he was breakfasting with the two Burnes's: before he fell, he had killed six men with his own hand. Capt. Drummond is protected by Osman Khan, Kariezi-Umeer, chief of the domain, the first stage from Cabul towards the Kohistan. Capt. Mackenzie, political assistant to Capt. Mackeson at Peshawur, came up to Cabul some time since; and when Lieut. Milne (in the Commissariat) was sent to Khelat-i-Gilzie Mackenzie took his place in the Shah's commissariat. He was located in the fort divided into two by the range of Commissariat godowns, one side inhabited by Brig. Anquetil, commanding the Shah's forces, the other by Mackenzie, who (the Brigadier being in cantonments) held out in both, with some sappers and miners, a few of the Shah's 6th Regt, and 130 Juzailchees: the latter are good men, and mostly Usufzyes. In this fort were stored 8000 maunds of ottah and wheat. Capt. Trevor hopes to defend his tower as long as it is not fired. Another report states that Trevor, his wife and one child, have

[1] Warburton commanded the Shah's artillery. He had not long before married an Afghan's wife, a niece of the exiled Dost Mahomed.

[2] The rupee was worth approximately two shillings. Since a lakh was one hundred thousand, a lakh of rupees was roughly £10,000.

escaped, whilst his six other children have been murdered. Another, that he has escaped, but that his wife and seven children are all murdered.

The Kuzzilbash quarter of the city is said to be all quiet. Naib Shureef's son has been killed in some of the scuffles in the city. Abdoolah Khan, Amenoolah Khan and a few other Dooranee chiefs, are said to be the instigators of the insurrection.

The King (who resides in the Bala Hissar) says if the rebellion is not over tomorrow morning he will burn the city,—by no means an easy task: the houses are all flat-roofed and mud-roofed. It is true Cabul has been burnt three times before, and therefore what has been may occur again. By throwing shells into the houses you may fire them; and the individual house fired, being ceiled with wood, blazes fiercely until the roof falls in, and the mud and dust smother the fire without danger to the adjacent buildings. The King had also declared that if the Meer Akor (who protected the man that stabbed Sturt) does not give the assassin up, he will hang the Meer Akor himself. It appears a very strange circumstance that troops were not immediately sent into the city to quell the affair in the commencement; but we seem to sit quietly with our hands folded and look on. On the breaking out of the insurrection, the King sent Campbell's[1] Hindostanee regiment into the city, with some guns, who maintained an arduous conflict for some time against the rebels; but being wholly unsupported, were obliged eventually to give way, when the greater part of them were cut to pieces and several of their guns were captured.

The state of supineness and fancied security of those in power in cantonments is the result of deference to the opinions of Lord Auckland, whose sovereign will and pleasure it is that tranquillity do reign in Affghanistan; in fact, it is reported at Government House, Calcutta, that the lawless Affghans are as peaceable as London citizens; and this being decided by the powers that be, why should we be on the alert?

Most dutifully do we appear to shut our eyes on our probable fate. The Shah is, however, to be protected, whatever may be the fate of the English in the city; and Brig. Shelton is sent with the Shah's 6th, some of the 44th Queen's, and three horse artillery guns under Capt.

[1] William Campbell was a Eurasian mercenary who had served under a variety of Indian rulers and was now in Soojah's employment. After the restoration of Dost Mahomed to the throne of Afghanistan, Campbell re-entered his service, in which he died in 1866.

Nicholl, to the Bala Hissar. The King, as he well may be, is in great consternation. At about 9 a.m. Capt. Sturt arrived at Siah Sung from the cantonments, bearing orders from Maj. Gen. Elphinstone for the 54th N.I., Capt. Nicholl's three horse artillery guns, and a company of the 44th, accompanied by the Shah's 6th regiment, to hold themselves in readiness to march at a moment's notice to the Bala Hissar. As they had all been on the *qui vive* since daybreak, they were ready in an instant, and eagerly expecting orders to march, when a note came from Capt. Lawrence (the Envoy's military and private secretary) dated Bala Hissar, 10 a.m., telling them, 'Stay where you are—all is quiet; you need not come.' This caused great suprise, as the firing was brisk in the city. After waiting another hour under arms, the Brigadier ordered Sturt to go in and see what was going on; this he gladly did, and, accompanied by eight suwars of the Shah's 2nd cavalry, went to the Bala Hissar. In half an hour a suwar returned, saying he had been badly wounded entering the palace gates, and bearing an order for an immediate advance of the troops. 'Forward' was the word; and, anticipating an attack on the city, the troops gladly set out, and arrived unopposed in presence of the King, when to their sorrow, instead of receiving *hookm* to enter the city, the Shah almost rudely inquired why they had come! After standing under arms another hour, firing being heard towards the Shor Bazaar, the Brigadier sent Lieut. Melville of the 54th to inquire what was going on. On going down to the gate toward the city, he found the fugitives from Campbell's regiment flying in, and reporting that their regiment was entirely cut up: this he reported to the Brigadier, who ordered him to take the light company down to the city gates, and whilst taking charge of that position to protect as best he could the retreating regiment. On arriving there, Lieut. Melville placed a section as a guard and took the remaining three to the entrance of the Shor Bazaar, and formed them up facing the street: he had not been there more than five minutes, when he observed a disorderly rabble retreating at a quick pace towards him, pursued by a large body of Affghans, whilst others from the tops and windows of the houses kept up a brisk fire upon them.

Immediately after the colours had gained the rear of his detachment, Lieut. Melville retreated slowly, facing the enemy, toward the gate, pouring in volley on volley; but, owing to the protection afforded the rebels by the walls, it is to be feared with but little effect. On reaching the fosse, he formed his men up again, to allow the two guns to pass to his rear; but the Affghans made a rush and the golundaz of the Shah took to a disorderly flight. As the idea of rescuing them with three sections was entirely out of the question, and the fire was becoming very hot, Melville sent Lieut. Macartney (of the Shah's service), who in the meantime had come to his assistance with one company of the Shah's 6th to man the walls over where the guns were left, and prevent the enemy carrying them off; this being done, Melville got a few of the golundaz to go back and spike one of the guns, after which he retired inside, having lost one subadar and three men wounded and one man killed. On arriving inside, he placed the men on the ramparts; and being accidentally bayoneted in the thigh, he was released from duty, making over charge of the men to Macartney.

It being found impracticable to bring in the guns, from the carriages being broken, the European horse artillery, who had been sent out for that purpose, came back; and some guns having been mounted on the wall and brought to bear on them, they were so broken by shot as to be perfectly useless: and it may be here remarked, that to the day the troops left the Bala Hissar, notwithstanding frequent attempts were made by the enemy, they never succeeded in gaining possession of them.

The King, who had been in a great state of excitement during the day, on hearing of the loss of his guns, and that 200 of Campbell's regiment had been killed or wounded, was excessively agitated; the more so that, immediately on the rebellion breaking out, almost all the Pesh Khedmuts and Shah Guzees had deserted him. He ordered a dinner for the officers in the evening; as, to their extreme disgust, they were obliged to stay the night in the fort, neither men or officers having an article of any sort or kind beside what they wore. The 5th cavalry who had accompanied the detachment to the Bala Hissar, had, after taking all the baggage from Siah Sung to cantonments, remained in the latter place.

The King, sitting with the British officers around him, was anxious to obtain their advice in the present crisis, and particularly asked that of ——;[1] whose conduct was represented on the emergency as pitiful and childish in the extreme, not having a word to say, nor an opinion to offer.

In cantonments all was confusion and indecision. The Envoy mounted his horse and rode to the gateway, and then rode back again—the best thing he could do; for had the Affghans either killed

[1] The pitiful and childish —— is presumably, once again, Brigadier Shelton.

him or taken him prisoner, it would have given them a decided advantage on their part.

Sir William and Lady Macnaghten had vacated the residency before 11 o'clock a.m., and came into cantonments; a circumstance which was no doubt soon known to the insurgents and must have given them an idea that we greatly dreaded an attack from them, which was threatened at night. The guns were placed in battery, and the walls manned with double sentries. The Kohistanees are reported to have 5,000 men assembled at Deh Hadji in the Kohistan. The villages about the Lake are all in a state of insurrection. The whole force from the Siah Sung cantonments are come in: the Shah's 6th, the 5th cavalry, Anderson's horse and Skinner's are in the Mission Compound; the escort in cantonment. Lawrence has kindly promised in case of an attack to come over to us; but we are so anxious about Sturt that we do not think much of danger.

Two Sipahees were cut down near the gate of the Commissariat Fort today; another was killed who only attempted to cross the road. We have good news today from Sale at Gundamuk, dated the 1st. They were all quite well, and supplied with all that they required.

November 3rd: At three in the morning the drums in cantonments beat to arms, in consequence of a large body of men coming over the Siah Sung hill; they proved to be the 37th from Khoord Cabul, who, about half-past 2 p.m. yesterday, received an order to march on its receipt to Cabul. Poshteens[1] arrived about an hour afterwards in safety, with no other guard than a couple of suwars; however, before the regiment was ready to move off its ground, the Ghilzyes had taken possession of the mouth of the pass, and were with some difficulty dislodged by two companies of the 37th, and two guns of the Shah's mountain train; the latter under under Lieut. Green. The order received by Major Griffiths to march the detachment under his command on receipt of the order, was accompanied by a note from Capt. Paton, Assistant Quarter-Master-General, telling Major G. that all Cabul was in insurrection, etc. The Laird of Pughman (who had held the pass from the time Sale left Bhoodkhak), with all his followers, joined our forces as soon as the reached his post and marched into Cabul with them. . . .

---

[1] 'Sheepskin' or 'fur pelisse', according to Lady Sale. These sheepskin jerkins served as greatcoats and blankets; when the battalion was on the march they might, as here, be carried on the regimental transport.

. . . I observe I have mentioned the Laird of Pughman,—a sobriquet applied to a good man, and a true one to the Shah and us. His proper name was the Syud Mahommed Khan; and for the good service he did in the Kohistan[1] with Sale's force he obtained the honorary title of Jan Fishan Khan, or the nobleman who is the exterminator of his sovereign's enemies. It is a difficult sentence to render into English.

This day there was a great talk of the Kohistanees being expected to arrive and attack us. The double sentries are loaded to-day, as also the sentries placed round the ammunition and stores.

In the evening the rebels appeared in considerable numbers near Mahommed Khan's Fort, and between that and the Commissariat Fort, situated 300 yards from the cantonments. We have only three days' provisions in cantonments: should the Commissariat Fort be captured, we shall not only lose all our provisions, but our communications with the city will be cut off.

This fort (an old crazy one, undermined by rats) contains the whole of the Bengal commissariat stores, valued at four lakhs of rupees, including about 12,000 maunds of ottah, wheat and barley, and all the medical stores, etc.[2]

No military steps have been taken to suppress the insurrection, nor even to protect our only means of subsistence (the Godowns) in the event of a siege. The King, Envoy and General appear paralysed by this sudden outbreak: the former is deserted by all his courtiers, and by even his most confidential servants, except the Wuzeer, who is strongly suspected of having instigated the conspiracy; and suspicion attaches to his Majesty again. It is here necessary to observe, that several months ago letters calling on all true Mussulmans to rise against the Kaffirs (English unbelievers) were widely disseminated: they bore the King's signature; but Sir William Macnaghten always insisted that they were forgeries of a very peculiar description, that

[1] The Kohistan was the name given to the mountainous region some fifty miles north of Cabul. In the previous autumn a small force under General Sale had given battle there to the Amir Dost Mahomed. The Political Officer in Kohistan at the time Lady Sale is writing, was Major Eldred Pottinger, the 'Hero of Herat'. His warnings of trouble stirring in the region had been contemptuously dismissed by Macnaghten.

[2] While the cantonments were under construction the Chief Commissioner Officer had begged for storage space inside the perimeter. Sir Willoughby Cotton had replied that 'no such place could be given him, as they were far too busy in erecting barracks for the men to think of commissariat stores'.

papers bearing the veracious signature had had their contents washed out, and these seditious writings inserted. The Shah of course said, 'An enemy had done this;' and, as dead men tell no tales, much of the obloquy was allowed to rest on Moolah Shekoor, who had paid the penalty of other state crimes.

In Affghanistan the English act as they do in all other countries they visit,—keep to themselves, and even (generally) employ only servants brought with them. The Envoy kept but few Affghans in his employ: he had a news reporter, at 150 rupees a month, who had the credit of concocting splendid untruths; an old moollah picked up at Kandahar, who, I believe, receives 200,—a man greatly in Sir William's confidence; there is also an old cossid. These people adhere to the Envoy, and flatter him into the belief that the tumult is *bash* (nothing), and will shortly subside.

This day there was a grand bustle, getting guns into all the bastions. Capt. and Mrs. Trevor and their seven children, came into cantonments. Trevor's Hazir Bashes brought them in safe,[1] but they had to walk through the river, and to carry the children, saving only the clothes they had on. As they escaped at one gate their tower was taken possession of by the rebels from another.

That the insurrection could have been easily crushed at its commencement, is evident from the circumstance that on the 2nd of November a considerable number of chiefs went to Capt. Trevor's house to lend him assistance. . . .

It is further worthy of remark, that Taj Mahommed Khan went to Sir Alexander Burnes the very day before the insurrection broke out, and told him what was going on. Burnes, incredulous, heaped abuse on this gentleman's head. . . . . .

Two of the Shah's mountain train guns, under Lieut. Green, and 400 of the 54th N.I., were sent, escorted by cavalry, to take ammunition and carcasses to the Bala Hissar, as also bedding for the men.

There is a report that the city is about to be fired.

A large party bearing the religious flag (green) came towards the rear gate; they fought with much *jee:* but one of our guns played on them, and then the cavalry dashed out and cut them up. Lieut. Le Geyt, of the Shah's service, with a small party of Anderson's horse,

---

[1] A courageous trooper, stretching out his bare arm to protect Mrs Trevor from a blow from an Afghan sword, had his hand lopped off; unmoved, he escorted her to the safety of the cantonments, the blood pouring from the stump.

feigned to fly, and drew a party after them, on whom they turned and dealt destruction.

During this day many projects were entered into for the purpose of putting down the rebellion, but none were put into practice. The Wuzeer went into the town, accompanied by some troops; but soon returned, having made no impression. The King wrote to Sir William Macnaghten, proposing that a free pardon should be offered to all offenders, and that all should be forgiven and forgotten if the leaders of the insurrection would come to his durbar, and acknowledging their faults, return to their allegiance. This, of course, was never carried into execution.

November 4th: Our guns from the south bastion opened early, and played almost all day on Mahmood Khan's fort, and on any body of Affghans that showed themselves. Lieut. Warren, who held the Commissariat fort with fifty men, wrote to the General to say that, unless reinforced, he could not hold out; that he was surrounded by the enemy, who he feared were mining the walls, and they were preparing ladders for the escalade; adding also that some of his men had already left him.

In the evening, a party of cavalry and infantry were sent to aid him in evacuating his position. Capt. Boyd, the Bengal Commissariat officer, on hearing the object of this force from Capt. Grant (Assist. Adjt. Gen.) proceeded in person to Gen. Elphinstone, accompanied by Capt. Johnson, (the Shah's Commissariat officer). They urgently entreated him to recall them, and instead, to send such reinforcements as were required to hold a position of such vital importance; pointing out the certain destruction of the whole force in cantonments, in the event of the capture of all our supplies. The General acquiesced in their views, and promised to issue the order for reinforcements. The above detachment was very shortly obliged to return to cantonments, having suffered most severely in men and horses, who were fired upon from behind every face and from every loophole of Mahommed Shureef's fort,[1] without their being able even to see an enemy. Previous to this detachment going out, a party of Europeans, under Capt. Robinson, went down the Kohistan road to effect the same object. Capt. Robinson (H.M. 44th) being killed,

[1] A small fort about 200 yards from the south-western angle of the British cantonments. It commanded the approach from the cantonments to the Commissariat Fort and had already been occupied by Afghan insurgents.

this small party was obliged to retire, having suffered severely. The whole of this occurred within 250 paces of the south bastion. In the evening no reinforcements had been sent to Warren, and the two heads of the Commissariats, Johnson and Boyd, again went to the General, to entreat he would not lose any more time in sending aid to that officer, and informed him there were but two days' provisions left in cantonments; pointed out the great fears entertained that we could not procure supplies from the surrounding country, with the enemy in force in the neighbouring forts, and the consequent destruction of our force from famine, unless the Godown fort were taken possession of at all hazards. The General conceded to these opinions. As Mahommed Shureef's fort commanded the only gate of the Commissariat fort, it would be requisite first to take possession of that fort. The Political authorities had no persons from whom they could obtain information! For a reward of fifty rupees one of Johnson's servants proceeded to the fort, and brought back intelligence (in about half-an-hour) that he saw twenty or thirty men with lighted matchlocks sitting on either side of the wicket: he judged, from the silence that prevailed, there were but few then within, and affirmed there were none on the road. Johnson subsequently sent another man, who confirmed the reports, but did not see any lights near the wicket. All this was made known to General Elphinstone, who determined on taking possession of the fort, and Capt. Boyd volunteered to carry the powder to blow the gate. The General, however, afterwards listened to other advice from other of his staff officers, who were averse to the proceeding, as involving too much risk! During this time another letter was received from Lieut. Warren by the adjutant of his regiment, stating that unless he was immediately reinforced, he must abandon his position, as many of his guard had gone over the wall to cantonments, by which his force was much weakened. Capt. Boyd and Johnson left the General about midnight under the impression that Mahomed Shureef's fort would be immediately attacked and the Commissariat one reinforced.

A letter was written by order (by Capt. Bellew)[1] to assure Lieut. Warren that he should receive reinforcements by two o'clock in the morning. Capt. Mackenzie held his (the King's Commissariat) fort until his ammunition was entirely expended, and then cut his way through the town; but in doing so was wounded in three places. Strange to say, this officer owed his life to beating a woman! He told

[1] Deputy Assistant Quartermaster-General of Elphinstone's force.

his people to abandon their property and save their lives. A woman put down her child to save her pots and pans; and expostulation being of little effect, and time most precious, Mackenzie drew his sword to strike her with the flat of it, by which means he had it in his hand when he was attacked immediately afterwards.

Trevor's tower has been burnt. Had reinforcements and ammunition been sent to Trevor's tower and Mackenzie's fort, they might have held out for ever against any force the rebels could have brought against them. The Hazir Bashes refused to stay to defend them, because they saw they must be sacrificed, and that no reinforcements were sent. Had they arrived, the Kuzzilbashes would have declared openly in our favour, with Khan Shireen Khan at their head; but unless supported by us, they dreaded giving offence to the insurgents.

Another party has been sent out with guns; it is said they are to fire the city, but most likely it will be a mere demonstration. Such it has proved. The guns were sent to take possession of the Lahore gate; they got not quite to Mahmood Khan's fort, and had to come back again.

The enemy have now possession of the Commissariat fort, the fort opposite the Bazaar fort, or Mahommed Shurref's and the Shah bagh; the two latter posts appear to have been left unoccupied for the enemy's especial advantage.

The only mortar we have being a five-and-half inch one, had little more effect than a pop-gun of large calibre.

A gun has been sent to attempt to blow open the gate of the Shah bagh, and thence to the city.

A large party of horsemen have shown themselves coming down the Siah Sung hill: the cavalry are sent to look after them. Mahmood Khan's fort is occupied by the enemy, who are to be shelled out, it is said; but we have been throwing shells into the small fort opposite the Bazaar[1] (Mahommed Shureef's) since 12 o'clock, and now at 4 they are still at it, and seem to have done nothing.

A Kulassy of Capt. Maule's has just come in from the Kohistan half-naked: he reports that the Kohistanees are all up; that Maule and Wheeler were killed at Kar Durrah, and that they were overpowered.

After we had, as we thought, settled poor Sturt for the night, between 8 and 9 o'clock, Capt. Lawrence came to see him and ask his advice. Sturt wished to have communicated with the General on the defence of the cantonments, and, ill as he was, he had written a

[1] i.e. The cantonments bazaar, situated at the south-western corner.

letter to him; but thinking that advice from so young an officer might not be relished, he, notwithstanding my remonstrances on the subject, tore it up. About 10 o'clock, Capt. Warburton, the Shah's Topshee Bashee and Lieut. Eyre, Deputy Commissary of Ordnance, came; and as they had received information that there are men posted outside the gate of the captured fort, with matchlocks all ready, the plan in agitation of blowing open the gate with a bag of powder would not answer: they, therefore, with Sturt, decided on getting the two nine-pounders into the bastion, and on setting to work forthwith to cut the embrasures to fit them; and between 2 and 3 o'clock in the morning was fixed upon as the time to commence playing on the fort to breach it, and at the same time to throw in a proportion of shells to create confusion. The place to be taken by assault. If this does not succeed, we shall probably have to retreat to Jellalabad. Sturt strongly advises the troops all being thrown into the Bala Hissar, and the cantonments being abandoned until we get up reinforcements; but the cry is, How can we abandon the cantonments that have cost us so much money?

The enemy's forces are estimated at from 1,500 to 2,000. Brig. Shelton is expected in from the Bala Hissar, where they are said to be short of provisions. Here we got six seers of ottah for the rupee yesterday, but today none is procurable. The servants are to get half rations from the commissariat tomorrow.

At the Bala Hissar two companies!!! were warned for service under Capt. Corri, 54th, for the purpose of entering the town to cause a diversion during the expected attack which it was understood there was about to be made from the cantonments. However, it was, as usual, only one of the theoretical plans so often talked of, and so little practised. Conolly, Troup, and Hay had gone there for the purpose of assisting with counsel; but there was 'great cry and little wool' and nothing was done.

The enemy were busied in hundreds all day in carrying off our stores, all which we plainly saw from cantonments.[1] The troops retired by order of Gen. Elphinstone, to my no small surprise, for the enemy had begun to run out from a broken bastion; but when they found our men retreating, they took courage, and no more left the fort, on which shot and shell kept playing all day. After stating this,

[1] 'The godown fort', wrote the Paymaster, Captain Johnson, 'was this day something similar to a large ants' nest . . . each man taking away with him as much as he could carry—and to this we were all eye-witnesses.'

it is unnecessary to add that Sturt's suggestions had not been acted on.

When the 44th retreated from Mahommed Shureef's fort, all were in amazement; the 37th asked leave to go and take it, but were not, permitted to do so. The Sipahees are grumbling at short allowance, and not being allowed to do anything. The 37th were anxious to be employed in recovering the Commissariat fort, though no actual proposition to that effect was officially made to the General.

On this day, a report was carried to the King and Conolly that the rebels had mined from the Shor Bazaar to immediately under H.M.'s palace, which said mine was to be sprung the same evening. The King instantly left the palace, and took up his abode at the Gate of the Haram Serai, where he remained during the rest of the siege; and all day, seated at a window commanding a fine view of cantonments, telescope in hand, watched anxiously the course of passing events in that place. He was at that time quite sunk into a state of despondency, and would gladly seize any opportunity of asking the opinion of any of the officers as to what was likely to be the issue of the struggle. He put off for the time all the insignia of royalty, made the officers sit by him on chairs, and seemed quite *gobrowed* (an expressive eastern term, to be rendered something between dumbfounded and at one's wits' end). The Shah's conduct in the particular of the chairs is the more worthy of remark, as he had been in the habit of keeping the officers for hours standing with folded hands silently in his presence, and then ungraciously dismissing them without even a passing remark. He now sent to each Sahib a warm silk resais and a pillow, which were very acceptable, as they were all starving with cold.

November 6th: Major Kershaw, Lieut. Hobhouse, and eleven soldiers of the 13th Lt. In. (who had been left at Cabul in consequence of illness) this day volunteered their services.

Sturt, having fretted himself half-mad at everything going wrong, determined, weak and ill as he was, to go out and do his duty. He is the only engineer officer at Cabul. He was unable to dress, but went out in his shirt and pyjamia [*sic*] to the works. Although he was out himself a little after 6 o'clock, he could not get things or people into their places until 10. General Elphinstone gave him permission to make any arrangements he considered as safe from chance of failure for taking the small fort; but when he had with great exertion got three nine-pounders and two twenty-four pound howitzers at work (the latter across the road), Major Thain was sent to him to desire he would be careful not to expend ammunition, as powder was scarce! there being at the time a sufficiency for a twelvemonth's siege! However, Sturt made no alteration in his proceedings, and by 12 o'clock an excellent breach was made, the bastion being thrown down and a great part of the curtain, so that ladders were not required: the gate was blown in at the same time by Capt. Bellew, Assist.Adjt.-Gen.[1] There was a small crack in the rampart near Sale's bastion, of which I used to take advantage, as a stepping-stone to enable me to see what was going on; and from my position I saw a storming party ascend the breach, under a heavy fire, with a commendable steadiness and great alacrity: they quickly drove the enemy from their stations, who then escaped through the wicket into the Shah's garden. The storming party was commanded by Major Griffith, of the 37th N.I., consisting of the light company of the Queen's 44th, Lieut. Hobhouse and ten men of H.M. 13th Lt. Inf., one company of 5th N.I., one company 37th N.I.; in all about 150 men. Lieut. Raban, 44th, killed while waving his sword on the highest point of the breach: Mr. Deas, 5th, wounded; I believe we had nineteen killed and several wounded; amongst the latter, one of the 13th. The flag taken from the enemy was waved on the crest of the breach by a Sipahee of the 37th, who captured it, and who was promoted for the act. He and a havildar of the same corps, though belonging to the rear company were, with Lieut. Raban, the first into the fort. But few of the enemy were found killed; but it is difficult to estimate the numbers of their slain, as they are so particular regarding Moslem burial that they always, when practicable, drag the bodies away. Great numbers escaped to the hills behind, which were quickly covered with horsemen, from 2,000 to 3,000 men. A party of Anderson's horse charged straight up the hill (just to the left of the gorge leading to the lake) in most gallant style, and drove the enemy along the ridge to the extreme left. Meantime, the 5th cavalry rode along the foot of the hill to the left, and charged up at that end; by which manoeuvre the enemy were hemmed in, in the centre of the two cavalry corps, when a very severe encounter took place. From the top of our house we saw everything distinctly; the gleaming of their swords in the sun, and the fire of their pistols and matchlocks: fresh horsemen came pouring on to the assistance of the enemy from the back of the hill; they buried our cavalry and Anderson's horse, who, overpowered by numbers and a most galling

[1] A slip on Lady Sale's part. Bellew was D.A.Q.M.G. The Assistant Adjutant-General was Captain Grant.

fire, were forced along the ridge to the spot whence the first charge took place.

The Affghans have many advantages over our troops; one consists in dropping their men fresh for combat; each horseman takes a foot soldier up behind him, and drops him when he is arrived at the spot he is required to fire from. Their horsemen are either gentlemen or yeomen (as we should denominate them), all well mounted, and their baggage ponies can manage the hills much better than our cavalry horses; in fact, the Affghan horses seem to me to climb about with as much unconcern as goats do. As regards pistols, we are on a par, as most of theirs have been presents from the Posha Khana [*the armoury*]; but their juzails carry much further than our muskets, and, whilst they are out of range of our fire, theirs tells murderously on us.

A standard bearer with a white flag was killed; he was evidently a person of some consequence, from the great anxiety evinced to obtain possession of his body. There were two red flags in another division.

Capt. Anderson distinguished himself, killing four men with his own hand; he rode up the gorge to challenge the enemy again, but they had the advantage of position, and would not come down.

The enemy continued to crown the heights: our guns were out of range, and the shot fell short. We had infantry out in skirmishing order, but the whole was little more than a very exciting and provoking spectacle; for we made little impression, although the whole of our cavalry was out: so cavalry, infantry, guns and all, came back again, and soon after the enemy came down the hill, some evidently returning to the Shah bagh, and others dispersing more to the left, and probably returning to the city.

Lady Macnaghten told me to-day that Sir William had written to inform Sale that we had been in siege since the 2nd, and to request his return with the force under his command; to leave the sick and wounded in safety at Gundamuk, under charge of the troops there. To this the General[1] assented, and signed the letter; but afterwards he said it would be abandoning the sick and baggage, and refused to recall Sale's brigade.

I was asked if I could send a letter from Sir William to Sale, through Sturt's influence with the natives; but if, with secret service

[1] i.e. Elphinstone. This little incident is typical of the confusion caused by a command divided between the Politicals and the military.

money at his command, the Envoy cannot bribe a messenger, how are poor people like us to do so?

Sir William has given one of the Kuzzilbash chiefs 50,000 rupees to raise a diversion in our favour, and has promised him two lakhs more if he succeeds.

The insurgent chiefs have set up a king, and a wuzeer; they went to the mosque, and read the fatcha or prayer, for the reigning monarch. Several of the Moollahs refused to recognise the name of Shah Zeman; they said they would allow that of Shah Shoojah as a legitimate monarch. There was a long and wordy dispute, but Shah Mahommed Zeman seems at present to possess most power in Cabul. This is not the blind Shah Zeman, Shah Shoojah's brother, but a relation of the Ameer Dost Mahommed. He is an old man, and said to be the son of an elder brother of Dost Mahommed's, and used to be called the Nawaub. He has struck coin in his own name.

Abdoollah Khan has sent a messenger to treat with the King, who replied that he would receive no such low person and that some person of respectability must be sent. The King is also said to have seized the man who stabbed Sturt, and to have declared his intent to put him to death; but just now I believe he dares not do so.

This day there was a report that Sir Alexander Burnes and his brother were still living, but that the people in whose power they were, were treating for a very large ransom.

Capt. Warburton left two guns in the city at his house; the Affghans have taken possession of them (six-pounders), and use them against us either with their own balls, or ours returned to us in that manner. They hammer our nine-pound shot into an egg shape. One of them that fell in Sturt's compound attracted attention, as we all supposed that they could not be hammered to fit other guns.

This day, General Elphinstone wrote to the Envoy to state that we were in want of ammunition, requesting him to endeavour to make arrangements with the enemy!

Capt. Bellew told me that the General has at length agreed that Sale's brigade shall be recalled. Had we more men, a brigade might be sent out on the hill, to punish the enemy who defy us there.

The men are greatly harassed; their duty is very heavy, and they have no cover night and day, all being on the ramparts. The weather is cold, particularly at night.

There was a good store of grain in the captured fort, but very little of it was brought into cantonments by the Commissariat, though a great deal found itself into the Bunneahs' shops, or was carried off by the Sipahees and camp-followers.

A great quantity of wheat has been brought in today and yesterday from the villages, and we are promised further supplies.

A note from Thain mentions that Sale has been sent for, but from the very cautious wording of the order, it appears doubtful whether he can take such responsibility upon himself as it implies. He is, if he can leave his sick and wounded and baggage in perfect safety, to return to Cabul, if he can do so without endangering the force under his command. Now, in obeying an order of this kind, if Sale succeeds and all is right, he will doubtless be a very fine fellow; but if he meets with a reverse, he will be told, 'You were not to come up unless you could do so safely!'

There has been much talk of bringing Brig. Shelton from the Bala Hissar, into cantonments, to aid with counsel and prowess; the plan is, however, for the present abandoned.

The troops in the Bala Hissar are better off than we are, as there are yet some supplies in the shops there, though at an exorbitant rate.

Despatches have been sent for reinforcements from Kandahar. If Gen. Nott's brigade had not proceeded on their way to the provinces further than the Kojuk pass, they are to return.

Accounts have been received that Codrington's corps at Charikar is surrounded. Capt. Rattray, the political agent there, and Lieut. Salisbury, killed. Capt. Codrington and the other officers wounded, as also Major Pottinger, political agent.[1]

There has been great talk of withdrawing the troops from the Bala Hissar into cantonments; but if this were done, the King, with his 800 ladies (wives, daughters etc., and their attendants), would follow and we should be soon starved out. If we make an inglorious retreat into Hindostan, he will still accompany us; and as we brought him to the country, we must stand by him.

When there was first an intention of building for the army at the Company's expense, Capt. Sturt gave it as his decided opinion, (which opinion is on record in the letter book of his office, in a letter to Sir A. Burnes,) that the garrisons should be placed in the Upper Bala Hissar, from whence (with plenty of ammunition and food, which might always be procured from the city, either purchased from friends or taken *zubberdust* from the enemy) we never could be dislodged. A

1 Charikar was an outpost in the Kohistan. Captain Codrington's wound was mortal and he died at Charikar.

large outlay (I write from memory, and therefore do not name the sum) was expended in commencing barracks, bombproofs, etc.; and last, not least, a new wing was added to a palace for the Envoy, and another, to make all square, was laid out, when the King sent to say he would neither have the Envoy nor the troops in the Bala Hissar: so all the money spent was thrown away, and the King had the new wing and the whole palace thrown down because it was originally erected by the Dost.

The camp was pitched at Siah Sung, but that site wouldn't answer for a cantonment for many reasons detailed by Sturt in his public letter, which I propose appending to my Journal.[1] I shall, therefore, only notice two of them,—the distance from good water, and the whole spot being commanded by the heights that surround it, except on one side, which is a morass, and from that cause not particularly healthy at some seasons.

There was ground on the further side of the city, but that would not answer, as should an insurrection occur in Cabul, it would cut off our communication with Jellalabad.

Eventually the King gave up a garden or orchard, the present site of cantonments, with water at hand, good and plentiful, and always procurable by digging two feet for it in any direction.[2]

Sturt urges the absolute necessity of our now withdrawing our forces from the cantonments into the Bala Hissar, but is still met by the cry of 'How can we abandon the good buildings and property?'

The ammunition might be buried and concealed, the guns spiked etc., but a great deal of the former might be sent into the Bala Hissar by the cavalry carrying each man a proportion on his horse nightly, and many of the latter might be taken to the citadel.

To Sergt. Deane of the engineers' department, the army are very greatly indebted for his great personal exertions in getting in grain. He is a particularly intelligent man, and very superior to his present station in life; and the fluency with which he speaks Persian enables him to pick up information[3] and also to go about at times in disguise for the same purpose.

[1] This letter was lost, together with all the rest of the documents of the army. [F.S.]

[2] But, as Lieutenant Eyre wrote, 'likewise full of impediment, to the movements of artillery and cavalry, being in any places flooded, and every where closely interlocked by deep water cuts. . . . Our cantonment at Cabul, whether we look to its situation or its construction, must ever be spoken of as a disgrace to our military skill and judgment.'

[3] Deane, like Captain Warburton, had married an Afghan wife.

31

If we can only continue to obtain provisions as we have done for the last two days, we shall be able to hold out on half rations, and in another month, it is said, the Kohistanees cannot touch us for the snow, which fell heavily on the hills last night.

We had rain here late in the evening, and at night; and this morning I saw a great increase in the snow on the hills.

In the Bala Hissar, Lieut. Melville having recovered from his wound sufficiently to do his duty, was sent down to take charge of the Lahote gate of the fort, which was now the only opening into the Bala Hissar, the others having been built up with almost solid masonry.

The troops there were isolated in a fort closely besieged, actually without a single case of amputating or other surgical instruments amongst them, and hardly a grain of medicine!—most culpable negligence, as they might easily have been sent from the cantonments, though a little foresight would have suggested their being taken there with the troops; and they might easily have been got ready during the time they were under arms—more than an hour—before they marched.

There has been constant firing for the last day or two on the city side of the fort, and the enemy have made several unsuccessful attempts to carry off the two guns that are lying beneath the walls. Food is already scarce in the bazaars and although plenty is stored up in the private houses of the natives, yet in the shops the price of two seers of wheat or two and a half is a rupee.

The Sipahees complain bitterly of the severity of the weather, particularly at night, and above sixty men are in hospital at the Bala Hissar already, beside the wounded; they are attacked with pneumonia, which carries them off in the course of a couple of days. The King sent strict orders to Melville at the gate, to allow no one to pass either in or out without a pass from either the Wuzeer or Conolly, except the surwans in charge of the grazing cattle which go out at 8 a.m. and return at 2, protected by a resallah of the King's Sikh regiment: in case of an alarm from without, a flag is ordered to be waved from the ramparts, on which signal all the cattle are immediately to come in. The above mentioned resallah are, without any exception, the worst set-up and the most disorderly body of troops calling themselves a regiment that can be imagined: their horses are ill-conditioned, their arms and accoutrements nominal, as each man dresses as he pleases, a stick with a bayonet on the top being the sole offensive weapon of many of them. And this is the imperial guard of the monarch of Affghanistan! Besides this regiment his majesty has with him in the fort, of his own troops (not reckoning those of the subsidiarised force), his orderly regiment (Campbell's), 400 Juzailchees, and 500 of another Hindostanee regt. The orderly regiment are certainly better men of the sort (not being the Company's soldiers) than are usually met with, although they did run away in the city on the 2nd., but it was not until they had lost 200 men and fought gallantly. Campbell himself is the King's right hand man.

From an idea of an insurrection being about to take place among the Arabs (who compose a large portion of the inhabitants), a proposal was set on foot for turning all the Affghans, etc. out of the Bala Hissar, and taking all provisions found for the use of the troops both there and in cantonments. This, as well as every other energetic measure proposed, was knocked on the head, either by the King or the politicals, and, instead of turning out all useless hands, an order was issued to allow no woman to pass the gate unless supplied with a pass, as an idea had got afloat that they were about to turn out their wives and children ere a general massacre of the troops took place. However, in lieu of an insurrection, food becoming very scarce, all the natives became clamorous for permission to leave the fort, and go into the city with their wives and children,—'a consummation devoutly to be wished', and to ensure which it had been good policy to have paid them a high price for their houses and grain, etc. This, the King positively refused to allow, but ordered a Shah-Gazee to join Melville at the gate, and having examined them one by one to see that they carried no arms, to allow females to pass; but no man to go on any account. In this way, in three days were passed out 750 women and their children, which was at least a good riddance!

November 7th: I did not go to bed till after Mr. Eyre went away this morning: he came at a little after midnight in consequence of some frivolous objections of the General's, based I believe mostly on Capt. Bellew's doubts as to whether the trees in the garden next the Commissariat fort were planted in lines parallel to the wall or not. Now Bellew always has an 'observation' to throw in, or 'begs to suggest' something. He had acknowledged he had never been in this garden, although Sturt had; neither could he be made to understand that it was the custom of the country to plant the trees in lines parallel with the outer walls: neither could he comprehend, that even if a tree intervened, a shot would destroy it from the heavy nine-pounders. These trees were not gigantic English oaks, the growth of a century; but fruit trees.

The heavy iron nines would now have proved their utility against the fort, but the old objection of the difficulty of transporting them over bad roads still exists; an iron nine cannot be as portable as a brass six-pounder, but the eighteen pounders would not have given much more trouble than the nines did on the march up, and would have done us good service had we them here. Capt. Abbott wrote for 3 eighteen-pounders; the military board made it a case of arithmetic, and sent 6 nines; and as they had to be taken up the hills by hand, a little more manual labour would have transported the others also over the Afghanee mountains.

I often hear the Affghans designated as cowards: they are a fine manly-looking set, and I can only suppose it arises from the British idea among civilised people that assassination is a cowardly act. The Affghans never scruple to use their long knives for that purpose, *ergo* they are cowards; but they show no cowardice in standing as they do against guns without using any themselves, and in escalading and taking forts which we cannot re-take. The Affghans of the capital are a little more civilised, but the country gentlemen and their retainers are, I fancy, much the same kind of people as those Alexander encountered.

The Juzailchees were sent out to skirmish: they attacked the Shah bagh, and cleared the west end of it; they then joined Major Thain, who, with a squadron of horse and two companies of infantry, attacked a garden beyond it, drove the enemy out with great slaughter, and burnt the garden house. Lieut. Eyre at the same time, through a small opening in the wall of the Shah-bagh, immediately under the captured fort, played with a six-pounder upon the gate of the garden. Not being supported, however, these advantages were lost, and the enemy being re-inforced in great numbers, the above troops were forced to retreat, having lost a considerable number of men; *par exemple*, fifteen of the Juzailchees out of ninety-five were left on the field. I have not the actual numbers of the Europeans and Sipahees who were slain.

The gun was saved with great difficulty, and here a great fault was committed in sending one gun only. In the Marquis of Hasting's[1] time an order was published prohibiting a single gun being sent out,

[1] Governor-General, 1812–23. The reason for the order was that a single gun was liable to be so overworked that it would become too hot to fire.

in consequence of the disastrous consequence attending it being un-supported during the Nepalese war. But all seems confusion here. Those who, at the head of affairs, ought to have been directing every-thing, appear to be in consternation. General Elphinstone from his first arrival in the country was in ill health, which gradually increased on him, till his mind became nearly as much enervated as his body; and so conscious was he of his own state, that he had written to Government to give up the command, and also to Gen. Nott at Kandahar to come up and take his place until a new commander of the forces was appointed.

We are now in circumstances which require a man of energy to cope with them. Major Thain is said to be a good adviser, but un-fortunately it is not always in the multitude of counsellors that there is wisdom; and so many proffered their advice and crossed his, that Thain withdrew his, and only now answers such questions as are put to him.

November 8th: At four in the morning a sharp firing was heard, for which at the time we could not account, but afterwards found that it proceeded from the captured fort, which the enemy had attempted to mine and re-capture. They had succeeded in making a large hole, but being repulsed they set the fort on fire. At daybreak, finding Sturt's servant still in the verandah, and knowing that his master was to have been up at half-past four, I went to the door to inquire, and found that the General, or rather his advisers, had decided that nothing was to be done.

The enemy are using our guns against us, throwing shot into cantonments from Mahmood Khan's fort.

Our men are so over-worked that it is intended to give them rest to-day.

Sturt went out early this morning, and found the garden next the Commissariat fort unoccupied; he immediately took the sappers under Lieut. Laing with fifty of the Juzailchees under Mackenzie to cover them, and sent for two companies of Sipahees as a covering party whilst they pulled down the wall, which was quickly accom-plished.

There is a report that we are to be attacked in cantonments to-night. Sturt went to Gen. Elphinstone and Brig. Anquetil, who both gave him *carte blanche,* and desired that all his instructions should be obeyed. He has accordingly placed 15 guns in position. We have only two artillery officers in cantonments that are available, now Waller is wounded; they are Eyre and Warburton. We have no laboratory men,—no other engineer officer than Sturt, who, weak as he is, has to do everything.

When we came into cantonments last November, Sir Willoughby Cotton commanded the forces in Affghanistan; and Sale, as the second here and commandant in cantonments, had the troops paraded and their posts assigned, in case of any sudden attack. These troops (the 1st brigade), who knew their posts, are now far from us, and no arrangement of a similar kind has been made since their departure; so Sturt has had the officers told off to their several stations, has paraded them at them, and goes his rounds before he goes to bed to see that they are all at their posts.

It is said that Mohun Lull[1] has named the man who killed poor Sir Alexander Burnes; he also writes that there are only 500 Kohistanees in the city, and that otherwise all is going on well in the Kuzzilbash quarter of the city, where he resides.

It was reported to-day that the city was on fire, but it proved to be a village fired by the Kohistanees.

Conolly writes from the Bala Hissar, accounting for the firing we heard this morning. An attack was made on the Bala Hissar, which was repulsed: the enemy were seized with a panic, fancied they were attacked from the rear, and began to fight amongst themselves; cries of *Aman* were heard in the cantonments by several persons besides myself. Conolly also writes that he has not only heard that we are to be attacked to-night, but that the enemy are making up bhoosa bags with which to fill up the ditch.

Sturt is gone to lie down to recruit his strength, knowing that I never dose now till daylight, but sit up to watch passing events, and give the alarm if need be, and have kept my nightly watch ever since the insurrection commenced. Our troops as yet are staunch; and if we are attacked, and succeed in repelling the enemy, we shall be able to keep our own until Sale's brigade arrives.

The enemy showed to-day on the heights, in force about 3000; but we cannot cope with them, so content ourselves by throwing shrapnell at them. Eyre threw some with great precision; the distance

[1] Burnes's *munshi* or private secretary, a highly intelligent Indian who remained in Kabul after the insurrection and supplied the British with useful information. Macnaghten used him as a go-between in negotiations with the Afghans. Lady Sale is quite inconsistent in her spelling of his name.

was, however, very great, and we consequently did little execution. We also greatly feel the want of laboratory men to cut fuses, etc.

Sturt asked for a party to occupy the village of Behmaru, but it was not given. The Envoy was anxious to secure this place, but all was in vain; and as we neglected our advantages, the enemy availed themselves of them, and Meer Musjudee threw himself and 1,000 followers into it. We have thereby lost 900 maunds of ottah, which was paid for.

Two forts near the village are in our possession.

An attack expected at about 3 o'clock this afternoon.

Brig. Shelton came in from the Bala Hissar with six companies of the Shah's 6th, one horse artillery gun, and one of the mountain train.

The people in cantonments expect wonders from his prowess and military judgment. I am of a different opinion, knowing that he is not a favourite with either his officers or men, and is most anxious to get back to Hindostan. I must, however, do him the justice to say that I believe he possesses much personal bravery; but, notwithstanding, I consider his arrival as a dark cloud overshadowing us. Most glad shall I be to find that, by his energy, the General is roused up to active measures. It is perhaps, a part of his complaint (but, nevertheless, equally unfortunate for us), that Gen. Elphinstone vacillates on every point. His own judgment appears to be good, but he is swayed by the last speaker; and Capt. Grant's cold cautiousness, and Capt. Bellew's doubts on every subject, induce our chief to alter his opinions and plans every moment.

At the Bala Hissar they began to be much cramped in their correspondence with cantonments which became very limited; a hurkaru stealing out at night, and returning with an answer early in the morning, being now the only means of communication; and the same man never went for more than five days without being either killed or confined.

The Affghans, having persons who can read English, French, and Latin, were aware of all our secrets.

Mohun Lull and the Naib Shureef were our newsgivers from the city, and always gave intelligence of the arrival of any new chief or body of troops; also doing, or saying they were doing, all in their power to enter into some sort of terms. The King is gradually getting worse and worse, and has quite lost all his self-possession. He has warned the females of his zenana (amounting in number to 860) that in the event of the cantonments falling into the hands of the rebels he should administer poison to them all! At least these are the reports he gathered from his few immediate attendants; how far they may be relied on as true, or whether they are merely set afloat to blind us to his own share in the insurrection, it is difficult to say.

Brig. Shelton made over the command to Major Ewart, 54th N.I., and left the Bala Hissar at 4 a.m., and arrived in cantonments before day break without meeting any opposition on the road.

On this day the men at the Bala Hissar were put on half rations in consequence of the large supplies of ottah required to be sent to cantonments, and which Capt. Kirby is getting stored as fast as he can.

Ammunition, by the directions of the Major-Gen., is now beginning to be thrown into the Bala Hissar, under charge of Capt. Walker, commanding detachment of 4th local horse, who has orders to bring back all the ottah he can collect in time to return before daylight; but, owing to the men (who are half starved in cantonments) always, immediately on depositing their loads, leaving their ranks to forage for themselves, not more than half the loads usually arrived.

We now began to bombard the city in earnest from Nicholl's battery,[1] beginning at eight o'clock every evening and continuing until eleven, firing at intervals of about ten minutes from the $5\frac{1}{2}$ inch mortar, and the nine-pounder. The effect was beautiful to us in the cantonments; but it is to be feared that was almost the only effect it had, as, from all we could learn, four or five were the usual average of victims, being a very small number for so great an expenditure of ammunition. Amenoolah Khan's house was the principal object of attack, and one or two shells went completely through it; but as, immediately on the shelling commencing, he and all his family left it for some other residence, the loss of a few of his horses was the utmost injury he suffered.

Regarding Brig. Shelton's view of affairs, it may be remarked that, from the first of his arrival in the country, he appears to have greatly disliked it, and his disgust has now considerably increased. His mind is set on getting back to Hindostan; and it is worthy of remark that from the first, on going into the Bala Hissar, he desired Capt. Nicholl to fill all the ammunition boxes, as fast as it was expended, with flour (ottah), to be ready for provision in case of retreat.

November 10th: Having bullied us with impunity yesterday, the enemy

[1] Captain Nicholl's Horse Artillery were posted in the Bala Hissar.

again showed themselves on the hills, and rushed with a shout into the village of Behmaru, which they occupy and vacate as the whim takes them. They also lined the Siah Sung hills, came down to the river, and kept up such a heavy fire that we could not keep our gun outside the rear gate and we had to bring it in.

The enemy are in possession of several forts near us. The 44th and part of every corps were out under Shelton, but considerable delay took place, and it was only on the Envoy assuring the General that he would take the responsibility of the act on himself that the troops were sent out.

They attacked the Rikabashees' fort. By some blunder, Bellew did not go to the gate, but blew in the wicket. Lieut. Bird of the Shah's 6th, and a few others, got in, when the enemy's cavalry charged, and the 44th turned—'Sauve qui peut.' Here Shelton proved a trump. Cool and brave, he with much difficulty succeeded in rallying the men, to save those inside, and when they did return they fought like lions. It was a very fearful affair as witnessed by nearly all in cantonments; and the men, both Europeans and natives, in the second attack behaved with undaunted courage. Bird's account of the affair is, that when they got in they experienced a most decided opposition, but the enemy rushing out at the opposite gate, they took advantage of it, when abandoned by their comrades, to close the entrance securing the chain with a bayonet. The enemy, seeing the success of their own charge outside, rallied, and, cutting a hole in the door with their long knives, they got out the bayonet and opened the gate again. Bird and one Sipahee, 37th, and one or two others retreated to a room in which there were two horses, and through a small opening kept up a sharp fire, luckily killing the few who saw them enter, and afterwards picking off all who passed in their way. Above thirty were thus killed, fifteen of whom fell to Bird's share, and six to that of the Sipahee of the 37th, for which the Sipahee was afterwards promoted, by Bird's especial request to Major Griffith. Col. Mackrell went to the door, to look as if relief was coming, disregarding Bird's advice to remain with him coolly and steadily till they got re-inforcements. The Colonel was wounded and fell, and the cavalry cut him up dreadfully. He was wounded in both legs, one below the knee, the other on the thigh; he had three cuts in the back, two toes cut off, and three or four cuts on the arm, which was taken off immediately after he was brought in. Poor man! He said 'This is not battle, it is murder!' He still lives, but is not likely to survive [*nor did he*]; better he had been shot at once. To

39

persons accustomed to a civilized warfare, these details must be revolting. Even a dead enemy is never passed without a cut at the body. They cry 'Aman' themselves, but never show mercy to Kaffirs.

Capt. MacCrea was in the fort all but one arm, by which they seized him and dragged him out: his was a very similar fate, but his sufferings were less protracted, for he was dead when found, with, I believe, his skull cloven.

Poor Westmacott of the 37th was cut to pieces near the Kirkee. We must have killed a great number of the enemy. Mr. Bird says he himself saw above 100 killed, but that as fast as a man fell, others came and dragged him away. Major Scott in vain tried to rally the 44th: excited to tears he called for volunteers to follow him, when a private, named Stuart was the only man who offered to go, and for which, on its reaching the Envoy's notice, he was, by Sir William's earnest entreaty to Shelton, promoted sergeant.

When the storming party came up the second time under Shelton, a cruel scene took place. The enemy could not have had less than 150 killed and wounded. We had ourselves fully that number. There were 26 killed and 28 wounded of the 44th; above 50 killed and wounded of the 37th. I did not hear the number of the Shah's 6th, and have not access to records; not that they are kept very correctly, for Sturt was never returned as a wounded officer.

The conduct of the 37th is highly spoken of: they drove the enemy (who had got on the top of a bastion) with their bayonets clean over the side, where they were received on the bayonets of the 44th.

The dreadful slaughter of our men is attributable to a desperate rush of Affghan cavalry. It is supposed that some very influential person was in the fort, and has been killed. A body, richly dressed, was found, but the head was carried away. This they do when they cannot take the body, as the head then receives Mussulman burial, which the Affghans are very particular in observing. A horse was taken, and a sword that was much bent; both are said to have been recognised as having lately been in possession of Moollah Mobend of Zoormut. Four other forts were taken, from which the enemy ran on the capture of the Rikabashees'.

Shelton led the troops out toward the Siah Sung Hill, where the enemy was in force, and where Eyre did great execution with two horse artillery guns. The troops remained out till dark, when, having completely overawed the enemy, they returned. Three times the sappers were ordered (and as often countermanded) for the purpose of blowing up these forts and firing them. At length it was decided to keep the Rikabashees' fort; and to occupy it. There is known to be a large store of boussa and lucern there; and we hope also to find grain. Zulfar Khan's fort was also occupied by us. These forts were not above 400 yards from cantonments. The furthest fort is memorable as the spot where a murder was committed not long ago, and was perhaps 1,000 yards distant; of this the four bastions were blown up, and the place itself fired. As Brig. Shelton has always been supposed to be greatly disliked by his men, it has excited much astonishment that the men of the 44th were all enquiring after the 'little Brig.', as they call him. They say they are ready to be led to any work there may be for them to do.

This event has already produced its effect. Khojeh Meer of Behmaru has sent his salaam to know our pleasure. The Envoy's reply was, 'If you wish to keep your two forts, sell us grain.'

The events of to-day must have astonished the enemy after our supineness, and shown them that, when we have a mind to do so, we can punish them.

Our spirits are raised and depressed by the barometer of public events. Could anything have roused us at first to action, the insurrection had been crushed in the bud. When the 44th turned and fled to-day, the Gen. asked the Envoy if he was prepared to retreat to Jellalabad as to-night [sic]; but Sir William replied that he would do his duty, and never desert the King; and, if the army left him, would die at his post!

Now we are uppermost we hold up our heads, and hope not to have to sculk into the Bala Hissar without baggage. Were Sturt's advice taken, we should nightly send ammunition there, and, when a sufficiency is conveyed, all make one bold night march in very light marching order, just what we can carry on our horses. In there, we can be lodged (not comfortably, I grant) in the houses of the inhabitants, who would be well paid for vacating them. They have laid in their stores for the winter, which would be bought at any price—and then we might defy all Affghanistan for any time. However, it seems hopeless to think on such subjects, for those who with a great end in view might be brought to abandon public works and property for a time will not consent to part with their own! A horse, with a handsome silver-mounted saddle, etc., has been brought in by Lieut. Vanrenen, who sold it for 120 rupees, to someone who fancied it because it was supposed to have belonged to a chief.

Sturt's recovery and energy appear little short of miraculous; he nearly possesses the power of ubiquity. He cannot yet mount his own horses, and must astonish my little Cape horse, for he gallops him the whole day from bastion to gate, and gate to bastion, laying guns, and off like a shot; his aim being to show the enemy that all our batteries and gates had guns in position, which we could fire nearly simultaneously,—for they know how weak we are in artillery officers.

General Nott may be here with his brigade in three weeks; we have plenty of ammunition, and if we can get grain we may hold out till they arrive.

November 11th: Two regiments were sent to cover the foraging party collecting grain from the captured forts. 600 maunds of wheat have been brought in, boussa, etc.; this gives us three and a half days' provisions.

Bad news from Candahar. A party of the Shah's troops under Lieut. Crawford, who were escorting state prisoners, are said to have been attacked and cut to pieces, and it is feared that Capt. Sanders (Engineers) was with them. Capt. Skinner is reported to have been killed in endeavouring to escape out of the city in women's clothes. A dog of Col. Dennie's, and another of Major Kershaw's, having come into cantonments, has caused much excitement: as we have not heard from Sale's camp for some time, we think it may be a proof that they are on their way back. . . .

Neither of these last two rumours was correct. Skinner was being safely hidden in Kabul by Afghan friends. Despite the return of the dogs, Sale's Brigade was still marching away from the capital and on towards India.

November 11th: We hear that to-morrow night the enemy intend to take the cantonments and that they have fifteen ladders to escalade with, and bags filled with boussa to cross by filling up the ditch. Our men are all in high spirits.

Meer Musjudee has sent to Sir William to say he will come in to treat; his vakeel was in cantonments yesterday. The Ghilzyes have been (it is said) brought off by the Envoy. It was a re-inforcement of 1,000 Ghazees that joined the enemy yesterday at the Rikabashees' fort; it is supposed that they suffered very severely in the action.

November 12th: Arrangements have been made by Sir William with Meer Musjudee, who is to receive 60,000 rupees if he brings in

Codrington's regiment; he, poor man, has died of his wounds.[1] The expected attack on the cantonments has not taken place, but there was a good deal of firing all night, and shells were thrown from one o'clock at Mahmood Khan's fort.

November 13th: The Ghilzye chiefs expressed a wish to treat: however that might be, the enemy showed themselves on their favourite heights (Behmaru); they are supposed to be re-inforcements from Zoormut. They took two guns up with them which they played upon cantonments. On this Brig. Shelton was sent with a force against them. It was with great difficulty the Envoy persuaded the General and the Brigadier to consent to a force going out; and it was late before the troops were ready.

There were three columns; two companies of the 37th led the left column under Thain, with the 44th in the centre and Shah's 6th in rear. The right column was under Scott, the reserve under Major Swayne.

Civilians and women are fond of honour and glory and perhaps do not sufficiently temper valour with discretion.

It appears that the Affghans attribute our forbearance, whatever may be its motive, to fear, which gives them courage to beard us lions in our den.

The General again (as in the late attack on the Rikabashee fort) asked the Envoy if he would take the responsibility of sending out the troops on himself; and on his conceding, the force was sent. The Envoy had also much angry discussion on this point with Brig. Shelton.

But all these delays of conference lost much time, and it was between four and five p.m. before operations commenced.

The Affghan cavalry charged furiously down the hill upon our troops in close column. The 37th N.I. were leading the 44th in the centre, and the Shah's 6th in the rear. No square or balls were formed to receive them. All was a regular confusion; my very heart felt as if it leapt to my teeth when I saw the Afghans ride clean through them. The onset was fearful. They looked like a great cluster of bees, but we beat them and drove them up again.

The 5th cavalry and Anderson's horse charged them up the hill again and drove them along the ridge.

[1] Codrington's battalion of Gurkhas, part of Shah Shoojah's army, had been annihilated at Charikar.

Lieut. Eyre quickly got the horse artillery gun into the gorge between the Behmaru hills and that to the left (the gorge leading to the plain towards the lake): from this position he soon cleared that plain, which was covered with horsemen. There was another stand made at the extreme left; but we were successful on all points, captured both guns, brought one of them in, for which we had spare horses in the field; and having no means of bringing the other away, it was spiked, upset, and tumbled down the hill.

The enemy had taken these guns up the hill with the King's elephants; but unfortunately they had sent the animals back, or they would have been fine prizes for us.

Brig. Shelton, perhaps not considering the lateness of the hour, deferred his return to cantonments until the shades of evening had closed over the troops; and it being impossible to distinguish friend from foe, we could not assist with our guns from cantonments, which in daylight would have swept the plain, and have prevented the enemy from following up our return from cantonments.

The enemy cut in between cantonments and our men, and their horsemen came up close to Sale's bastion. Our anxiety was very great, for all this time our front was attacked (it is said by 400 men); the firing was sharp and long-continued. The Brigadier did not get back until 8 o'clock; and it was some time after that before all was quiet. When the men of the 37th were upbraided for turning, they replied, 'We only retreated when we saw the Europeans run, and knew we should not be supported.'

We moved into Sturt's house this evening, as Brig. Shelton was grumbling about the cold in a tent.

November 14th: We had a quiet night; which was a great blessing, as Sturt was suffering very much from the wound in his face.

The chiefs complained that we broke faith with them yesterday in attacking them when they had expressed their wish to treat: however, we were not the aggressors, for we did not do so until they had fired at us. To-day they have requested we will not fire on the hill, which has been agreed to; they are (they say) busy searching for swords and anything they can find, also picking up balls of all kinds.

The Affghan cavalry yesterday were not inclined to make a second charge: Col. Chambers invited an attack, which they declined. Their infantry seems to be contemptible in the plain, but they fight hard when cooped up in the forts. They fire from rests; and then take excellent aim; and are capital riflemen, hiding behind any stone sufficiently large to cover their head, and quietly watching their opportunities to snipe off our people. There is also a peculiarity in the Affghan mode of fighting,—that of every horsemen carrying a foot-soldier behind him to the scene of action, where he is dropped without the fatigue of walking to his post. The horsemen have two and three matchlocks or juzails each, slung at their backs, and are very expert in firing at the gallop. These juzails carry much further than our muskets. . . .

The enemy are evidently spreading false information, through persons professing to be travellers. No travellers are on the road now. Cossids are scarcely procurable; the few that have been sent to recall the brigade have not succeeded in their attempt. The man who went on the 6th was stopped and his letter read by a man who was educated at Loodianah. The enemy have another sçavant, who imbibed literature at the college of Delhi. There is also a prisoner, a Mr. Tierney, in the city; whether he assists them or not we do not know. . . .

November 15th: Our camels are dying fast: we see several dragged away daily; and as they are only just thrown without the gate, the air is tainted by their carcases.

Major Pottinger and Mr. Haughton have made their escape from the Kohistan; the former has a ball in his leg; the latter has lost his hand, and is severely wounded in the back and neck. During the time they were beleaguered in Charikar, they were, in common with the Sipahees of the Shah's 4th regiment (Ghoorkhas), subjected to great misery from the want of water; the allowance for the last four days being one wine glass full per diem for each man: the horses they rode on had not had a drop to drink for ten days, nor food for five.

The site of the cantonments was badly chosen. In addition to there being no water, which of itself rendered the site unfit for a military post, their position was completely commanded on two sides by the enemy; who, having cut off their supply of water from above, gave the few defenders no rest by night or day. Added to these trying circumstances, the garrison were encumbered with their wives and children, who had been encouraged to come up from Hindostan in great numbers. It is affirmed that they did so by permission of Lord Auckland; it being supposed that they would have no wish to quit the country with their families settled along with them.

The not being allowed to bring up their families, even at their own expense, was always considered as a heavy grievance by the Europeans; but, in their instance, the wisdom of the refusal has been proved. But to return to the Ghoorkas; harassed by the enemy, and encumbered by their families, they sank into a state of perfect apathy; not so the Punjabee artillerymen who served the guns. Part of these deserted to the enemy; and, on the following day, had the insolence to return for the purpose of seducing away their comrades. It was in trying to arrest some of these that poor Haughton was so dreadfully wounded: perceiving his intentions, the Jemadar of artillery (a Punjabee snatched Lt. Rose's sword from him, and with it cut off Haughton's hand. It was with great difficulty that Pottinger and Haughton effected their escape. Somewhere between Akterae and Istalif during the night, they strayed from the other officers. Finding themselves separated from the rest, they determined to make the best of their way, secreting themselves in a hollow during the day, and travelling all night; but Haughton's wounds, particularly those in the neck and back, prevented his urging his horse beyond a walk. On arriving at Cabul, they decided on going straight through the city in the night; they were challenged, and Pottinger gave a Persian reply; which the guard evidently judged a doubtful one, as it was followed by a volley being fired at them, but fortunately without effect, and they pursued their way to cantonments, arriving at the gate in such a state of exhaustion that had they had a mile further to go they never could have sat on their horses. From them I heard the particulars of Maule's, Rattray's, and Wheeler's deaths. They were sitting together, I believe, at breakfast, when some of their own men attacked them: they are said to have set their backs against the wall and defended themselves until they were deliberately shot.

It is also reported that the enemy say they cannot meet us in the field, but they will starve us out of the country. The Envoy has information that we are to be attacked to-night on three faces of the cantonments; this is the first night of the moon: Sturt's Affghan servants say that, if an attack is made, it will not be for three nights to come, as at present they are all feasting. . . .

November 16th: A report has come in from the Bala Hissar that Sale has gone on the way to Jellalabad, which Brig. Shelton told me he believed, on the principle of 'Being out of a scrape, keep so'. Most people believe the report to be a ruse of the enemy, to shut out hope of relief coming to us. We, however, doubt Sale's ever having received the order to return.

The city seems to be much quieter, and some ottah and grapes were brought very early this morning to sell. The King has written to say he wishes to offer terms to the rebels; but Sir William says that they must first be sent for his approbation, lest his Majesty should offer too much.

A quiet night, as far as regarded hostilities,—with plenty of rain.

November 17th: We had a gloomy day, with rain at intervals.

Another report that the 1st brigade is gone on to Jellalabad; coupled, however, with its being only to deposit their sick in safety, and that a force of 10,000 men have arrived there to our assistance from Peshawer.

Jubbar Khan (a brother of the Dost's) has been appointed Wuzeer to Zeman Shah Khan, who has coined rupees in his own name.

This has been a good grain day: at 12 o'clock we had got in 400 maunds, at two Cabul seers the rupee, and otta at one. The Cabul seer is equal to the amount of six Hindostanee seers. The Affghans continued to bring in grain and ottah all day.

November 18th: Accounts received from Jellalabad by a cossid, who brought the letter to Sir William which he had torn in three pieces for the better concealment of its contents; on seeing the enemy he swallowed another small one; he was searched, but brought in the torn letter without discovery. He reports that after Macgregor gave him the letter, he delayed his departure a little; that there was a grand *Larye* at Jellalabad; that Sale had thrown his forces into the fort there; that the enemy had come down with 40,000 men, and Sale had sallied out and beat them, pursuing the enemy eight or ten miles to Futteabad.

My letter, containing a precis of goings-on here from the 2nd to the 8th inclusive, had reached Sale and was the only detail of events that had been received; it was sent on to the Commander-in-Chief, and a copy of it to Lord Auckland.

It had been wished that this blow below should be followed up here by another; but the council at the General's was as usual both divided and wild. One plan was to sally out, sword in hand and attack the town,—a measure that must have been attended with great loss on our side, even if victorious; with the pleasing certainty of all who were left in cantonments having their throats cut during the absence of the troops.

The next proposition was the taking of Killa Mahmood Khan. But nearly the same objection existed there. With a large force, and much probable loss, we might take it; but we could not destroy it quickly, and could not afford troops to garrison it. It is rather fortunate that the last mentioned attack was not made: for a few hours afterwards we had certain information that, instead of 200 men, the enemy have nearly all their infantry there.

November 19th: In the course of the day we got in a good deal of grain; but the General appears to be kept in a deplorable state of ignorance. Although reports are sent in daily, he scarcely knows what supplies are in store, or what is our real daily consumption. Affairs are curiously carried on: for instance, the Shah's 6th indent for six maunds daily; the 37th, a much weaker corps, for about twenty! These indents are all signed by authority! The quantity required is easily calculated as each fighting man gets a half seer of wheat, and each camp follower six chattahs per diem. There is much roguery going on in the regimental bazaars, where the chowdrys make money in connection with the Bunneahs.

They say the 6th have a full bazaar from loot at the forts taken lately, and do not require to draw for their followers: the 37th have 5,000 registered camp followers, and other corps much in the same proportions.

The Affghans are highly indignant at Pottinger and Haughton having ridden through the town. It certainly appears to us very wonderful that they did so in safety.

The enemy have sent to the Kohistan for the guns that are at Charikar, and on their arrival propose giving us battle. A plan was laid to sally out from the Bala Hissar towards the city and destroy an Hamaum exactly in front of the Ghuznee gate. In this place reside a barber and a blacksmith, two of the best shots in Cabul, who have picked off many of our men. They completely commanded the loopholes with their long rifles; and although the distance is probably 300 yards, yet they seldom fail to put a ball though the clothes or into the body of anyone passing them. It was sufficient for the loophole to be darkened, for it to be fired at; and it became an amusement to place a cap on the end of a pole above the walls, which was sure to be quickly perforated by many balls.

I believe this plan was never put into execution, and only like many others, proved a source of speculation and conversation.

November 20th: Camels and tattoos are dying fast, and the air is most unpleasantly scented at times.

It is now rumoured that the reason Sale's brigade does not come up is, that the two regiments refuse to do so. This I do not believe; they may have been annoyed at the thoughts of returning; but I will never believe they refuse to aid us in our extremity, if they have the power to do so; and I consider the report to be of a piece with Brig. Shelton's expression that Sale's brigade was safe and would keep so.

November 21st: The enemy uncommonly quiet; said to be employed in manufacturing powder and shot, and hammering such of our shot as they pick up to fit their guns.

At dinner time, Brig. Shelton sent to Mr. Eyre, stating that the Envoy had information that 80,000 foot and 10,000 horse were coming to set fire to our magazine with red hot balls! How these balls were to be conveyed here red hot is a mystery, as the enemy have no battery to erect furnaces in: but nothing is too ridiculous to be believed; and really any horrible story would be sure to be credited by our panic-stricken garrison.

It is more than shocking, it is shameful, to hear the way that our officers go on croaking before the men: it is sufficient to dispirit them, and prevent their fighting for us.

There is said to be a kind of republican council in the city, composed of twelve chiefs, to whom the people at present pay obedience. I wonder what the new King, Zeman Shah Khan and his Wuzeer think of this new power.

A man of Warburton's artillery has deserted, as also a havildar of Hoskin's regiment; the latter was received by Zeman Shah Khan with great honour, and told that all good Mussulmans were welcome; a house and shawls were given to him.

Our useless expenditure of ammunition is ridiculous. At the captured fort last night the garrison popped away 350 rounds at shadows, probably of themselves: however, we have plenty of it; 13 lakhs made up, and 900 barrels of powder, shot, bullets, etc., in store in profusion.

Shelton croaks about a retreat; and so much is openly said of our extremity, that were we obliged to fall back on Jellalabad, it is more than probable that there would be much desertion among the Mussulmans.

It is difficult to ascribe the just cause to the inactivity of the enemy: if they feared us, they would disperse; and if they mean to starve us, why do they allow us to get in supplies in the quantities they do? That something is in agitation there can be no doubt; and the most plausible idea is, that the enemy think that by keeping us on the alert for so long for nothing, that we shall all relax in our vigilance, and give them the opportunity to attack the cantonments with success.

Sturt has in vain suggested that a picket of infantry and cavalry with a couple of guns be sent at daybreak up the hill towards Siah Sung, to cut off the supplies we see daily going into the town.

By purchasing them, we might induce the people to supply us largely, and at all events prevent the enemy obtaining them. I have no patience with those who say, 'Oh, it is not ottah, it is only charcoal.' Now our foes require charcoal as much as we do food, for they cannot make their gunpowder without it; and wood is very scarce in the city, for the poor people who used to bring it in on donkeys have ceased to do so, lest it should be taken for nothing.

November 22nd: A party was sent to occupy the friendly village of Behmaru; but, as usual, delay was the order of the day, and it was deferred until the enemy had taken possession, though not in great force.

On the troops arriving there under Major Swayne of the 5th,[1] the enemy evacuated it: he, instead of allowing the men (as they themselves wished) to enter the village, kept them under hedges, firing pot shots, on which the enemy re-occupied the position. The troops returned, having done nothing.

The Ghilzye chiefs say they have sworn on the Koran to fight against us; and so they must fight, but that they will not fight hard. This is what they have told Sir William through their emissaries. He is trying to treat with all parties: but the sanctity of an oath is evidently but little regarded; and what faith can we put in their assertions?

We have just heard that Capt. Woodburn, with 130 men, returning to India, was enticed into a fort at Shekobad, a few marches on this side of Ghuznee, where they swore on the Koran to be our

---

[1] i.e. 5th Native Infantry, one of the Company's regiments. The only British battalion at Kabul was the 44th, the 13th Light Infantry having departed with Sale.

friends, and where the whole party were massacred. Poor Woodburn was represented as a strong man, who took four or five Golees to kill him! There is a report to-day that two regiments coming from Candahar have been cut up.

Grand dissensions in military councils. High and very plain language has been this day used by Brig. Shelton to General Elphinstone; and people do not hesitate to say that our chief should be set aside—a mode of proceeding recommended a fortnight ago by Mr. Baness the merchant.[1]

The poor General's mind is distracted by the diversity of opinions offered; and the great bodily ailments he sustains are daily enfeebling the powers of his mind. He has lost two of his best advisers in Paton and Thain; the former confined by his wound, the latter declining to offer advice, from disgust at its being generally overruled, by the counsel of the last speaker being acted on.

There is much reprehensible croaking going on; talk of retreat, and consequent desertion of our Mussulman troops, and the confusion likely to take place consequent thereon. All this makes a bad impression on the men. Our soldiery like to see the officers bear their part in privation; it makes them more cheerful; but in going the rounds at night, officers are seldom found with the men. There are those that always stay at their posts on the ramparts, and the men appreciate them as they deserve. To particularise them would be too openly marking the rest, but their names will, I trust, be remembered to their honour and advantage hereafter. Amongst those, Capt. Bygrave, the Paymaster General, was conspicuous: he never slept away from his post (the battery near his house) for a single night, and took his full share of fatigue, without adverting to his staff appointment.

Col. Oliver is one of the great croakers. On being told by some men of his corps, with great *jee*, that a certain quantity of grain had been brought in, he replied, 'It was needless, for they would never live to eat it.' Whatever we think ourselves, it is best to put a good face on the business.

The enemy are erecting sungahs on the heights above Behmaru.

A few hundred yards from the cantonments lay the small village of Behmaru,

[1] Baness seems to have been a man of bold enterprise. He volunteered, if given just twelve or fifteen men, to go out and drive the Afghans away from the cantonments, and was extremely angry with the British generals when this spirited offer was refused.

from which the British paymasters had been buying grain to replace the stores lost in the Commissariat Fort. Afghan insurgents from Kabul now occupied the village to put a stop to this source of supply and began to harass the garrison with a dropping fire from two small guns they had posted on the hills above the village. Spurred on by Macnaghten, Shelton reluctantly led out a force to drive away the insurgents. The débâcle which Lady Sale now describes was a grievous blow to the garrison's morale; and Shelton's conduct of the battle finally convinced the Afghan leaders that there was little to fear from British generalship.

November 23rd: We had firing of one sort or another all night. From the Bala Hissar they were shelling the city and there was much firing from our ramparts.

At about two in the morning, in consequence of a resolution arrived at the preceding evening to submit no longer to the insults of the enemy, (who by occupying Behmaru greatly annoyed our foraging parties, and almost precluded our attempting to drive them off the hill immediately above the village, whither they were accustomed to resort in great numbers for the purpose of bravado, and also probably to prove our strength or weakness), Brig. Shelton marched out of cantonments with seventeen weak companies: I believe many of them did not muster above forty men; those from the 44th were under the command of Major Swayne of the 5th N.I.; those from the 37th and Shah's 6th under Major Kershaw of the 13th. All the 5th were employed under their own Colonel (Oliver). One squadron of regular cavalry, and two detachments of irregular horse; one six-pound gun under Sergt. Mulhall, and 100 sappers and miners under Lieut. Laing.

This force ascended the hill immediately above Behmaru, dragging the gun with them with great difficulty, and thence up on the knoll overhanging the village. From thence they perceived that the village was in the possession of the enemy, who were discernible as they slept around their watch-fires. A few rounds of grape from the gun quickly roused them; and they sought cover in the houses and towers from which they replied to our cannonade and musketry by a sharp and pretty well-sustained fire of juzails. Both officers and men were most anxious to be led against the village, to take it by storm, but the Brigadier would not hear of it; and our men were helplessly exposed to the fire from behind the walls, which the enemy quickly loopholed for that purpose. After waiting until day dawned, and losing the opportunity of taking the enemy by surprise, a party was ordered under Major Swayne of the 5th, who instead of at once leading his men through the principal entrance of the village, went to a small kirkee, which he reported himself unable to force, though this was afterwards done by a few men pulling it down with their hands and kicking at it; and after remaining there a considerable time came back having lost several of his men killed and wounded.

The enemy (as daylight dawned) were seen leaving the village in small parties: to cut these off, Walker was sent down to the plain on the north west side of the hill leading to the lake, with his irregular horse. At this time large bodies of the enemy were descried ascending the hill, near the road by which they used to issue from the city, and separated from that occupied by our troops only by a narrow gorge leading to the plain and lake beyond. To meet and oppose these, Brig. Shelton, leaving three companies of the 37th, under Major Kershaw, to maintain their original position, marched the remainder of the force along the ridge towards the gorge, taking with him also his solitary gun!

I had taken up my post of observation, as usual, on the top of the house, whence I had a fine view of the field of action, and where, by keeping behind the chimneys, I escaped the bullets that continually whizzed past me. Brig. Shelton having brought forward skirmishers to the brow of the hill, formed the remainder of his infantry into two squares, the one about 2,000 yards in the rear of the other, the intervening space being crammed with our cavalry, who from the nature of the ground, were exposed to the full fire of the enemy without being able to act themselves.

The number of the enemy's foot men must have been upward of 10,000 (some say 15,000), and the plain, on the N.W. of the hills was swept by not less than 3,000 or 4,000 Affghan cavalry, whose rapid advance obliged Lieut. Walker to retreat up the hill, by which the enemy were enabled to throw fresh reinforcements and ammunition into the village of Behmaru; a circumstance which rendered it difficult for him to hold his ground.

The fight continued till about 10 o'clock, by which time our killed and wounded became very numerous. In spite of the execution done by our shrapnell, the fire of the enemy told considerably more than ours did, from the superiority of their juzails and jingals over our muskets.

They fought also from behind sungahs and hillocks, whilst our men were perfectly exposed; our troops also labouring under the disadvantage of being drawn up in square, from an apprehension of an attack from the Affghan cavalry.

The vent of the gun became too hot for the artillerymen to serve it.[1]

At this time, that is at about half-past 9 or 10, a party of Ghazeeas ascended the brow of the hill, by the gorge, where they planted three standards close to each other, a red, a yellow and a green one. It is possible that the Brigadier might not have seen their advance; but when they had nearly attained the summit, they had an evident advantage over us, as their shots generally told in firing up at our men, whose persons were wholly exposed, whilst only a few of their heads were visible to our troops, and the old fault of firing too high most probably sent all our shots harmlessly over their heads, for to hit them it was requisite to fire on the ground. When they fairly appeared above ground, it was very evident that our men were not inclined to meet them; every field-glass was now pointed to the hill with intense anxiety by us in cantonments, and we saw the officers urging their men to advance on the enemy. Most conspicuous were Mackintosh, Laing, Troup, Mackenzie, and Layton; who, to encourage the men, pelted the Ghazeeas with stones as they climbed the hill; and, to do the fanatics justice, they returned the assault with the same weapons. Nothing would do,—our men would not advance, though this party did not appear to be 150 in number. At length, one of the Ghazeeas rushed forward waving his sword over his head: a Sipahee of the 37th darted forth and met him with his bayonet; but instead of a straight charge he gave him a kind of side stroke with it, and they both fell and both rose again. Both were killed eventually; and the Ghazeea was shot by another man. It was very like the scenes depicted in the battles of the Crusaders. The enemy rushed on: drove our men before them very like a flock of sheep with a wolf at their heels. They captured our gun; Sergeant Mulhall received three wounds; poor Laing was shot whilst waving his sword over the gun and cheering the men. It was an anxious sight, and made our hearts beat: it lasted but for a few minutes. (Brig. Shelton says, that when

[1] Because of this very possibility there had for years been a standing order in force in India expressly forbidding less than two guns to take the field under any circumstances. Lieutenant Eyre thought that taking out a single gun on 23rd November was 'the first and perhaps the most fatal mistake of all'. Cf. p. 34.

our men ran, he ordered the halt to be sounded, at which the troops mechanically arrested their flight, and fell into their places!)

They ran till they gained the second square which had not broken; and the men finding a stand, turned about, gave a shout and then the Ghazeeas were, in their turn, panic-stricken, abandoned the gun, but made off with the limber and the horses.

On this we retook the gun without resistance. One of the artillery-men had a wonderful escape; he had clung on to, and under the wheels, and never quitted it. Once more in our possession, the gun was instantly re-opened on the enemy; but our men had an antipathy to the brow of the hill and would not advance as quickly as they might have done, until some successful shots from the gun and three splendid ones which were made by Serjeant Wade from the Kohistan Gate; one of which struck Abdoollah Khan's horse, and caused him to fall off,[1] on which the people surrounded their chief, and were occupied in carrying him off; they fled to the other hill, and I believe never stopped until they got into the city. All appearing to be over, I hastened home to get breakfast ready for Sturt, everyone supposing that the enemy were routed, and that Brig. Shelton was coming back with the troops.

At this time I was standing on the ramparts, and heard the Envoy, in my presence, ask the General to pursue the flying troops into the city, which he refused, saying it was a wild scheme and not feasible.

Had Shelton returned to cantonments, or thrown his force into Behmaru, all had gone well, and we had remained masters of the field.

The enemy had, as I before mentioned, a large body of cavalry on the other side of the hill, on whom our men kept firing.

At about half-past twelve, just as we had finished our breakfast, the enemy gradually came up the hill, and their fire was so severe that our men in square could scarcely fill up the gaps as their comrades fell, and our whole force, both horse and foot, were driven down the hill, and our gun captured—a regular case of *sauve qui peut*.

All would have been sacrificed but for four circumstances; first, a well-directed fire kept up from the Mission Compound by part of the Shah's 6th. A charge made by Lieut. Hardyman with a fresh troop of

---

[1] Abdoolah was, in fact, mortally wounded, but it was never certain that Wade's shot was the fatal one. It was widely believed that Abdoolah had been shot by a traitor of his own side, bribed by Mohun Lal. There was sufficient doubt about the matter for Lal to refuse the promised reward to the self-proclaimed assassin.

the 5th cavalry, being joined in it by Walker, who had collected about twenty of his Irregulars. It was in going too far across the plain, in driving the Affghan Horse back towards the hills, that poor Walker received his mortal wound in the abdomen. Major Swayne was wounded in the neck while in the square. A party of about fifty of Mackenzie's Juzailchees,[1] under Capt. Trevor, lined some low walls on the plain in front of and to the left of the old Musjeed, whence they kept up a steady discharge. Two of these men, seeing a wounded Sipahee wave his arm for help, gallantly dashed into the midst of the enemy and brought him off.

Perhaps the greatest safeguard of our troops was the conduct of Osman Khan, who suddenly stopped the pursuit and led his men back.

Perceiving our defeat on the hill, the troops at the captured fort and those at the Musjeed deserted their posts, and were with difficulty persuaded to go back to them. The troops all scuttled back as hard as they could. The General went outside the gate (and took great credit to himself for doing so) to rally them, as he called it; but there was little chance of doing that while they were under our walls. I was amused at hearing him say to Sir William, 'Why, Lord, Sir, when I said to them "Eyes right", they all looked the other way.'

Shelton, in taking up his position as before described, had both his flanks exposed, as also his rear. The men were formed into two large squares when attacked by infantry, and in these squares were men of different regiments all mixed up together: they had never been practised to it: no man knew his place.

Whilst in this square a reward of ten rupees was offered by the Brigadier to the first man who volunteered to go with him to take the enemy's flag in the gorge. Capt. Mackenzie shouted 100 for the flag. After some hesitation, a havildar of the 37th came forward; but as no other followed him, he was told to return to his place. The enemy then came on, and the whole square rose simultaneously and ran. The 44th had, I believe, fifty-eight wounded; the loss of the 5th I did not ascertain; the 37th had eighty killed and wounded ten. Of officers, Col. Oliver,[2] Capt. Mackintosh, and Lieut. Laing were

[1] Afghan riflemen recruited for the Shah's service. They stood by their British officers with magnificent loyalty throughout the campaign and fought against fellow Afghans without a qualm, and indeed with obvious relish.

[2] Oliver, having pessimistically concluded that the battle on the Behmaru hills must end in headlong flight, remarked that he was too stout to run and therefore the sooner he got shot the better. He then walked slowly towards the enemy and was shot dead.

killed; Walker mortally wounded; Swinton, Evans, Major Swayne, Hawtrey, Bott and Mackenzie wounded.

The three companies of the 37th that were out under Major Kershaw suffered severely; they were amongst the last to leave the hill. The grenadier company returned with only a Naick and two men!

The misfortune of the day is mainly attributable to Shelton's bad Generalship in taking up so unfavourable a position, after his first fault in neglecting to surprise the village, and occupy it, which was the ostensible object of the force going out.

Had he remained above Behmaru, he might have retreated into and occupied that place, in which the enemy had but few men at first, and who might have been easily dislodged. Shelton tries to lay all the blame on the Sipahees. He says they are timid, and that makes the Europeans timid also; but he has been told some home truths. On asking Capt. Troup if he did not think that the 44th had behaved nobly, that officer plainly told him he considered that all had behaved shamefully.

The troops certainly were wearied out; and, having been out since two in the morning, it appears wonderful to me that at half-past twelve they were not too weary to run; however, they had one great inducement to do so. Osman Khan was heard by our Sipahees to order his men not to fire on those who ran, but to spare them. A chief, probably the same, rode round Kershaw three times, when he was compelled to run with his men; he waved his sword over his head, but never attempted to kill him; and Capt. Trevor says his life was several times in the power of the enemy, but he also was spared.

Another great fault committed was in taking only one gun; a second would have supported the first: with only one, as soon as it was fired the enemy could rush upon it; as they did.

November 24th: A person has come in from Osman Khan (who is a nephew of the Ameer Dost Mahommed) and Shumshir deen Khan, offering us terms: they propose that we should leave the country, giving hostages that we will send the Dost back to them. They say they do not wish to harm us, if we will only go away; but that go we must, and give them back the Dost; that Akbar Khan (his son) will be here to-morrow with 6,000 men; and that if we do not come to terms, they will carry the cantonment; and that they are ready to sacrifice 6,000 men to do so.

What Sir William and the General's council of war (Shelton,

Anquetil, and Chambers) mean to do we know not; but our situation is far from pleasant.

General Elphinstone has written to the Envoy today; requesting him to negotiate with the enemy, in consequence of the impossibility of our going to the Bala Hissar, and Shelton concurs in opinion that we cannot fight our way in: also stating we have upward of 700 sick, and the scarcity of provisions.

Akbar Khan has directed, that when the cantonments are taken, the officers, their wives and families are to be made prisoners, as hostages for his father. If once in his power we might be safe; but these Ghazees are fanatics and would cut us into mincemeat.

Poor Oliver's head and one hand were cut off when his body was found: the latter was probably done to obtain a diamond ring which he always wore. The heads of all the Europeans were taken away, and will, no doubt, be exhibited as trophies!

November 25th: The Big-wigs are angry at anything having transpired regarding the letters that have come in from the chiefs; and say it is all a mistake. Be that as it may, a guard of honour was turned out, on the arrival of two men who refused to parley with Lawrence and Trevor, and said they must see the Envoy and General. It proved to be Sultan Khan[1] and his private Meerza. They held their conference with the Envoy in the officer's guard room of the rear gate-way.

The new king, Zeman Shah Khan, has written to the Envoy to say that he has accepted the throne, not from his own wish, but to prevent greater ills arising.

There was a very long and unsatisfactory conference with the ambassador. He and his secretary rode sorry yaboos, and were only attended by their saces. If their array was thus humble, their demands were sufficiently exorbitant; and the terms they offered such as could not be accepted, even by persons in our condition. They require that Shah Shoojah be given up to them, with his family; demand all our guns and ammunition; and that Gen. Sale's force should move to Peshawer before we march from this place.

Akbar Khan[2] has arrived; we heard the firing in honour of his

[1] Probably Sultan Jan, a nephew of the exiled Dost Mahomed.

[2] Dost Mahomed's favourite son, and the only member of the Dost's family who had refused to obey his father's advice to surrender to the British. 'This man', wrote Eyre, 'was determined to exercise an evil influence over our future fortunes. The crisis of our struggle was already nigh at hand.'

arrival in the city. He is reported to have brought in an accession of 6,000 men to the force, which was before estimated at 10,000 horse and 15,000 foot. The new arrivals are probably Uzbeks, and not far removed from rabble; but even a mob may from numbers succeed against us.

The subadar of the native artillery has gone off, as also three of Skinner's horse: these men are all said to have families in the city.

In the evening there was a great crowd of Affghans; some hundreds of them, all armed to the teeth, round the cantonments. They came in the most friendly manner, saying all was settled, *jung-i-kalus*. The men of the 44th went out of cantonments amongst them unarmed, were shaking hands with them, and receiving cabbages from them, un-checked by Lieut. Cadett, the officer on duty on that face, who seemed to think that this friendly meeting was a very fine affair: however, the circumstance got reported, and the adjutant got the men in.

This appears very like a ruse on the part of the enemy, to throw us off our guard, and surprise us. It was suggested to the adjutant to examine the cabbages, as it was possible that outer leaves might cover bladders of spirits; and that, having intoxicated the men, they would when they were drugged make an attack on us: however, nothing suspicious was discovered.

We saw a fire on the hill this evening, supposed to be a party watching our movements, towards the Bala Hissar.

There can be no doubt that the enemy have spies in cantonments, and there are so many Affghan servants, that it is perhaps difficult to prevent their passing in and out.

Two men of suspicious appearance were prowling about the Envoy's tent, and Lawrence desired a chuprassy not to molest them, but quietly to dodge them, and to report progress. This he did, and stated that the men walked all over the cantonments, looked at every-thing and then walked out at the gate! So much for surveillance.

Great care is taken of the fire-wood in store in cantonments, and much discontent prevails because fires are not allowed. The Hindo-stanees feel the severity of the weather, to which they are exposed day and night; and the want of fuel adds much misery to their privations in being put on short allowance of food. There is at this time a com-plete winter stock of firing laid in; added to which, on emergency, the trees of the orchard might be cut down.

Capt. Sturt was urgent, both with Gen. Elphinstone and Brig.

Shelton, that the men might have fires at night to enable them to warm themselves and dry their frosted clothes when coming off duty: but no order was given in consequence of his suggestions.

November 26th: Negotiations with the enemy broke off.

To-day, the Affghans lined the hills; some thousands of them, with many horsemen. They afterwards came down to the plain, and we expected an attack upon the cantonments. On their nearer approach, they were found to be mostly unarmed; some had sticks, some sticks with a knife tied on the end of them: they were merely the shop-keepers come out to look at us. The Affghan knife is a very formidable weapon, about two feet long, and thicker, stronger and broader than a sword, and as sharp as possible.

Some of these men went up to the breach of the captured fort, and asked, as the *jung* was over, if they might not return and live there. And on being told, 'No', they said, 'Very well; we will go away to-day, and come again to-morrow, and see if we may come then.'

One well-dressed man inquired if the volunteer regiment (37th) was there; and being replied to in the affirmative, said, 'I want my horse back that I lost the other day; have I any chance of getting it?'

All this coming close to our works, and spying, ought to have been stopped.

Sturt called out to them in Persian, and warned them off, or he would open the guns upon them. Some respectable people begged, for God's sake he would not do so; for they were not warriors, but had come out to see sights and amuse themselves.

Sturt saw a man meanly dressed on foot stealing up close to the walls, and called out *'Pesh Burro'*; on which he raised his hand, telescope fashion to his eye, and showed the end of a note. He was passed on to the gate, and admitted into cantonments; and was said to be the bearer of a letter from Akbar Khan. However, this is denied, or even that any letter came.

Whenever the political horizon clears a little, mystery becomes the order of the day. 'Out of the abundance of the heart the mouth speaketh'; and when overwhelmed with perplexity, the directors of events here are not so close. However, events do transpire, and we know that treaties are on foot with the Ghilzye chiefs; though that, too, is denied to-day.

Sleet in the morning; and in the afternoon snow, which soon froze.

November 27th: We had a quiet night; and it continued tranquil till the middle of this day; when the horsemen again took post on the hills, and escorted infantry to the right, and down into the village of Behmaru, into which we threw some shells.

The negotiations are now come quite to a close. The enemy's demands were modest, considering that they were the first to treat, it is said. They require, in addition to giving up the King and his family into their hands, all our guns and ammunition, muskets, bayonets, pistols and swords. The married men, women and children to be given as hostages; and then—we are to trust to their generosity. To this the Envoy sent a chivalrous reply—that death was preferable to dishonour,—that we put our trust in the God of battles and in His name bade them come on.

The King is in an awful state of alarm; for he has been told that we have been making terms for our free exit out of the country, paying for the same five lakhs of rupees; and leaving him to his fate, poor man! He is certainly to be pitied (if not at the bottom of it all)[1] fallen from his high estate, and believing us to have abandoned him.

Jan Fishan Khan is the only chief who stands by him; and he has had his forts and property destroyed; his wives and children, he hopes may have been saved by some of his neighbours; but as yet he only knows the fate of one young boy who was burned alive. He had one wife with him in Cabul when the insurrection broke out, and urged her to fly to Pughman for safety; the old chief told me, her reply was worth a lakh of rupees, 'I will not leave you; if you fall, we die together; and if you are victorious, we will rejoice together!'

There was an absurd report to-day, that the enemy had sent us back the gun they captured on the 23rd, with the horses; and the gullibility of John Bull was proved by many persons leaving an auction of some of the deceased officers's property, to go to the Kohistan gate, and find it was all nonsense.

November 28th: Shelled the village of Behmaru, whence the enemy annoyed us by firing on our yaboos sent out to endeavour to procure grain.

This day we had both rain and snow.

A Hindu merchant has offered to bring grain and lay it at the gate

[1] The British suspicion that Soojah had been playing a double game and was the real instigator of the rebellion seems to have been baseless. But the cry of '*nous sommes trahis*' has always been a welcome face-saver.

of Mahommed Shureef's fort in the night. We are not to speak to his people; and are eventually to pay him at the rate of one Cabul seer for the rupee, and we are bound to take 200 kurwars. Also on every hundred maunds being delivered, we are to lay down a bag of 1,500 rupees as a present. He says many would assist us, but are afraid; that as he is the first in the market, he expects to make his fortune.

November 29th: The horses are hard up for grain: those for the artillery have not been much looked after since Lieut. Waller was wounded; and one of them is averred to have eaten his comrade's tail! That he bit it off there is no doubt.

November 30th: Amongst other political barometers, the manner in which persons are spoken of indicates whether affairs are going on well or ill: just now things are looking up again. A few days ago people spoke of 'The Macnaghtens'; and then they became again 'Sir William and my Lady'; and today they have left their refuge in a tent in cantonments, and are gone into the great house again, which they think will have a good effect, and tend to quiet people's minds.

The politicals are again very mysterious, and deny that any negotiations are going on, etc., but letters come in constantly; and we know they are treating with the Ghilzyes.

Sturt proposes to hut the men on the ramparts, and give them plenty of firewood. As yet they are not allowed any fires, except for cooking their food. He also wishes to have the city shelled, both from the Bala Hissar and the cantonments, particularly to annoy the quarter where the gun-powder-makers reside.

December 1st: The enemy's confederacy is said to be breaking up; they are now quarrelling regarding the partition of power which as yet they have not. One says he will be the chief of Cabul, another of Jellalabad, etc. The plan proposed for the capture of cantonments by the enemy is, to send 200 bildars in front to cut down the ramparts; next come the infantry, and then the horse. I suppose we are to stand still and look on.

Akbar Khan is said to be very ill.

A man of the Ghoorka corps has come in.[1] He says the men are wandering up and down the country, and that some have taken refuge

[1] A straggler from the garrison of Charikar (p. 45). Neither Rose nor Grant was ever seen again.

in forts; that poor Rose, in a fit of despair, put an end to his existence by shooting himself; and that Dr. Grant when he last saw him, was wounded in the leg.

The people of the city are said to be discontented. They have no firewood; the people who used to bring it in are afraid to do so lest they be plundered.

December 3rd: The attack intended for yesterday has been postponed to to-day, we hear; but there seems to be little likelihood of one.

Khojeh Meer [*the headman of Behmaru*] says that he has no more grain: we only got 50 maunds in to-day. He also says that the moollahs have been to all the villages, and laid the people under ban not to assist the English, and that consequently the Mussulman population are as one man against us. He says he expects himself to have to run for his life to Peshawer whenever we go away. Khojeh Meer has a difficult part to play: his pecuniary gain in siding with us is great; but being the father-in-law of Meer Musjudee, who married the Khojeh's daughter, he, of course, lets the enemy occupy the village whenever they please. As far as we are individually concerned, Khojeh Meer has been very civil to us: he sells us grain whenever we can manage to send an Affghan servant on a yaboo to purchase it. Sturt has been kind to the man; and he evinces his gratitude by writing to say that he will get us what supplies he can. Much more grain might have been procured, had we not foolishly tried to drive hard bargains with Khojeh Meer. It has been intimated to the Envoy that the enemy's troops who lately got one rupee daily for each horsemen, and eight anas for each foot soldier, have not had any pay for four days, and that they are grumbling at it. . . .

Orders were this day issued, that the arms and accoutrements, discipline, etc. of the various corps, should be attended to! Consequent on this order, the 5th have been very busy cleaning their musket barrels,—a most unusual exertion. The arms used to be placed against the rampart, and of course the barrels were rusty and the powder damp.

A committee is ordered to assemble to-morrow to value all useless horses in the Bazaar which are to be destroyed; so there will be plenty of cheap meat, as tattoos and camels have for some time past been eaten: even some of the gentlemen eating camel's flesh, particularly the heart, which was esteemed equal to that of the bullock. I never was tempted by these choice viands; so cannot offer an opinion regarding them.

Brig. Shelton sent to tell Sturt that one of the bastions of the captured fort was on fire, and to request he would send bildars to dig the place and lay on fresh earth. He went accordingly to see what was the matter, and came back very angry, as the guard had been burning the defences he had put up.

December 4th: Two chiefs have been treating with the King: they propose that he throws off the Feringhees, on which they will render their allegiance to him. His Majesty, however, thinks it unsafe to break with us.

December 5th: The enemy assembled in small parties on the Siah Sung Hill; also, but not in great force, on the other hills.

In the morning they attacked a foraging party sent by the cavalry, and surrounded them in a fort. At length they took an oath on the Koran not to hurt them; and a trooper, notwithstanding the remonstrances of the rest, came out: he talked with them, shook hands with them, and they seemed very friendly. They then desired the camp followers to come out; but they distrusted them, and called to the trooper to return to them: as he was doing so they shot him. The grass cutters had amongst them one old musket, with which they shot two of the enemy: further operations were suspended by the arrival of a reinforcement, when the enemy disappeared instanter.

Sturt has again to-day narrowly escaped being shot. The enemy seem to know and to lie in wait for him, and he never shows his head above the rampart without a ball whistling close to it. The Affghans are good shots when they fire from their rests; and as the ammunition is the property of each individual, they do not throw it away as we do ours. Their gunners appear to be inferior, as they fired at the captured fort at a distance of 300 yards, yet did not hit it.

December 6th: Sturt was out till one o'clock this morning. Between twelve and one he crept round the fort and got into the enemy's mine: they had worked in about eight feet. He blew up the mine, which fell in and destroyed the covered way they had made and shook down part of the garden wall.

At daybreak not a vestige remained of the bridge; which, however, the General is still very anxious to rebuild, and has sent to inquire if Sturt can do so. Without materials or workmen, and the enemy on the spot, it is as impossible as useless to attempt it.[1]

The enemy were out to-day, but not in great force. They have got a Russian seventeen-pounder of brass, which they have brought in from the Kohistan, and have planted it in the road, near and on this side of Mahmood Khan's fort. From this they have been firing at us all day, and the balls fall many of them in the gardens of Messrs Eyre and Sturt's house. We have picked up three cannon balls close to the door of the verandah.

Lieut. Hawtrey of the 37th N.I. was on duty at the captured fort[2] to-day with 100 men—forty of these were of the 44th, the rest from the 37th. Suppose this to be the fort:

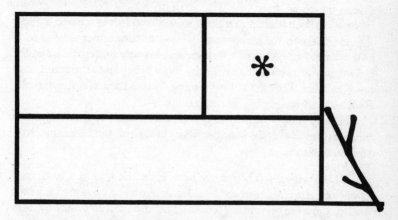

a small room upstairs, to which there was no outlet, the window being blocked up with mud. In this room were six of the 44th. The Affghans planted their crooked sticks, which served them for scaling ladders; got up one by one; pulled out the mud, and got in. A child with a stick might have repulsed them. The Europeans had their belts and accoutrements off, and the Sipahees the same. They all ran away as fast as they could! The 44th say that the 37th ran first, and as they were too weak they went too. Hawtrey says there was not a pin to choose,—all cowards alike. After he was deserted by the men, he himself threw

[1] This was a bridge which the British had erected over the Kabul river to shorten the route between the cantonments and their detachment on the Siah Sung hills.

[2] A small fort, known as Mahomed Sheriff's fort, less than 300 yards from the cantonments; it had been occupied by insurgents at the start of the insurrection, but had been captured and garrisoned by the British a few days later.

six hand grenades before he followed them. One man of the 44th was an exception, and he was shot whilst assisting Hawtrey in throwing these missiles.

Lieut. Gray, 44th, was wounded in the arm earlier in the day, by a man who climbed up and fired through a loophole at him. He thoughtlessly left his post to return to cantonments and get his wound dressed; and the men endeavoured to excuse themselves by saying their own officer was not there to direct them. It was the most shameful of all the runaways that has occurred. The men (all agree) were not dressed when the enemy entered. The 37th had three men left dead in the breach, and two were wounded, which certainly looks as if they had defended themselves. We lost 6,000 rounds of ammunition in this fort.

Brig. Shelton wished that the garrison who had evacuated the fort should re-take it. For this purpose he got the men under arms as soon as they could be collected together, and kept them, regardless of the inclemency of the weather with the snow lying on the ground, until three or four o'clock in the morning, when they were eventually dismissed, nothing being attempted.

The least thing seems to-day to create alarm. The following note accompanied by a six-pounder shot, was sent by order of Brig. Shelton to Sturt.

'Dear Hogg[1]—The enemy have planted a gun in a bastion of one of their forts, near the road leading to the Kohistan gate of the city, and have been firing it at the Magazine fort since one o'clock. Two or three shots struck the rear face. I send you one that fell in the room above the gateway, after passing through the wall.
'Yours, W. Grant.'

General Elphinstone wrote again to the Envoy to-day, urging him to treat for terms with the enemy.

At near 9 a.m. Sturt left us with an intention of blowing up the captured fort, which the men seem to have taken a dislike to, and to be determined not to defend it. He had not been gone more than a few minutes, when quick firing commenced: the enemy had come down evidently in force along the south-eastern face of cantonments. There was a blaze of light from Mahmood Khan's fort to our rear

---

[1] Lieutenant Hogg of the 44th, later killed during the retreat. The object of Captain Grant's communication remains a mystery.

gate: it did not last long, but it was a very anxious time; for our north-eastern portion of rampart is occupied by the 5th, and I distinctly heard Bygrave using no gentle language whilst he kicked the men up and out of their tents. Lieut. Mein (13th) was also active in assisting to do the same but with very little success; all the drums beating to arms and the hallooing and shouting for the General and the Brigadier, were noise enough to have aroused the dead. Lieut. Deas was on the rear gate guard; and had a rush been made at it by the enemy, there did not seem to be anyone to oppose them.

Yesterday when Sturt was talking to the General and the Brigadier about the captured fort, he mentioned that Capt. Layton commanded there that day, and that he wished he should remain and retain it as a permanent command, it being a place for which an officer should be selected, and he considered him as well fitted for the command. Shelton, with a sneer, asked if Layton would like to stay there? To which Sturt replied, 'I do not know what he would like, but I know that I should wish him to do so.' Capt. Layton's courage and steadiness were too unimpeachable for the sneer to affect his character as a soldier. The Brigadier's dislike of him arose from his not being a man of polished manners, and rather ungrammatical in his language.

After all had gone wrong, the Brigadier told Sturt that he had told him to order Capt. Layton to remain, and appealed to the General whether he did not; to which Elphinstone hesitatingly replied, yes. On Sturt saying that he never understood such an order, and that their recollections of the conversation were different from his; that he (Sturt) was wide awake at the time; the Brigadier lying on the floor rolled up in his bedding, and either really or affectedly half-asleep. On this the General hedged off evasively by saying, he did not think what was said amounted to an order!

Now when Sturt mentioned the circumstance to me yesterday, I asked him whether he thought they would select an officer as a permanent commandant, and his reply was, 'God knows.' Besides if it was to be, it would have been notified in Orders, being a decided innovation on the daily relief of the fort.[1]

'One example is as good as a million': these circumstances show how affairs are carried on. The General, unsettled in his purpose, delegates his power to the Brigadier, and the Brigadier tries to throw off all responsibility on the General's or anybody's shoulders except

[1] Lady Sale is still referring to Mahomed Sheriff's fort. See p. 65.

his own: and the General is, as in the present instance, too gentleman-like to tell him that he deviates from the exact line, and thus takes on himself the evasion.

Sturt came home quite disgusted; vowing that if those dear to him were not in cantonments, they might blow them up for what he cared.

The General peremptorily forbade the camp followers trying to take away the piles of the bridge that remained; so the enemy, who are hard up for wood, came down in great numbers, and did it for us. To-day we have seven days' provisions left.

December 7th: Sturt was anxious to take the recaptured fort; and as it appears that the men are determined not to keep it, he proposed to blow it up, and to call for volunteers for that purpose.

The 44th say they wish to wipe out the stain on their name, as do the 37th. Hawtrey's company volunteer to go with him, and take it without the assistance of any other troops.

In sending the Sipahees to that fort, the sixty men were taken six from each company, so that very few could have had their own officer, European or native, havildars, jemadars, or even their own comrades. It was certainly a particularly bad arrangement.

The General wished to know from Sturt whether the fort was practicable and tenable; at least this was the message brought by Capt. Bellew: to which Sturt said but one reply could be made—'Practicable if the men will fight: tenable if they do not run away!' but that he considered that the great object was to destroy it; as he more than doubted the willingness of the troops to garrison it, although daily relieved.

Akbar Khan sent in, offering us terms to go out, bag and baggage: but this was before the fort was taken, and he will now probably rise in his demands, which have not transpired. No reply has yet been given, as hopes are entertained of the arrival of Gen Nott's force before we are quite starved: beside, as Zeman Shah Khan has not given up the power to Mahommed Akbar Khan, he may not be able to guarantee our safety.

December 8th: Had Sturt's wish been complied with, long ago we should have been safe in the Bala Hissar, with plenty of provisions, and might have set all Affghanistan at defiance until an army could have arrived from the provinces.

This morning both Sturt and Warburton heard the booming of very distant artillery, and several other persons did the same. Ghuznee is only about eighty miles from us: so that the firing might be from thence: but it is confidently asserted that the Kandahar force must be near; and three days are given as the period for their arrival.

Hopes of relief from Kandahar were illusory. In response to Elphinstone's plea for help General Nott with no great enthusiasm, had sent off one brigade under Brigadier Maclaren, telling him that 'in my own private opinion I am sending you all to destruction'. A few days later Maclaren returned to Kandahar, saying that snow was falling in the passes and it was impossible to get through. Nott made no further attempt to relieve Kabul.

A letter was sent by the General to the Envoy, finding fault with the site of cantonments, adverting to our want for provisions, etc.; and also urgently pointing out the necessity of the Envoy's negotiating with the enemy for the best terms he could get from them. This letter was signed by the four members of the council of war,—Major-General Elphinstone, Brig. Shelton, Brig. Anquetil, and Col. Chambers. Anquetil appended to his signature, 'I concur in this opinion in a military point of view.'

December 9th: Another letter, much of the same tenor, from the General to the Envoy.

Letters received from Jellalabad.

Sale had written to the Commander-in-Chief to say that reinforcements for this country must be much greater than those now on their way; that there must be a strong siege train, engineer officers, with all *materiel*—light infantry, British infantry, and dragoons; and had stated that the whole country was in insurrection, and up against us. In a postscript, he mentions that on the day he wrote the first, they had sallied and entirely defeated the enemy.

Treating is still going on. We have only three days' provisions!

We had Sturt's yaboo paraded this morning, who did not seem to feel the smallest inconvenience, notwithstanding that he had been knocked down by a nine-pounder shot yesterday. The ball struck the rampart and rebounded on to his neck, which was protected by such a mane as would not be believed on description, being of the very shaggiest of those in this country.

At one this morning Sturt was roused up to examine a wall that Brig. Shelton wished to have pulled down, and was kept out, with

Capt. Hawtrey and fifty men for an hour. It proved to be a mare's nest, and the party were sent on a harassing duty for no purpose.

The 44th have asked for a court of inquiry, and it is to sit tomorrow: but there is but too much evidence to prove that the Europeans were the first to run away from the captured fort. The artillerymen in the bastions all assert that they were so, and also the first into cantonments; and the rest of the regiment have cut that company; and men are generally good judges of their comrades' conduct.

Capt. Hay was this day sent with a message of consequence to the King, attended by an escort of fifty horse. He went out of cantonments at a brisk trot, and forded the river. The enemy kept an excellent look-out; they were immediately in pursuit, but our party got safe into the Bala Hissar. It was a beautiful sight to see Hay with his cap pulled down on his brows, his teeth set, neither looking right or left, but leading his men with the air of a man ready and expecting to encounter the worst and fully determined to do his *devoir*. We were all very anxious about him, and were delighted to hear that he had got back safe, for they were fired on in returning, and ten horses without riders were the heralds of their return. One man is missing, and we hope he may yet find his way in, as it is very dark, and the enemy may miss him.[1]

To avoid the enemy, they had to make a detour out of the road some miles, and the men got dismounted by their horses stumbling and falling into ditches, etc. There was much anxiety relative to the purport of the message. It was supposed to be an urgent entreaty from the Envoy to the King, that the latter would come into cantonments for the purpose of retreating with the army to India: whatever it was, it produced an order for the immediate evacuation of the Bala Hissar by our troops.

This day orders have been issued to deprive all camp followers that are not mustered of their grain rations; but those who will take meat are permitted to have it in lieu. We have commenced giving our servants two sheep a day. Between Sturt's servants, mine, and Mr. Mein's (who is staying with us) we muster forty.[2]

[1] The gallant Hay was killed at Gundamuk on 13 January 1842, the last day of the retreat.

[2] An excellent example, of which Lady Sale is quite unconscious, of the hordes of servants and camp-followers, who would fatally encumber the British retreat. As we already know (p. 48), a single battalion might have as many as 5,000 registered camp-followers.

Sturt was told yesterday that two of his sappers were going to desert, and he had the circumstance reported; but the General and Capt. Bellew would not put them into confinement, because their plan being overheard was not considered as a sufficient proof of their intentions: so they ordered them to be watched and the end of the story is, that to-day they are not to be found. A second case of most excellent surveillance.

December 11th: Early this morning, a convoy went to and returned from the Bala Hissar, having conveyed bags there to be filled with grain.

An armistice; and chiefs came to treat with the Envoy: they met on the plain; and whilst the negotiations (which were lengthy) were carrying on, the enemy were busy throwing up works and placing guns in position.

As we have only two days' provisions, terms have been accepted. As far as I can learn, four political hostages are to be given—Pottinger, Trevor, MacGregor, and Conolly—to insure the return of the Dost.

Akbar Khan is to go down with us. They say they will give us carriage, and we are to be off on Tuesday. The 54th from the Bala Hissar are to come in to-morrow morning.

December 12th: The troops from the Bala Hissar have not come in, at the desire of the chiefs; who have now decided that they wish the Shah to remain, and only require us to go. They wish the King to strengthen their allegiance by giving his daughters in marriage to the chiefs, and receiving theirs in return.

They were anxious to have our ladies as hostages, but it was refused.

The Kuzzilbashes have everything to lose, should the Dost return, and the Barukzye power come in.[1]

December 13th: Another letter from Gen. Elphinstone, urging the Envoy to treat with the chiefs.

A report prevalent that it is wished the force should remain; which is, however, discredited.

[1] The Kuzzilbashes were the descendants of Persian mercenaries imported in the eighteenth century by Shah Soojah's grandfather, Ahmed Shah, founder of the kingdom of Afghanistan. As Lady Sale correctly implies, they were pro-British simply because of their hostility to Dost Mahomed and his Barukzyes. Had they seen any hope of firm leadership by the British, they would almost certainly have come out in open support.

A curious scene occurred to-day. The men are to leave their old muskets, and take fresh ones out of the magazine. Without any order or arrangement the Europeans, Sipahees, and camp followers all got into the midst of the stores, and helped themselves to whatever came in their way; it was a regular scene of plunder.[1]

December 15th: There is a very evident change in politics. 'The good King', as Sir William used to call him, is now thrown over by us, as he refused to deviate from his accustomed hauteur towards his nobles, or to admit of his daughters marrying the chiefs they proposed.

Shah Shoojah has also set his seal to a proclamation calling on all true Mussalmans to fight against the Feringhees.[2]

A small quantity of ottah was brought in to-day.

Negotiations are still going on.

The chiefs are very anxious to have all the married men and their families as hostages for the Dost's safe return.

Two days since the King was to have come into cantonments, in rather light marching order, to accompany us to the provinces. At that time it was decided that Osman Khan (head of the Barukzyes now in the country, and at present Vizier) should remain at Cabul: and it being expected that the expulsion of our force would be a scene of bloodshed and disaster, a running fight all the way down, Sturt said, that if he could see Osman Khan himself, and make his own terms with him for our safety and protection in his own house, he would not object to being one of the hostages, and keeping his wife and mother with him: he authorised Capt. Lawrence to say as much to the Envoy. To his great astonishment he heard that his name had been proposed to the chiefs without any further communication with him, and with a state of politics wholly different from those under which he would have acquiesced in the proposition. In the first place, Shah Shoojah is not going with our army; but is doing all he can to raise a party against us,[3] and sits at a window of his palace in the Bala Hissar, whence he distributes shawls, khelluts, and bhoodkhees to the

---

[1] 'A scene of disgraceful confusion and plunder', says Vincent Eyres 'an instance of the unsteadiness of the troops, and of the recklessness that now began to extend itself amongst all ranks of the force.'

[2] This was almost certainly untrue and the proclamation a forgery. Soojah, placed in an impossible position, seems to have remained loyal to his British allies. The converse, unfortunately, is not true.

[3] Another injustice to Soojah; see note on p. 61.

Ghazeeas. In the second place, Osman Khan is one of the chiefs who it is now decided are to go down with the Envoy.

Sturt's having talked imprudently to a friend, and its being taken advantage of, prevents his interfering in the affair; but I am not so tied, and have represented (through friends) to the General in a military point of view that he ought to object to Sturt's being taken as a hostage, on the plea that should there be anything to do on the way down, through the Khyber or in the Punjab, he is the only engineer officer we have;—a circumstance which the General acknowledges escaped his recollection, but he quickly remedied the ill by writing to the Envoy on the subject: and time must show the result.

Determined not to put his wife and myself in the enemy's power, he wrote to the Envoy as follows:

'My dear Sir William,

'Within the last hour a report has reached me, that myself, Lady Sale, and Mrs. Sturt, had been proposed to the Cabul chiefs as hostages, in exchange for Capt. Trevor.

'I have a very distinct recollection of having told Lawrence to mention to you that I had no objection to such an arrangement *under certain terms*; but not having been made acquainted with the fact of such a proposition having been made, or further consulted on the subject, I write in much anxiety to inquire if there is any foundation for the report, and if there is, to be made acquainted with the arrangements proposed, under which I can be expected to acquiesce in them as far as regards Lady Sale and Mrs. Sturt; for myself I am ready for any circumstances likely to benefit or aid in bringing negotiations to a satisfactory conclusion. I trust you will ease my mind upon that point, for reports have reached me from several quarters, all of which are more vague than satisfactory.

'Very truly yours,

'J. L. D. STURT.

'15th December, 1841'.

This elicited a reply from Sir William stating that he was much hurried by business, and did not recollect whether Sturt's name had been mentioned to the chiefs or not; but it was of no consequence, as no ladies were to be sent as hostages; etc. The letter was evasive and diplomatic; and it did not inform us whether Sturt was to be sent from us or not. It was, I believe, unfortunately thrown amongst a heap of papers which Sturt was destroying, for I could not find it afterwards.

December 16th: The impudence of these Affghans is very great! Yesterday some men who were looting our people close to the gates were warned off, and they replied, that we might keep within our walls; all *without* belonged to them.

To-day, a well-dressed man, one of Akbar Khan's personal attendants, was attacked by them close to the walls, and stripped of his garments.

Mr. Baness, the merchant, was standing talking to some of the Affghans by the gate; a man snatched his watch from him, ran up to a suwar, knocked him off his horse, mounted it, and galloped off.

This day Sturt was fortunate in purchasing a bag of otta sent in to him by Taj Mahommed; whose man brought another which our servants were purchasing.

In a moment there was a cry of otta; and the garden was filled with camp followers and Sipahees. I never saw such a scene: the joy of those who got a handful for a rupee, the sorrow evinced by those who were unsuccessful, and the struggles of all to get close to the man! The gentlemen had to stand with thick sticks to keep the people off. There was no weighing; at first the man gave two handfuls for a rupee, but the quantity soon diminished in consequence of a great demand for it.

To prove our good faith and belief in that of the chiefs, we are to-day placed entirely in their power.

They know that we are starving; that our horses and cattle have neither grain, bhoosa, nor grass; they have pretty well eaten up the bark of the trees and the tender branches; the horses gnaw at the tent pegs. I was gravely told that the artillery horses had eaten the trunnion of a gun! This is difficult of belief, but I have seen my own riding-horse gnaw voraciously at a cart wheel. Nothing is satisfied for food except the Pariah dogs, who are gorged with eating dead camels and horses.

To show how strangely military matters are conducted at present; we were taking our evening walk on the ramparts, when a Sipahee quite out of breath came up, and asked for the Brigade Major, saying that he was sent from the Rikabashees fort[1] to ask for the order to give it up, as the men were waiting outside the gate ready to march off, and the Affghans were also waiting to march in; as we plainly saw,

[1] A small fort only 300 yards or so east of the cantonments. It had changed hands more than once in the earlier fighting, but it had now been agreed to hand it over to the Afghans, who, during the truce, were regarded as 'our allies'.

when we stood near Bygrave's bastion. I do not attach any blame to the General in this; but to those whose duty it was to issue the orders and see them executed.

Our allies, as they are now called, will be very magnanimous if they let us escape, now that they have fairly got us in their net. It is said the Bala Hissar will be attacked to-morrow by those who are neither the King's nor our friends; though they are now termed allies instead of enemies.

December 17th: Both otta and bhoosa brought in to-day; but not more than for the day's consumption, and only for the commissariat. Camels were brought in, and some sold to the commissariat for 140 and 150 rupees each. We offered 1,000 rupees for eight camels; but for so few they insisted on receiving 200 for each. The plunderers were, as usual, outside attacking all who passed, friend or foe, and were fired on from the magazine fort: the garrison there were also firing.[1]

Sturt was standing at the rear gate, when a man inquired if he was an officer; and, on his asking why he wished to know and what he wanted with him, said, half drawing his sword, 'to fight'.

It is said that our departure depends on the King's reply, which was expected to be given to-day. He is either to go with us to Loodianah, to remain here, or to go on a pilgrimage to Mecca.

In the city Zeman Shah Khan now reigns.

The people say that, as soon as we go, there will be dreadful fighting; not such as they have had with us, but chupaos on each others houses, sword in hand, and cutting each other's throats; that we shall be attacked all the way to Khoord Cabul, but that not after that, as that part of the country belongs to Ameenoolah Khan, whose son goes with us.

Nothing decided regarding Sturt, but it is said he will have to remain.

December 18th: When we rose this morning the ground was covered with snow; which continued falling all day.[2]

Two men of the 54th have made their escape out of the Bala

---

[1] The magazine fort had also been handed over to the Afghans.

[2] This was to prove fatal to the British. Winter had now set in in earnest, and in the final retreat the snow would kill as many as the Afghans.

Hissar; they passed a rope through one of the loopholes and let themselves down. They say the King has been tampering with them, offering to give them 15 rupees a month, and to promote all the non-commissioned officers; but that not one has accepted his offers.

This day we bought camels at 150 rupees each.

December 19th: More strange things have occurred. Brig. Shelton wrote privately to Akbar Khan for forage for his own use, and obtained ten loads of bhoosa. He made the man who brought it a present (writing to Sir William that he wished to have a pair of pistols or a chogah of small value from the Tosha Khana[1] to present to a respectable native), and the present was sent with a bill attached to it for 30 rupees. On its arrival, Shelton left the room to receive it, and during his absence the Affghan appropriated to himself a sword which had been a gift to the Brigadier from Shah Shoojah. On this he applied to the Envoy for its restoration, which brought the whole story to light; and occasioned the Brigadier to receive an admonition for having, unknown to the Envoy, entered into correspondence with one of the chiefs.[2] The General, having heard the former part of the above story, wrote to the Envoy to ascertain if he also could not obtain forage from Akbar direct; but Sir William was extremely indignant at any attempt at correspondence being entered into with any of the chiefs by individuals, and peremptorily forbade it; having the courtesy to add that he was in expectation of obtaining some for himself, of which he would permit General Elphinstone to have a part.

The chiefs are evidently fearful that we are getting in supplies to a greater extent than they wish.

We had been fortunate enough to purchase some otta and barley for our servants and cattle. A servant of Akbar Khan's came into our verandah and wanted to take it away by force; but I saw what was going on, and called Sturt, who took him by the collar, and expedited his departure by a kick; to the great astonishment of sundry Affghans at such indignity being offered to the servant of a sirdar.

Snow fell again to-day.

In a letter from Gen. Elphinstone to the Envoy to-day, he observes,

---

[1] *Sic.* Presumably a misprint for 'Posha Khana', i.e. 'Armoury'.

[2] Nearly a year later this episode would lead to Shelton's conviction by a court martial; but, fortunately for him, the admonition saved him from any further penalty.

'that the force is not in a state to act in any way necessity might require; but he hoped that it would be better disposed to-morrow!'

December 20th: Taj Mahommed Khan[1] came again to see Sturt; and through his servants we got some new cheese.

Taj Mahommed assures us of the intended treachery of Akbar; and says the force will be annihilated, and is most anxious that we should accept such protection as he is willing to afford us somewhere in the hills until the return of the English;—for that a strong force will be sent to retake Cabul, and avenge the meditated destruction of our army, is a general opinion amongst the thinking Affghans, several of whom, as well as Taj Mahommed Khan, obtained written testimonials of their friendship towards the English, that they may hereafter produce them for their advantage. We can only thank him for his good intentions. It is difficult to make these people understand our ideas on military subjects; and how a proceeding, which was only intended to save a man's life, conjointly with that of his wife and mother, can in any way affect his military honour. Certain it is that we have very little hope of saving our lives.

The Envoy seems to fear treachery on the part of the chiefs, and evidently wants to break the treaty. If he does so, it must be by a simultaneous attack on the three forts we have given up to our 'allies',[2] and also on Mahommed Khan's fort. It would, if successful, give us a decided advantage, and perhaps alarm many into siding with us; but the plan is too late a one. Sturt was applied to for a sketch of operations, which he gave, for the attack on Mahommed Khan's fort, but was of opinion we were too weak and our men too dispirited to attempt it. On this subject he received a letter from the General, of which the following is a copy:

'My Dear Sturt,
'I do not know whether Thain has written to you the substance of a conversation I had this day with the Envoy. He thinks it possible we may be driven to hostilities, and asked with the view

---

[1] Taj Mahommed was an Afghan of some distinction who showed himself consistently friendly to the British. On the night before the murder of Burnes he had come secretly to the Residency and warned Burnes of the plot against his life; but the warning had been contemptuously rejected (p. 21).

[2] i.e. the Rikabashees fort, the Magazine fort, and another little strongpoint known as Zulfa Khan's fort.

to the recapture of the magazine (fort) whether we had ladders,
or the means of making them. I hope they will not drive us to this,
although things look very ill and very like treachery.

'Yours,

'W.K.E.'

'20th Dec.'

The chiefs rise daily in their demands; and to-day required that we
should send the guns and ammunition that were to be left at once into
Mahmood Khan's fort.

They now will not give up Trevor; because, as the Envoy wishes
to get him back, they take it for granted he is a person of consequence.
The affair of the sword has made the same impression regarding
Brig. Shelton, whom the chiefs have demanded with Capts. Grant and
Conolly. Trevor is with them, and Drummond and Skinner are still
detained in the city.

Sturt has proposed to the General that we break off all treaty, and
openly retreat to Jellalabad; directing Sale to remain there, and the
whole force to await the arrival of troops, either at Jellalabad or
Peshawer; not to leave our sick as was intended, with Zeman Shah
Khan, but to take all officers' and other private baggage for them and
the ammunition, allowing a small portion for women and children.
The staff and sick officers to be allowed a riding horse, the others to
march with their men. This is a public-spirited proposition of his; for
we had succeeded, at great expense, in obtaining carriage for his most
valuable property, which, by this arrangement, must be abandoned,
and for which it was possible he would not receive any recompense.

Thursday is, at present, said to be the day for our departure.

December 21st: The hostages are decided on,—Airey, Pottinger,
Warburton and Conolly, who are to start immediately for the city.

The Envoy met Osman Khan and Akbar Khan in conference.

December 22nd: The waggons, ammunition, etc., given up to our
'allies'.

Lady Macnaghten's carriage and horses given to Akbar Khan.

The troops were kept under arms for two hours about nothing.
Some cavalry horses were sent out to be shot: the Affghans wished to
take them away, but the guard (37th) bayoneted one man, and shot
another; on which they dispersed.

The Affghans say, that if, when we retook the gun on the hill, on the 23rd of last month, we had pursued to the gates of Cabul, they would never have made head against us again. They say they cannot understand Shelton's conduct on the hill on that day; and that, if our Generals can do no more, the Affghans have nothing to fear from them. This is nearly verbatim what has been remarked before, but I am not attempting to shine in rounded periods; but give everything that occurs as it comes to my knowledge: and this was the saying of an Affghan gentleman, and also of several of the lower classes, who came both to-day and often to see Sturt, to give him warnings, which alas! were by those in authority slighted.

A general opinion prevails amongst the Affghans that a force will be sent up against them; and many persons are getting letters to prove who are our friends.

Macgregor[1] writes that for reasons of the utmost consequence, it is impossible for Sale's brigade to leave Jellalabad. Yesterday there was a grand discussion in the chief's durbar. One party objected to the departure of the English, urging that *coute qui coute*, they should be killed: the Nawaub Zeman Shah Khan said, 'If that is your opinion, I shall go into cantonments; after that, do as you will: for me, I will never lend myself to any act that is contrary to good faith.' Our friends in the city seem to think that this chief's character is not understood by our chiefs in cantonments. Zeman Shah Khan does not wish our departure; but he fears his followers, and dares not openly say what he thinks.

The Envoy, in taking the party of Akbar Khan, and in giving him money, has given him the means of doing much harm. Before he received money from us he had no power, and was not a person of any consequence; now he is in force with the disadvantage of possessing a very bad disposition; and until the Nawaub said, 'If you put difficulties in their route to Jellalabad I shall go into cantonments', he did everything in his power to embarrass the council. At present, all appears *couleur de rose*.

It is said that yesterday Akbar Khan went to Osman Khan's house, and swore on the Koran that he would do whatever the Nawaub desired. This act, they say, decided everything; and it was settled that the troops should march on Tuesday the 4th, Osman Khan to go with the army; he appears to be a good and intelligent person. The son of the Nawaub also goes, but he is not considered a shining character,

[1] The Political Officer attached to Sale's brigade.

though he is a good person. It is believed that Shah Shoojah will have a strong party after the English depart; but the Nawaub's faction treat this opinion with ridicule.

December 23rd: Humza Khan is a Ghilzye chief, now in Mahmood Khan's fort. He was the Governor of the Ghilzye country; and, when the insurrection broke out in the end of September at Bhoodkhak he was sent by the King to suppress it: instead of which he organised the rebel force.

On the return of this chief to Cabul, he was put in irons in prison, and was to have been sent to the fortress of Ghuznee; he obtained his release when the insurrection of the 2nd of November took place. This said Humza Khan has proffered to the Envoy, for a large consideration, provisions, if we will hold out; but his reputed bad character for faith renders him perhaps unsafe to deal with: besides, it may be a mere *ruse* to ascertain whether we are sincere or not in regard to the treaty we have made. There are said to be 2,000 men in Mahmood Khan's fort at present.

Our sick men were placed in doolies to-day, preparatory to their removal to Zeman Shah Khan's house in the city; but their departure was delayed.

Some of our ammunition waggons were taken away by the allies; as also shrapnell and eight inch shells.

Capt. Skinner came in at eleven last night with two Affghans; one, I believe, was a half brother of Akbar's, by name Sultan Khan. At one this morning they returned to the city on important business.[1] Moussa Khan was also sent into the city early this morning on some affair connected with negotiations.

The 54th, Shah's 6th, and some guns are ordered for a secret service; which the staff officer who gave this order said was to attack Mahmood Khan's fort, and from thence to bring away Amenoollah Khan, dead or alive.[2] This force was ordered on an especial requisition of the Envoy's. I was present at mid-day, when Capt. Lawrence told

[1] Skinner was the innocent go-between in a plot devised by Akbar Khan to test Macnaghten's good faith. Macnaghten failed to pass the test and now he was to be dramatically murdered by Akbar almost in full view of the cantonments. Lady Sale, in the fog of rumour surrounding the cantonments, not unnaturally failed at first to realize what was happening.

[2] This was the inducement with which Akbar had baited his trap for Macnaghten; note how the nature of the 'secret' service was at once disclosed.

Capt. Boyd that he was to purchase any quantity of grain and provision in his power, even to the extent of fifty days in supplies; and if it was not required, the loss would fall on the Government, should we go away and leave it behind. This conversation took place just previous to the Envoy going out to meet Akbar Khan, on the plain between the cantonments and the Siah Sung Hill.

I remarked that Lawrence styled the chiefs rebels instead of allies; which coupled with the order to the commissariat officer to lay in provisions, looked very suspicious.

About two o'clock we suddenly heard firing, and all went to the rear gate to see what the matter was; when I met Mr. Waller who informed me that the Envoy has been taken away by the chiefs.

The clearest account we have yet obtained was from Le Geyt,[1] who accompanied the Envoy. It seems, when he arrived at the burned bridge, the Envoy sent back all his escort except ten men.

Brig. Shelton having expressed a wish to be present at the conference, and not having joined the party, Le Geyt was sent back to hasten his arrival. The Brigadier said he was occupied, and could not go;[2] and when Le Geyt returned it was too late, and he met the escort, who said that Lawrence and Mackenzie had ordered them back.

Many shots were fired, and some of them came into cantonments. Le Geyt's saces, who had been desired to remain when his master returned to cantonments, now came up; and reported that on the Envoy's arrival he found the chiefs seated on a loonghee on the ground; that he sat there with them and discoursed, whilst Trevor, Mackenzie and Lawrence remained on their horses; that after a time two sirdars came and stood behind the Envoy who rose, as did Akbar Khan; that the Ghazeeas came and cut in between them and the cantonments, and firing commenced; that one of them drew Lawrence's sword from his side; that Akbar Khan took the Envoy by the hand, and led him, and all the gentlemen dismounted, towards the Yaghi fort; but it is generally believed that they are all safe, but taken into the city; however, great anxiety prevails regarding their fate, and that of Skinner, Conolly and Airey, who are in the city as hostages.

The regiments were got under arms, the walls manned, etc., but

[1] Lieutenant Le Geyt, Bombay Cavalry, was in command of Macnaghten's personal escort on this occasion.

[2] Shelton was supposed to command the troops who were to seize Mahmood Khan's fort and capture Amenoolah Khan; true to form, neither he nor the troops were ready and Macnaghten had therefore gone without them to his conference with Akbar.

nothing was done. Grant declared that it was impossible to say whether it was a piece of treachery on the part of the chiefs, or friendship to save the party from an attack by the Ghazeeas. The only thing is certain, that our chiefs are at a non-plus.

There is a general opinion in cantonments that faith has been broken on both sides, and that the Affghans have made the cleverest chupao.

Boyd has seven days' provisions; and says the bazaar can furnish seven more.

The bridge is taken up at the rear gate, and the camels that came in with grain have not been allowed to go out again. Neither is egress permitted to any respectable looking Affghan who is in cantonments.

The plain was at one time covered with people; but the horsemen seemed wending up and down trying to quiet them, and they gradually dispersed.

There was a great crowd about a body, which the Affghans were seen to strip; it was evidently that of a European,[1] but, strange to say, no endeavour was made to recover it, which might easily have been done by sending out cavalry.

December 24th: I received a note from Lawrence, enclosing one from Conolly (Sir William's nephew) to Lady Macnaghten, and had the sad office imposed on me of informing both her and Mrs. Trevor of their husbands' assassination: over such scenes I draw a veil. It was a most painful meeting to us all.

Numerous reports are current, that of to-day is that Sir William was taken to the city, and arraigned before a tribunal there for want of faith; and that Trevor suffered from the assiduity with which he executed the Envoy's orders. All reports agree, that both the Envoy's and Trevor's bodies are hanging in the public chouk: the Envoy's decapitated and a mere trunk; the limbs having been carried in triumph about the city.

A fallen man meets but little justice; and reports are rife that the Envoy was guilty of double-dealing, treating with Akbar Khan and Amenoollah Khan at the same time. In justice to a dead man, it should

---

[1] It was, in fact, the body of Sir William Macnaghten. He had been killed, almost certainly by Akbar's Khan's own hand, at the parley. The Afghan chiefs then strove nobly to save the lives of Lawrence, Mackenzie and Trevor; but Trevor had fallen or been dragged from his rescuer's horse and immediately killed by Ghazi fanatics.

be remembered that the only person supposed to know the object of the Envoy's going out on the 23rd was Skinner; who is now in the city. Sultan Khan [*Sultan Jan, Akbar's cousin*] was, I believe, the name of the person who came in with him, with a letter from Akbar Khan, on the night of the 22nd. In that letter, which was read by a friend of mine, Akbar proposed that he should be made wuzeer to Shah Shoojah; he was to receive thirty lakhs of rupees, down, and four lakhs per annum: our troops to remain eight months; and then only to go if the King wished them to do so. He urgently requested the Envoy to come and talk it over with him.

We must hold in mind that, although we had performed all promises made on our part, given up our wagons, ammunition, forts, etc., the treaty had never been signed by the chiefs; nor had they fulfilled a single condition which had been specified verbally, beyond giving us grain in small quantities. The sequitur is, that the Envoy was perfectly justified, as far as keeping good faith went, in entering into any arrangement by which the condition of the troops could be ameliorated and the honour of our country be insured. He only erred in supposing it possible that Akbar Khan, proverbially the most treacherous of all his country-men, could be sincere.

It was a part of Akbar Khan's plan to have Amenoollah Khan seized and brought to cantonments as a hostage.[1]

It was a most decided piece of treachery on the part of Akbar. They were seated on a bank together; Lawrence, a very spunky, active man, felt as if something was wrong; and when urged to sit, only knelt on one knee, that he might start up on occasion. But his pistol and sword were seized and his arms secured instantaneously, which rendered him powerless, and he was hurried away behind a chief on horseback; as was Mackenzie.

At that time, Akbar Khan had seized the Envoy by his left wrist, and Sultan Jan held him by the right; they dragged him down the bank, he exclaiming, 'Az Burai Kodar!' (For the love of God!). At the moment he was laid hands on, Mackenzie, Trevor and Lawrence were disarmed, and forced away *en croup* behind different chiefs. They saw no more of the Envoy alive. Sultan Jan uttering an opprobrious epithet, calling him a dog, cut poor Trevor down, as did also Moollah Momind. Mackenzie would have shared the same fate

[1] This was the story put to Macnaghten by Akbar to test his good faith; Akbar had no intention of sacrificing Amenoollah and the latter had agreed to his name being used as bait for the trap.

had not Mahommed Shah Khan, behind whom he rode, received the cut on his own arm, which went through his postheen. Lawrence's life was saved by hard galloping: but he received some blows. This account I had from the surviving principals in the tragedy; so it may be depended on as the true account. The body we saw from the rear gate was that of the Envoy.

The original treaty between Sir William and the chiefs has been sent in again; with three additional clauses:

To leave all our treasure:

To leave all our guns excepting six:

To exchange the present hostages for all the married men and their families; and General Sale's name particularly mentioned.

General Elphinstone said he might give the officers as hostages; but that their wives and families were not public property; and, unless the husbands consented, he could not send them.

Major Thain was accordingly sent round to ask all the married officers if they would consent to their wives staying; offering those who did so a salary of 2,000 rupees a month. Lieut. Eyre said if it was to be productive of great good he would stay with his wife and child. The others all refused to risk the safety of their families. Capt. Anderson said he would rather put a pistol to his wife's head and shoot her; and Sturt, that his wife and mother should only be taken at the point of the bayonet: for himself, he was ready to perform any duty imposed on him.

There certainly appears to have been a fatality about the events of yesterday. I have mentioned that Sir William applied to Gen. Elphinstone for two regiments and two guns for a secret service, which were in readiness, but never went out of cantonments: had they done so, it is more than probable that the surprise never would have occurred. Added to this, with his usual vacillation, Gen. E. wrote a note to the Envoy which never reached him, as it arrived at his house after his departure, and was not even opened at the time. In this note he stated that we were too weak to send two regiments out of cantonments; particularly as the magazine fort was now garrisoned by 400 men instead of 40, the number the allies had stipulated should be thrown into it: and that if two regiments and two guns were to go out, the safety of the cantonments would be endangered. The Envoy had only ordered ten of his escort to attend him. Lawrence had taken sixteen; but a part of these returned of their own accord, feigning orders from Lawrence and Mackenzie. They probably had some knowledge of what was in contemplation; for there can be no doubt that the Envoy was surrounded by spies and traitors. Persian notes, that have arrived, have on different occasions been offered for perusal by his chuprassies—who were unable to read themselves, and anxious to know the contents—to Capt. Trevor's eldest boys who could read the characters; but they, imagining it was pure curiosity, and having no turn of a diplomatic description, refused to read them; and the notes were probably taken to others who did so, and made bad use of what intelligence they contained.

As it appears extremely uncertain whether we shall get on with the treaty or not, we are busy making up hammocks to carry the sick. They are making up in Sturt's compound; so light that two men can carry a heavy man in one easily.

Reports are assiduously spread that the Envoy's and Trevor's deaths were the act of the Ghazeeas; and that Akbar Khan greatly regrets all that is past.

December 25th: A dismal Christmas day, and our situation far from cheering. A letter brought in from Conolly[1] to say, that the Nawaub Zeman Khan had interested himself greatly in the cause, and had procured the two bodies to be stolen, and that they hoped to be able to send them in at night. Trevor's had not been mutilated. It appears probable that the Envoy's death was not contemplated. Akbar wished to seize him, in hopes, by making him a hostage, to obtain better terms: but he is a man of violent passions; and, being thwarted, the natural ferocity of his disposition was evinced.

At night there was some firing, and the bugles sounded; all went to their respective posts, but the party of about 200 Affghans went away.

There was evidently great commotion in the city at the same time. A cossid came in from Jellalabad; but no news later than the 7th.

December 26th: The bodies were not sent in. The city is in great excitement; the Affghans fearing we shall not make the treaty good and force our way down.

It seems that the original treaty insured to the chiefs thirteen lakhs of rupees; and they insist on having it paid; not, as was stipulated, on

---

[1] Captain John Conolly, a young cousin of Sir William Macnaghten; he remained in the Bala Hissar throughout, acting in effect as liaison officer with Shah Soojah.

our safe arrival at Peshawer, but to be given now in bills on the Government, which there are people here who will cash for them on the spot. We are to be allowed to keep six yaboo loads of treasure; and all the rest is to be given to them before we go; or else the chiefs fear they will not get it, as their people would *loot* it all.

However, we are informed that the chiefs do not mean to keep faith; and that it is their intention to get all our woman into their possession; and to kill every man except one, who is to have his arms and legs cut off, and is to be placed with a letter *in terrorem* at the entrance of the Khyber passes, to deter all Feringhees from entering the country again. A Persian note, without signature or address, was brought by a common looking man to the officer on duty at the rear gate; giving information that the cantonments are to be attacked to-night. We also have information that the road to Jellalabad is likely to be clear; as the Ghilzyes are all come into Cabul to exterminate us and loot the cantonments.

The chiefs wish to force us to go down by another route, where our people say we are sure to be opposed.

Letters received from Capt. Mackeson, Political Agent at Peshawer, state that the advance with ammunition had reached Peshawer, and the 16th Lancers, the 9th and the 31st, were close behind.[1] It is, however, impossible that they can arrive here in time to save us from either a disgraceful treaty, or a disastrous retreat.

December 27th: The Council—Elphinstone, Shelton, Anquetil, and Chambers, with Major Pottinger—have ratified the treaty. No one but themselves exactly knows what this same treaty is; further than that it is most disgraceful! $14\frac{1}{2}$ lakhs to be given for our safe conduct to Peshawer; all our guns to be given up, save six; and six hostages to be given on our part; and when they are sent Lawrence and Mackenzie are to return.

December 28th: Lawrence has come in, looking haggard and ten years older from anxiety. It appears that the Envoy, when Akbar Khan took hold of him, grappled with him and threw him on the ground. Akbar

---

[1] This was not the 'Army of Retribution' which General Pollock would presently lead into Afghanistan to avenge Elphinstone's defeat, but the regiments already moving up to relieve units of the Kabul garrison in the normal tour of duty. In the event, in mid-January, they were trounced by the Afghans in the Khyber Pass and forced to retreat.

fired his pistol at him, and wounded him; and afterwards he was cut to pieces.

There has been great excitement in the city. Khan Shereen Khan refused to attend the Durbar; and Akbar's conduct has been generally condemned by the chiefs.

Naib Shureef paid for the interment of Sir A. Burnes's body; but it was never buried; and part of it, cut into many pieces, is still hanging on the trees in his garden.

The Envoy's head is kept in a bhoossa bag in the chouk; and Akbar says he will send it to Bokhara; to show to the king there how he has seized the Feringhees here, and what he means to do to them.

Our guns are brought down to the gate, to be ready for the Affghans to carry off to-morrow.

Conolly, Airy, and Skinner are in the city; and Warburton, Walsh, and Webb have been sent as the other three hostages, to make up the number, although the treaty is not yet signed by the chiefs. There is much doubt whether Mackenzie will be given up to us.

Many routes have been named for our downward march this morning. We were to go by Zoormut; but I believe we still go by Jellalabad.

Amenoollah Khan is now represented as our best friend amongst the chiefs.

Whether we go by treaty or not, I fear but few of us will live to reach the provinces.

Although there is plenty of carriage for the sick, it is to-day decided that they are to be left behind; and the medical men drew lots who were to stay; they fell upon Primrose of the 44th, and Campbell of the Company's service: the former exchanged with Dr. Berwick, the late Envoy's medical staff, who, with Mr. Campbell of the 54th are to go to the city with the sick men.[1]

Snow all day.

December 29th: Mackenzie and Skinner came in, in handsome dresses presented to them by Akbar Khan, who professed to them he had no hand in the Envoy's death: and, to prove his sincerity, wept for two hours.

Brig. Shelton has again had recourse to Akbar; and has obtained carriage from him.

[1] The exchange cost Primrose his life. He was killed in 'The Last Stand of the 44th at Gandamack'.

It is said it was the Envoy's intention to have superseded General Elphinstone, had Gen. Nott arrived: but no such measure would have been requisite, as the General had summoned Nott to take the command, and had, in fact, given it over to him from the 1st of November: so that it is a point of speculation as to who is our military chief; and whether, under existing circumstances, Gen. Elphinstone is empowered to treat with the chiefs regarding the troops.

To give an instance of the strange way in which matters are conducted here: Serg. Deane came and reported to Sturt that he had received orders to slope the banks of the canal, etc., without any reference to Sturt; who, of course, ordered his sergeants not to undertake any work without his orders. Sloping these banks would facilitate the passage of the enemy; who otherwise must cross the canal at the usual spots, either the ford or bridge.

Our sick sent to the city.

Snow all day.

December 30th: 500 Ghazeeas made a rush at the rear gate; and only desisted on finding the port-fire ready, which would have sent grape in amongst them. In revenge, they tore up the small bridge over the canal.

More of our guns were sent to the chiefs, who now dictate to us, delaying our departure, which is to be postponed according to their pleasure.

More sick men sent to the city to-day. As the camels and doolies that conveyed them there returned, they were attacked and plundered; the men were stripped, and had to run for their lives without any clothing, their black bodies conspicuous as they ran over the snow. The doolies and camels were all carried off. One of the hostages has written to me, dated midnight of the 29th, and tells me that they are all well in the city, and that from the appearance of affairs, we shall most likely go down unmolested: that the Nawaub Zeman Khan is very kind; and he or one of his sons is with them nearly all day: the room they inhabit is eighteen feet by ten, and all the hostages are together: it is very uncomfortable, being thus confined; this, however, must be the case for some time: even the court-yard below is not free from vagabonds. The night the Envoy was killed the Ghazeeas rushed even up to the door, determined on Conolly's and Airey's death; and it was difficult to get rid of them. The poor Envoy's hand was held up to the window, to show it to Conolly! Ameenoollah Khan seems to be well pleased. The King went to them the night the letter was written, and took his musicians with him, who played and sang till eleven o'clock: he is represented as a most fatherly old gentleman. This alludes to Zeman Shah Khan, and not to Shah Shoojah.

The Nawaub's second son, Soojah ool Dowlah, is to go down with us: he is represented as a very nice fellow, about twenty-two years old.[1] A postscript, added this morning, informs me that the chiefs are very well pleased; and do not wish us to go till all our arrangements are comfortably made, for their suspicions are now at an end.

Sturt received instructions from Capt. Bellew to scarp the banks of the canal, by way of rendering them easier for the camels to get over. 'To slope, I suppose you mean?' said Sturt. 'You may suppose what you please,' replied Bellew: 'but the General's orders sent by me are, to scarp the banks;—and now do as you like: and you are also to cut the rampart down, to make a free passage for the troops; as, there being but one gateway on the face, it would take a long time for the troops and baggage to pass out.'

When Sturt was first desired by the General to cut an opening, he proposed making two of twelve feet each, with twenty feet between them; this was objected to, as being too small; and he then said he would throw down the rampart between, which would make an opening of forty-four feet: but of course such a breach (for the rampart was to be thrown to fill the ditch, twenty feet wide) was a work only to be undertaken at the last hour; unless the General could give guns and additional troops to defend it.

In consequence of these messages, Sturt wrote to Grant to say, that unless we were to start instanter after the breach was made, or the General had the necessary means for its defence, it would risk the safety of the cantonments; particularly after what had occurred this morning. Grant, by the General's desire wrote to know what did occur; and then Sturt wrote an account of the attack of the Ghazeeas at the rear gate, our cattle having been carried off and the bearers plundered, etc.—upon this Grant, by the General's desire, wrote to say they did not know any of the circumstances; and begged nothing might be done to injure our defences.

Snow all day.

December 31st: The chiefs say they have no control over the Ghazeeas;

[1] This 'very nice fellow' not long afterwards murdered the unfortunate Shah Soojah.

that when they offend we may fire on them; that they will have the camels, taken from us yesterday, restored.

Now did they give us even camel for camel, it would be another matter: but, instead of that, fifteen of the worst of our own were brought back out of the thirty-six; and a present of 100 rupees was made to them for the trouble they had taken.

This morning, a number of camels laden with grain, etc. were plundered close to the rear gate. Verbal orders were sent by Brig. Shelton to fire on these people if absolutely requisite: but no written order to that effect has been given, and no one will take the responsibility upon his own shoulders. No orders of any import are transmitted in writing. Someone, anyone, is sent with a verbal message to the officer it concerns; and if anything goes wrong, what has he to show as his authority for acting as he has done? Amongst other orders, there is one not actually to fire, but to make believe they are going to do so; which has occasioned some ridiculous and harmless flourishes of port-fires.

There is still negotiation going on; and there seems to be some hints regarding Shah Shoojah's abdication. The Affghans do not wish to put him to death, but only to deprive him of his sight.

The chiefs are, we hear, to come into Mahmood Khan's fort with a large force tomorrow, to be ready to protect cantonments, and we are to march out the next day.

Thus ends the year. The bodies of the Envoy and Trevor have not been brought in; and we hope that the Nawaub Zeman Khan may be able to get them privately interred in his own garden.

Sergeant Williams, who died in consequence of his wound, was placed in the coffin, and buried in the grave prepared for the Envoy behind the barracks.

Snow has lain on the ground since the 18th of December.

Jan 1st., 1842: Negotiations are still going on.

The Nawaub Zeman Shah Khan and Osman Khan appear to be honourable men; as also Mahommed Shah Khan Ghilzye: the former, or his son, sits with the hostages day and night to insure their protection. The latter is the person who received the sword cut on his arm intended for Mackenzie, and thereby saved his life, on the 23rd of last month.

A party of fifty Affghan workmen, magnified by the General into 500, have been sent to work on the banks of the canal: they soon said they were cold and tired and would finish the rest to-morrow.

Two men came in to-day with a Koran to Sergeant Deane (who, from having an Affghan wife, has many acquaintances and friends amongst the people of Cabul): they report that Akbar Khan is false; that 10,000 Kohistanees are to attack us at Tezeen, and all the Ghilzyes at Soorkhab.

Offers have been made of provisions; but it is suspected that it is only to try our faith, and see if we will lay in provisions on the sly.

January 2nd: Before breakfast Sturt received the following note from General Elphinstone:—

'Dear Sturt,

'Are we to have the Affghan Bhildars again to-day? If so, they had better be employed on the other side of the river. Pottinger proposes our taking on the planks to cross the stream in the Khoord Cabul pass. He says 250 planks would do. He will explain this to you after breakfast. Let me hear what was done yesterday. We shall march on Tuesday, I think: that is the present arrangement. You must settle with Boyd about the bullocks for the bridge, which we must take on to the Loghur.

'Yours,

'W.K.E.'

There have been so many clever propositions during the siege that, if I succeed in saving my papers, many of the original letters will require to be appended, to prove that I do not use the traveller's privilege! To-day's is this. We make a bridge to cross the Cabul river; and carry on planks to the Loghur, in case that bridge should have been destroyed. Major Pottinger proposes that we carry 250 planks to be laid down in the Khoord Cabul, for crossing the streams, which occur on an average every 100 yards. Could we afford transport for these planks, the delay occasioned would render the journey through that pass one of about three days, as the stream is crossed about thirty times. One word regarding the carriage of these said planks. A camel would only carry two; thus 125 animals would be required; and we are unable to take the requisite quantity of ammunition, for want of carriage. Besides, why is this stream not to be frozen, as it is but a few inches deep anywhere?

There appears to be much commotion amongst the chiefs regarding the Envoy's death and Akbar's conduct; who still repeats that he did not kill the Envoy, but that it was done by the Ghazeeas. He threatens to attack us on the road; and Osman Khan says if he does he will fight him all the way down, taking, as his own party, 1,000 horse and 500 foot.

Aziz Khan is to be at Soorkhab ready to exterminate us. We hear from the city that Sale has been taking forts, carrying off women, and provisions, and greatly annoying the good people of Jellalabad.

January 3rd: The march, which was fixed for to-day, is again postponed. The Kohistanees have not received any part of the money given to the chiefs. They have sent an agent to Sturt to say that, if we wish it, they will bring the chiefs of Kardurrah into cantonments, with four others, as hostages; that we need not give them any money now, they know we have none, and are content with our promise. They wish us to remain quiet. They will give us provisions; and attack and fire Cabul within three days. They will also go down and bring up re-inforcements for us from Jellalabad. They assure us that the chiefs are false, and mean to attack us on the road. All this was represented to our chiefs by Sturt. The reply he received was, 'It was better to keep the matter quiet; as in the present state of things it might, if known, cause excitement.'

The 40,000 rupees given by us to the chiefs to raise 2,000 men at twenty rupees each, to protect us to Jellalabad, have not succeeded. They have kept the money, of course, but say they cannot get men to go at this season; and even if they could, the chiefs cannot afford to weaken their party by sending their followers away.

The thermometer to-day at sunrise was below zero; in the sitting-room with an enormous blazing fire, at noon, 40 degrees. Yesterday, with the same good fire, at 9 a.m., 11 degrees.

Another excellent project of Major Pottinger's. Among our various vacillatory measures, there is again a thought, now that the time for action is long past, to force our way into the Bala Hissar: but how are we to get our ammunition in? Erect a battery on the Siah Sung Hill (of course to be the work of fairies during the night), fire our shot from cantonments into the battery, where of course guardian sylphs would protect the lives of our men who were quickly to pick them up, and send them on, in like manner, into the Bala Hissar! No arrangement made for transporting the powder. The tale was told from where the conversation had taken place—at the General's. The narrator was Capt. Bellew. Both Sturt and I taxed him with joking;

but he assured us it was all true, and only another of the many strange events constantly occurring. Then ensued a long parley and military discussion on the point, its feasibility, and its having been tried in some peninsular warfare. But I never could get Bellew to explain how our men's lives in the battery were to be saved.

January 4th: I heard from Sale, dated 19th December. He acknowledged the receipt of my note, giving an account of operations up to the 9th inst. He was doubly anxious relative to our situation, from having heard only the day before that the Kandahar troops were near us, and all the cossids telling those at Jellalabad that we had plenty of provisions; and he still trusts in God that the Kandahar force may arrive in time to save us and prevent the necessity of terms disgraceful to our reputation in India.[1] He informs me of the arrival of the advanced guard of our cavalry at Peshawer with ammunition; and that the 3rd Buffs and 9th Foot had marched; with altogether six regiments of N.I. and some artillery, sappers, and engineer officers. The news from Cabul had not then had any effect on the chiefs about Jellalabad, whose followers are daily diminishing. Our troops were, nevertheless, as hard at work as ever, making the place as strong as possible. At that time, Mackeson had not sent them any money; of which they were in great want, not having a rupee to give the troops, and three months' pay nearly due. Extracts from my letter had been sent to Government and to the Commander in Chief. The original has been sent to my son-in-law, Capt. Brind; as Sale writes me that no other person gives them any idea of our position at Cabul.

The Affghans still tell us we are doomed; and warn us to be particularly cautious of our safety in going out of the cantonments. Taj Mahommed says that Mrs. Sturt and I must wear neemchees over our habits—common leathers ones—and turbans, and ride mixed in with the suwars; not to go in palkees or keep near the other ladies, as they are very likely to be attacked.

The chiefs are to come in to-morrow to take charge of cantonments before we leave them. Nawaub Zeman Shah Khan is also to come in to see the General.

Orders for the first bugle at 6, the second at 7. Sturt inquired if he was to make the breach, and when made, who were to guard it, etc.: to which the following is the reply:

[1] But no Kandahar force was on the way.

'My dear Sturt,

'If it is as well as before, the General thinks you need not turn out the sappers. The Brigadier says you are the best judge as to whether it is defensible or not.

'Yours truly,
'Wm. THAIN.

4th Jan. 7. p.m.

'The General wants to know if the planks which were sent have been removed. The troops are not to turn out at 6 in the morning as ordered, but wait till further orders.

'W.T.'

January 5th: Sturt employed in making the breach. The chiefs say we shall go to-morrow; Orders out for 7 and 8 o'clock.

Shah Shoojah has sent a message to ask if not even one officer of his force will stand by him. This message was, I know, delivered by Sturt himself to several; but circumstances admitted not of their further adherence. Indeed it is more than doubtful that the King was at the bottom of the insurrection, never dreaming that it would go so far.

II

The Retreat from Cabul

Thursday, 6th January 1842: We marched from Cabul. The advanced guard consisted of the 44th Queen's, 4th Irregular Horse, and Skinner's Horse, two H.A. six-pounder guns, Sappers and Miners, Mountain Train, and the late Envoy's escort. The main body included the 5th and 37th N.I.; the latter in charge of treasure; Anderson's Horse, the Shah's 6th Regiment, two H.A. six-pounder guns. The rear guard was composed of the 54th N.I., 5th Cavalry, and two six-pounder H.A. guns. The force consisted of about 4,500 fighting men, and 12,000 followers.

The troops left cantonments, both by the rear gate and the breach to the right of it, which had been made yesterday by throwing down part of the rampart to form a bridge over the ditch. All was confusion from before daylight. The day was clear and frosty; the snow nearly a foot deep on the ground; the thermometer considerably below freezing point.

By eight o'clock a great part of the baggage was outside the cantonments. It was fully expected that we would have to fight our way out of them although terms had been entered into with the Sirdar for our safe escort. . . .

We started at about half-past nine A.M. The advance party were not molested; there might have been 50 or 100 Affghans collected about the gateway to witness our departure. The ladies, collectively speaking, were placed with the advance, under the charge of the escort; but Mrs. Sturt and I rode up to Capt. Hay, and mixed ourselves with his troopers. [*i.e. with the 4th Irregular Horse*].

The progress was very slow; for the first mile was not accomplished under two and a half hours. There was only one small bridge over the Nullah, which is eight feet broad, but deep, situated about fifty yards from cantonments.

Great stress had been laid on the necessity of a bridge over the Cabul river, about half a mile from cantonments. In vain had Sturt represented over and over again, that as the river was perfectly fordable, it was a labour of time and inutility: with snow a foot deep, the men must get their feet wet. However, as usual, every sensible proposition was overruled; and Sturt was sent long before daylight to make the bridge with gun carriages. They could not be placed overnight, as the Affghans would have carried them off: he had therefore to work for hours up to his hips in water, with the comfortable assurance that, when his unprofitable task was finished, he could not hope for dry clothes until the end of the march, and immediately on quitting the water they were all frozen stiff. I do not mention this as an individual grievance, but to show the inclemency of the weather, and the general misery sustained.

The bullocks had great difficulty in dragging these gun carriages through the snow, and when the bridge was made it was proved to be an unnecessary expense of time and labour. The baggage might have forded the river with great ease, a little above the bridge, where it was not deep. Mrs. Sturt and I rode with the horsemen through the river, in preference to attempting the rattling bridge of planks laid across the gun carriages: but the camp followers determined not to go through the water, and jostled for their turns to go over the bridge. This delay was the origin of the day's misfortunes, which involved the loss of nearly all the baggage, and the greater part of the commissariat stores.

The troops had been on half rations during the whole of the siege: they consisted of half a seer of wheat per diem, with melted ghee or dhal, for fighting men; and for camp followers, for some time, of a quarter of a seer of wheat or barley. Our cattle, public and private, had long subsisted on the twigs and bark of the trees. From the commencement of negotiations with the chiefs, otta, barley, and bhoosa were brought in in considerable quantities; the former selling at from two to four seers per rupee, and the latter from seven to ten; but neither ourselves nor our servants benefited by this arrangement: it came to the commissariat for the troops. The poorer camp followers had latterly subsisted on such animals (camels, ponies, etc.) as had died from starvation. The men had suffered much from over work and bad feeding, also from want of firing; for when all the wood in store was expended,[1] the the chiefs objected to our cutting down any more of the fruit trees; and their wishes were complied with. Wood, both public and private, was stolen: when ours was gone, we broke up

[1] Hardly consistent with Lady Sale's remark on 25 November that there was 'a complete winter stock of firing laid in'.

boxes, chests of drawers, etc.; and our last dinner and breakfast at Cabul were cooked with the wood of a mahogany dining table.

When the advance had proceeded about a mile, an order was brought for a return to cantonments, as Mahommed Zeman Shah Khan had written to say the chiefs were not ready; but shortly afterwards a counter order arrived to proceed without loss of time.

When the rear guard left cantonments, they were fired upon from the cantonment then filled with Affghans. The servants, who were not concerned in the plunder, all threw away their loads, and ran off. Private baggage, commissariat, and ammunition were nearly annihilated at one fell swoop. The whole road was covered with men, women, and children, lying down in the snow to die.

The only baggage we saved was Mrs. Sturt's bedding, on which the ayah rode; and keeping her close to us, it was saved.

The Mission Compound was first vacated: and when the force from thence came into cantonments in order to pass through them, it was immediately filled with Affghans: who, in like manner, occupied the cantonments as our troops went out.

It was the General's original intention to halt at Begramee, close to the Loghur river, and about five miles from Cabul (reiterated was the advice of our Affghan friends—alas, how little heeded!—to push on at all risks through the Khoord Cabul the first day[1]): but the whole country being a swamp encrusted with ice, we went on about a mile further, and halted at about 4 p.m. There were no tents, save two or three small palls that arrived. All scraped away the snow as best they might, to make a place to lie down on. The evening and night were intensely cold: no food for man or beast procurable, except a few handfuls of bhoosa, for which we paid five to ten rupees. Captain Johnson, in our great distress, kindly pitched a small pall over us: but it was dark, and we had few pegs; the wind blew in under the sides, and I felt myself gradually stiffening. I left the bedding, which was occupied by Mrs. Sturt and her husband, and doubled up my legs in a straw chair of Johnson's, covering myself with my poshteen. Mr. Mein[2] and the ayah fully occupied the remainder of the space. We

[1] To get through the Khoord Cabul pass in the day would have meant a march of fifteen miles, something quite beyond the powers of Elphinstone's disorganized multitude.

[2] Lieutenant Mein, 13th Light Infantry, had been wounded in October during Sales' withdrawal from Kabul and had been bought back to the cantonments to convalesce. The 13th being dear to the heart of the 'Colonel's lady', Lady Sale had adopted him as a member of her household.

only went in all six miles, and had to abandon two H.A. guns on the road: we were also much delayed by the bullocks that dragged the planks, in case the Loghur bridge should have been destroyed. We had, however, positive information that it was all right; and so it proved.

Previous to leaving cantonments, as we must abandon most of our property, Sturt was anxious to save a few of his most valuable books, and to try the experiment of sending them to a friend in the city. Whilst he selected these, I found, amongst the ones thrown aside, Campbell's Poems, which opened at Hohenlinden; and, strange to say, one verse actually haunted me day and night:

> 'Few, few shall part where many meet,
> The snow shall be their winding sheet;
> And every turf beneath their feet
> Shall be a soldier's sepulchre.'

I am far from being a believer in presentiments; but this verse is never absent from my thoughts. Heaven forbid that our fears should be realized! but we have commenced our retreat so badly, that we may reasonably have our doubts regarding the finale. Nearly all Hopkins's corps, the Shah's 6th, deserted from this place; as also the Shah's sappers and miners, 250 in number.

We afterwards heard that 400 of Hopkins's men went back to Cabul the next day.

January 7th: Yesterday's rear-guard did not get up to our bivouac till two this morning, as there was no attempt to form any lines. As stragglers came up we heard them shouting out, to know where their corps were; and the general reply,—that no one knew anything about it.

During last night, or rather towards the morning, there was an alarm. Had it proved the enemy, we were perfectly defenceless; fortunately it was only camp followers, etc.

At daylight we found several men frozen to death, amongst whom was Mr. Conductor Macgregor.

The reason the rear-guard were so late was, that they did not leave cantonments till sunset. Previous to their quitting them, the Affghans had entered; and set fire to all the public and private buildings, after plundering them of their contents. The whole of our valuable magazine was looted by the mob; and they burned the gun-carriages to procure the iron.[1] Some fighting took place between the Affghans and our Sipahees. About fifty of the 54th were killed and wounded; and Cornet Hardyman, of the 5th Cavalry, killed. A great deal of baggage and public property was abandoned in cantonments, or lost on the road; amongst which were two Horse Artillery six-pounders, as before mentioned.

The officers of the rear-guard report that the road is strewn with baggage; and that numbers of men, women and children are left on the road-side to perish. Capt. Boyd's office accounts, to the amount of several lakhs of rupees, have been lost.

Two or three small tents came up to-day.

The men were half-frozen; having bivouacked all night in the snow, without a particle of food or bedding, or wood to light a fire.

At half-past seven the advance-guard moved off—no order was given—no bugle sounded. It has much difficulty in forcing its way ahead of the baggage and camp followers; all of whom had proceeded in advance as soon as it was light. Amongst them there were many Sipahees; and discipline was clearly at an end. If asked why they were not with their corps, one had a lame foot, another could not find his regiment, another had lost his musket: any excuse to run off.

The whole of what little baggage was left, was not off the ground ere the enemy appeared, and plundered all they could lay hands on.

As the mountain train, consisting of three three-pounders dragged by yaboos and mules, was passing a small fort close to our back-ground, a party of Affghans sallied out, and captured the whole. Scarcely any resistance was offered on the part of our troops, and the saces immediately absconded. Brig. Anquetil and Lieut. Green rallied the men, and retook the guns; but were obliged to abandon them, as the 44th, whose duty it was to guard them, very precipitately *made themselves scarce:* but this was not done until Anquetil and Green had spiked them with their own hands, amid the gleaming sabres of the enemy.

As the troops advanced on their road, the enemy increased considerably on both flanks; and greatly annoyed the centre and rear.

It was the General's intention to proceed through the Khoor Cabul pass to Khoord Cabul; and as it was not above one P.M. when the advance arrived at Bhoodkhak, having only come five miles, it was with dismay we heard the order to halt.

[1] Thus fortunately rendering useless the guns which Elphinstone had left behind in scupulous observance of the treaty with Akbar.

We left Cabul with five and a half day's rations to take us to Jellalabad, and no forage for cattle, nor hope of procuring any on the road. By these unnecessary halts we diminished our provisions; and having no cover for officers or men, they are perfectly paralysed with the cold. The snow was more than a foot deep. Here, again, did evil counsel beset the General: his principal officers and staff objecting to a further advance; and Capt. Grant, in whom he had much confidence, assured him that if he proceeded he risked the safety of the army!

On our arrival at Bhoodkhak, the enemy had very greatly increased around our position; and we heard that Akbar Khan was with them. Scarcely any baggage of either officers or men now remained. In a very small pall of Johnson's we slept nine, all touching each other.

We were also indebted to Johnson and Troup for food. They had a few Cabul cakes and some tea, which they kindly shared with us.

During this short march we were obliged to spike and abandon two other six-pounders, the horses not having the strength sufficient to drag them on. We have only two horse artillery guns left, with scarcely any ammunition.

Again no ground was marked out for the troops. Three fourths of the Sipahees are mixed up with the camp followers, and know not where to find the head-quarters of their corps.

Snow still lies a foot deep on the ground. No food for man or beast; and even water from the river close at hand difficult to obtain, as our people were fired on in fetching it.

Numbers of unfortunates have dropped, benumbed with cold, to be massacred by the enemy: yet, so bigoted are our rulers, that we are still told that the Sirdars are faithful, that Akbar Khan is our friend!!! etc. etc.; and the reason they wish us to delay is, that they may send their troops to clear the passes for us! That they will send them there can be no doubt; for everything is occurring just as was foretold to us before we set out.

Between Begramee and Bhoodkhak, a body of the enemy's horse charged down into the column (immediately after the 5th and 37th had passed); and succeeded in carrying off an immense quantity of baggage and a number of camels, without experiencing the least resistance.

January 8th: At sunrise no order had been issued for the march, and the confusion was fearful. The force was perfectly disorganised,

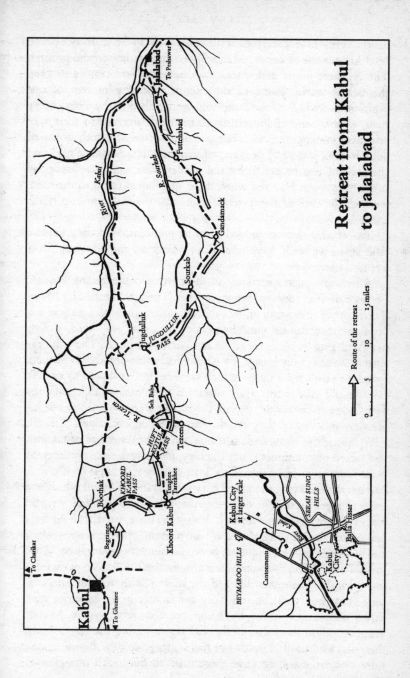

Retreat from Kabul
to Jalalabad

→ Route of the retreat

0   5   10   15 miles

Kabul

To Charikar
To Ghuznee

Begramee
Boothak
KHOORD KABUL PASS
Khoord Kabul
Tunghee Tareekhee
HUFT KOTUL PASS
Tezeen
R. Tezeen
Seh Baba
JUGDULLUK PASS
Jugdulluk
Sourkab
Gandamack
R. Sourkab
Futtehabad
River Kabul
Jalalabad
To Peshawar

Kabul City at larger scale

BEYMAROO HILLS
Cantonments
River Kabul
Kabul City
SEEAH SUNG HILLS
Bala Hissar

nearly every man paralysed with cold, so as to be scarcely able to hold his musket or move. Many frozen corpses lay on the ground. The Sipahees burnt their caps, accoutrements, and clothes to keep themselves warm. Some of the enemy appearing in rear of our position, the whole of the camp followers rushed to the front; every man, woman, and child, seizing all the cattle that fell in their way whether public or private. The ground was strewn with boxes of ammunition, plate, and property of various kinds. A cask of spirits on the ground was broached by the artillerymen, and, no doubt, by other Europeans. Had the whole been distributed fairly to the men, it would have done them good: as it was, they became too much excited.

The enemy soon assembled in great numbers. Had they made a dash at us, we could have offered no resistance, and all would have been massacred.

After very great exertions on the part of commanding officers, portions of their corps were got together. The 44th, headed by Major Thain, drove the enemy off to a short distance, and took up a position on a commanding height. The cavalry were also employed. Bullets kept whizzing by us, as we sat on our horses, for hours. The artillerymen were now fully *primed,* by having had some brandy given them from the 54th's mess stores, which were being distributed to anyone who would take them. They mounted their horses; and, with the best feeling in the world, declared that they were ashamed at our inactivity, and vowed they would charge the enemy. Capt. Nicholl, their immediate commandant, came up; abused them as drunkards, and talked of punishment: not the way, under such circumstances, to quiet tipsy men. They turned to Sturt shortly after their own officer had left them, having showered curses and abuse on them, which had irritated them dreadfully. Sturt told them they were fine fellows, and had ever proved themselves such during the siege; but that their lives were too valuable to be risked at such a moment: but, if need were, and their services were required, he would himself go with them. This, in a certain degree, restrained their ardour; yet still they kept on talking valiantly. These men listened the more readily to Sturt, because they knew him well: he was daily and hourly in the batteries with them, encouraging them by being ever foremost in the post of danger; and on those dreadfully cold nights during the siege, whilst there was a bottle of brandy to be had at any price, after his own small store was expended, he gave those men on duty each one glass to warm and cheer them—a comfort they fully appreciated, as they had long been without what was now become necessary, though it is in general the soldier's bane. For myself, whilst I sat for hours on my horse in the cold, I felt very grateful for a tumbler of sherry, which at any other time would have made me very unlady-like, but now merely warmed me, and appeared to have no more strength in it than water. Cups full of sherry were given to young children three and four years old without in the least affecting their heads.

When Major Thain took command of the 44th, he took part of the 37th N.I. with him. The 44th lines were nearest to the men who were firing into our camp; which was only saved by the promptness of Thain and Lawrence, who brought up the escort at a trot in the direction of the firing. He had to pass to the right of the 44th, and there he found about 150 of that regiment falling into their ranks. Major Thain was about 200 yards in advance, apparently reconnoitring the enemy, who were creeping up under cover of the ravines and hillocks, and keeping up a desultory fire on our camp. About this time a company of the 37th N.I. formed on Lawrence's right, and on Thain making a signal all moved forward, and drove the enemy off in good style. Anderson's horse were formed on the opposite face of the camp, with orders to keep back the camp followers, who were rushing towards the entrance of the pass. Major Thain appears to have acted on the spur of the moment; which is the only reason I can assign for his commanding the 44th. Lawrence was not under any one's order's; as the General, before quitting cantonments, told him that his escort would be an independent body.[1]

I am by no means certain that our chiefs pursued the wisest course. Had they, when the enemy first appeared, showed a good front, and dashed at them, they would probably all have scampered off as fast as they could. The Affghans never stand a charge.

The General and Major Pottinger soon discovered that Akbar Khan was there, and entered into communication with him: he agreed to protect the troops, on condition that he should receive hereafter 15,000 rupees; and that Pottinger, Lawrence, and Mackenzie should be given over to him as hostages for General Sale's evacuation of Jellalabad; but that the troops should not proceed further than Tezeen until information be received of the march of the troops from

[1] Even now the troops were ready to respond to proper leadership. Lawrence's men had assured him that 'we will follow you anywhere', and he believed that 'even at this, the eleventh hour, we might, if properly led, have driven the enemy like sheep into Caubul'.

that place. These disgraceful propositions were readily assented to; and the three officers went off to the Sirdar.

Capt. Lawrence received a note from Conolly, telling him to be cautious, to put overselves as little as possible in Akbar's power, and above all things to push on as fast as we could: but this note did not arrive until the conference was over, and all points adjusted.

We commenced our march at about mid-day, the 5th N.I. in front. The troops were in the greatest state of disorganisation: the baggage was mixed in with the advanced guard; and the camp followers all pushed ahead in their precipitate flight towards Hindostan.

Sturt, my daughter, Mr. Mein, and I, got up to the advance; and Mr. Mein was pointing out to us the spots where the 1st brigade was attacked, and where he, Sale, etc. were wounded.[1] We had not proceeded half a mile when we were heavily fired upon. Chiefs rode with the advance, and desired us to keep close to them. They certainly desired their followers to shout to the people on the height not to fire: they did so, but quite ineffectually. These chiefs certainly ran the same risk we did; but I verily believe many of these persons would individually sacrifice themselves to rid their country of us.[2]

After passing through some very sharp firing, we came upon Major Thain's horse, which had been shot through the loins. When we were supposed to be in comparative safety, poor Sturt rode back (to see after Thain, I believe): his horse was shot under him, and before he could rise from the ground he received a severe wound in the abdomen. It was with great difficulty he was held upon a pony by two people, and brought into camp at Khoord Cabul.

The pony Mrs. Sturt rode was wounded in the ear and neck. I had, fortunately, only *one* ball *in* my arm; three others passed through my poshteen near the shoulder without doing me any injury. The party that fired on us were not above fifty yards from us, and we owed our escape to urging our horses on as fast as they could go over a road where, at any other time, we should have walked our horses very carefully.

The main attack of the enemy was on the column, baggage, and

[1] i.e. in the previous October, when Sale's brigade had been attacked on its march from Kabul to Jellalabad.

[2] Major Eldred Pottinger asserted that Akbar Khan himself was shouting 'Slay them!' in Pushtu while ordering the tribesmen, in Persian, to stop firing, 'imagining that we should understand the last, and not the first'. Cf. p. 162.

rear guard; and fortunate it was for Mrs. Sturt and myself that we kept with the chiefs. Would to God that Sturt had done so likewise, and not gone back.

The ladies were mostly travelling in kajavas, and were mixed up with the baggage and column in the pass: here they were heavily fired on; many camels were killed. On one camel were, in one kajava, Mrs. Boyd and her youngest boy Hugh; and in the other Mrs. Mainwaring and her infant, scarcely three months old, and Mrs. Anderson's eldest child. This camel was shot. Mrs. Boyd got a horse to ride; and her child was put on another behind a man, who being shortly after unfortunately killed, the child was carried off by the Affghans. Mrs. Mainwaring, less fortunate, took her own baby in her arms. Mary Anderson was carried off in the confusion. Meeting with a pony laden with treasure, Mrs. M. endeavoured to mount and sit on the boxes, but they upset; and in the hurry pony and treasure were left behind; and the unfortunate lady pursued her way on foot, until after a time an Affghan asked her if she was wounded, and told her to mount behind him. This apparently kind offer she declined, being fearful of treachery; alleging as an excuse that she could not sit behind him on account of the difficulty of holding her child when so mounted. This man shortly after snatched her shawl off her shoulders, and left her to her fate. Mrs. M.'s sufferings were very great; and she deserves much credit for having preserved her child through these dreadful scenes. She not only had to walk a considerable distance with her child in her arms through the deep snow, but had also to pick her way over the bodies of the dead, dying and wounded, both men and cattle, and constantly to cross the streams of water, wet up to the knees, pushed and shoved about by man and animals, the enemy keeping up a sharp fire, and several persons being killed close to her. She, however, got safe to camp with her child, but had no opportunity to change her clothes; and I know from experience that it was many days ere my wet habit became thawed, and can fully appreciate her discomforts.

Mrs. Bourke, little Seymour Stoker, and his mother, and Mrs. Cunningham, all soldier's wives, and the child of a man of the 13th, have been carried off. The rear was protected by the 44th and 37th; but as they neared the pass, the enemy concealed behind rocks, etc. increased their fire considerably upon them. The companies that had been skirmishing on the flanks of the rear-guard closed in; and they slowly entered the pass, keeping up a heavy fire on the assailants, who had by this time got amongst the straggling camp followers and

Sipahees. Owing to a halt having taken place in front, the pass was completely choked up; and for a considerable time the 44th were stationary under a heavy fire, and were fast expending their ammunition. The 37th continued slowly moving on without firing a shot; being paralysed with cold to such a degree that no persuasion of their officers could induce them to make any effort to dislodge the enemy, who took from some of them not only their firelocks, but even the clothes from their persons; several men of the 44th supplied themselves with ammunition from the pouches of the Sipahees: and many proceeded to the front owing to their ammunition being expended. Major Scott and Capt. Swinton of the 44th, had also gone to the front severely wounded; and the command of the regiment devolved on Capt. Souter. Lieut. Steer, of the 37th N.I., with great difficulty, succeeded in bring to the rear a yaboo loaded with ammunition; but scarcely were the boxes placed on the ground, opened, and a few rounds taken out, than they were obliged to be abandoned; as, owing to our fire having slackened, the enemy became bolder and pressed upon the rear in great numbers. They had the advantage of being covered by our stragglers, which compelled our men to retire, firing volleys indiscriminately amongst them and the Affghans. At this time our men were dropping fast from a flanking fire from the heights; and, seeing it was useless to attempt to maintain a position in the rear, under such circumstances, with only about sixty men, they were withdrawn; and with difficulty forced their way through the crowd to a more commanding position where the rear-guard of the 44th was joined by Gen. Elphinstone, Col. Chambers, of the 5th Lt. Cavalry, with some troopers, and Capt. Hay, with a few of the Irregular Horse, and the only remaining gun, one having been abandoned in the pass. The 37th and the camp followers gradually passed to the front; but the Affghans were checked from following them.

After halting full an hour to let the stragglers, etc., get well to the front, they resumed their march; but, owing to the depth of the snow, the troops were compelled to assist the gun by manual labour, the horses being unable to get it on. In this way they reached the encamping ground, without molestation from the enemy.

On leaving Cabul each Sipahee had forty rounds of musket ammunition in pouch, with 100 spare loads—we have now not three camel loads left; and many Sipahees have not a single cartridge in pouch.

500 of our regular troops, and about 2,500 of the camp followers, are killed.

Poor Sturt was laid on the side of a bank, with his wife and myself beside him. It began snowing heavily: Johnson and Bygrave got some xummuls (coarse blankets) thrown over us. Dr. Bryce, H.A., came and examined Sturt's wound: he dressed it; but I saw by the expression of his countenance that there was no hope. He afterwards kindly cut the ball out of my wrist, and dressed both my wounds.

Half of a Sipahee's pall had been pitched, in which the ladies and their husbands took refuge. We had no one to scrape the snow off the ground in it. Capt. Johnson and Mr. Mein first assisted poor Sturt over to it, and then carried Mrs. Sturt and myself through the deep snow. Mrs. Sturt's bedding (saved by the ayah riding on it, whom we kept up close with ourselves) was now a comfort to my poor wounded son. He suffered dreadful agony all night, and intolerable thirst; and most grateful did we feel to Mr. Mein for going out constantly to the stream to procure water; we had only a small vessel to fetch it in, which contained but a few mouthfuls.

To sleep in such anxiety of mind and intense cold was impossible There were nearly thirty of us packed together without room to turn.

The Sipahees and camp followers, half-frozen, tried to force their way, not only into the tent, but actually into our beds, if such resting places can be so called—a poshteen (or pelisse of sheepskin) half spread on the snow, and the other half wrapped over one.

Many poor wretches died round the tent in the night.

The light company of the 54th N.I., which left Cabul, thirty-six hours previously, eighty strong, was reduced to eighteen files. This is only one instance, which may fairly be taken as a general average of the destruction of our force.

January 9th: Before sunrise, the same confusion as yesterday. Without any orders given, or bugle sounded, three fourths of our fighting men had pushed on in advance with the camp followers. As many as could had appropriated to themselves all the public yaboos and camels, on which they mounted.

A portion of the troops had also regularly moved off, the only order appearing to be, 'Come along; we are all going, and half the men are off, with the camp followers in advance!' We had gone perhaps a mile, when the whole were remanded back to their former ground; and a halt for the day was ordered, in accordance with the wishes of the Sirdar [*i.e. Akbar Khan*]; who had represented to the General, through Capt. Skinner, that his arrangements were not made either as regarded our security or provisions.

Skinner urged the General to show some mark of confidence in the Sirdar's promises; which he instantly did by sending Capt. Anderson to order back the troops and baggage.

Mrs. Trevor kindly rode a pony, and gave up her place in the kajava to Sturt, who must otherwise have been left to die on the ground. The rough motion increased his suffering and accelerated his death: but he was still conscious that his wife and I were with him: and we had the sorrowful satisfaction of giving him Christian burial.[1]

More than one half of the force is now frost-bitten or wounded: and most of the men can scarcely put a foot to the ground.

This is the fourth day that our cattle have had no food and the men are starved with cold and hunger.

Reports are prevalent in camp that the Irregular Cavalry, and the Envoy's escort, are about to desert to Akbar Khan; and also that the Affghans are tampering with our Sipahees to leave us and return to Cabul. The Subadar Major of the 37th N.I. has deserted: he was a Subadar Bahadur of the order of British India.

Shortly after Pottinger, Mackenzie, and Lawrence arrived at the Khoord Cabul fort with the Sirdar, he turned to Lawrence and said that he had a proposal to make, but that he did not like to do so lest his motives might be misconstrued; but that, as it concerned us more than himself, he would mention it; and that it was, that all the married men, with their families, should come over and put themselves under his protection, he guaranteeing them honourable treatment, and safe escort to Peshawer. He added, that Lawrence must have seen from the events of the day previous—the loss of Capt. Boyd's and Capt. Anderson's children, etc.—that our camp was no place of safety for the ladies and children. Lawrence replied, that he considered the proposition a most admirable one; and, Skinner coming in just then, he repeated what had passed to him, who replied, 'This is just what I was thinking of suggesting.' On which Lawrence begged he would go off and get the General's sanction, and bring them all without delay. Major Pottinger concurred entirely in the expediency of this measure.

Our present position is one of imminent peril. Immediately on Skinner's arrival about mid-day, we set off escorted by some chiefs to a fort about two miles distant, where Akbar Khan had taken up his

[1] 'The only man of the whole force who received Christian burial' (Eyre).

temporary residence. Capt. Troup, Brigade-major to the Shah's force, who was wounded, accompanied the party as did also Mr. Mein of the 13th, who, having been sent back with a year's sick leave to Cabul, after he was wounded in October, followed Mrs. Sturt's and my fortunes, not being attached to any corps, nor having any duty to perform.

There can be little doubt but that the proposition was acceded to by the General in the two-fold hope of placing the ladies and children beyond the dangers and dreadful privations of the camp, and also of showing the Sirdar that he was sincere in his wish to negotiate a truce, and thus win from him a similar feeling of confidence.

Overwhelmed with domestic affliction, neither Mrs. Sturt nor I were in a fit state to decide for ourselves whether we would accept the Sirdar's protection or not. There was but a faint hope of our ever getting safe to Jellalabad; and we followed the stream. But although there was much talk regarding our going over, all I personally know of the affair is, that I was told we were all to go, and that our horses were ready, and we must mount immediately and be off.

We were taken by a very circuitous route to the Khoord Cabul forts, where we found Akbar Khan, and the hostages. Mr. Boyd's little boy had been brought there, and was restored to his parents. Mrs. Burnes and young Stoker were also saved, and joined our party. Anderson's little girl is said to have been taken to Cabul, to the Nawaub Zeman Shah Khan.

Three rooms were cleared out for us, having no outlets except a small door to each; and of course they were dark and dirty. The party to which I belonged consisted of Mrs. Trevor and seven children, Lieut. and Mrs. Waller and child, Mrs. Sturt, Mr. Mein, and myself, Mrs. Smith and Mrs. Burnes, two soldier's wives, and young Stoker, child of a soldier of the 13th, who was saved from people who were carrying him off to the hills, and came in covered, we fear, with his mother's blood: of her we have no account, nor of Mrs. Cunningham, both of the 13th. The dimensions of our room are at the utmost fourteen feet by ten.

At midnight some mutton bones and greasy rice were brought to us.

All that Mrs. Sturt and I possess are the clothes on our backs in which we quitted Cabul.

Here I must divide the account. I shall go on with my own personal adventures; and afterwards, from the same date, follow up the fortunes of our unhappy army, from the journals of friends who, thank God! have lived through all their sufferings.

January 10th. Akbar Khan left us, to escort our troops. 500 deserters are said to have come in to him. It is reported that the thieves have nearly exterminated our force; and that four of Akbar's sirdars are killed. Akbar is expected back at night; and if the road is clear, we are to march at night and go thirty miles. Some officers are said to have taken refuge in a fort near this place. A letter came from the General, stating that he wished Capt. Anderson and Capt. Boyd to return: this was in consequence of a representation made to him that Anderson's making over the command of his corps to Lieut. Le Geyt, and going away, might have a bad effect on his men, who now showed symptoms of an inclination to leave us to our fate. But it was decided by the politicals that for those officers to return would have the appearance of their faith in the Sirdar's promises being shaken, and that it would be productive of much evil: they remained therefore with us. Here was another instance of the General's vacillation. Anderson, on his return from taking the message to bring the troops back, was ordered by the General to go off with the other married men and their families. Whatever may have been his own sentiments on the occasion, his opinion was never asked, and he had but to obey.

January 11th: We marched; being necessitated to leave all the servants that could not walk, the Sirdar promising that they should be fed. It would be impossible for me to describe the feelings with which we pursued our way through the dreadful scenes that awaited us. The road covered with awfully mangled bodies, all naked: fifty-eight Europeans were counted in the Tunghee and dip of the Nullah; the natives innumerable. Numbers of camp followers, still alive, frost bitten and starving; some perfectly out of their senses and idiotic. Major Ewart, 54th, and Major Scott, 44th, were recognised as we passed them; with some others. The sight was dreadful; the smell of blood sickening; and the corpses lay so thick it was impossible to look from them, as it required care to guide my horse so as not to tread upon the bodies: but it is unnecessary to dwell on such a distressing and revolting subject.

We hear that Akbar Khan offered to escort the army down, provided the troops laid down their arms; but that the General went on, upon his own responsibility.

We arrived at the Tezeen fort, where we were well treated; and where we found Lieut. Melville, 54th. He had, in guarding the colour

of his regiment, received five severe wounds.[1] He had fortunately seven
rupees about him; these he gave to an Affghan to take him to the
Sirdar, who dressed his wounds with his own hands, applying burnt
rags; and paid him every attention.

January 12th: We went to Seh Baba; and thence out of the road,
following the bed of the river, to Abdoollah Khan's fort. We passed
our last gun, abandoned, with poor Dr. Cardew's body lying on it,
and three Europeans close by it.

During the march, we were joined by Mr. Magrath, surgeon of the
37th N.I., and six men of the 44th. He had been wounded and taken
prisoner on the 10th, whilst endeavouring to rally a party of some
forty or fifty irregular cavalry, and bring them to the assistance of the
unfortunate wounded men, who were being butchered at the bottom
of the Huft Kohtul. On his coming up with this party, and again
ordering them to halt, to his great disgust he found Khoda Bukh
Khan, a Ghilzye chief, amongst them; to whom they were apologising
for not having gone over the day previous, as their comrades had
done. Mr. Magrath had several narrow escapes; and, when surrounded
by Ghilzye footmen with their long knives drawn, owed his life in a
great measure to an Affghan horseman, who recognised him as having
shown some little kindness to some of his sick friends at Cabul.

At night we had snow.

Our whole party, ladies and gentlemen, crammed into one room;
one side of which was partitioned off with mats and filled with grain.
Here an old woman cooked chupatties for us, three for a rupee; but,
finding the demand great she soon raised the price to a rupee each.

January 13th: We travelled over mountain paths, where the camels
found it difficult to get on with the kajavas, till we arrived at
Jugdaluk: near the Ghavoy there had been fearful slaughter, principally
of Europeans.

We found General Elphinstone, Brig. Shelton, and Capt. Johnson
here in tents.[2]

[1] Eyre, on the other hand, unsympathetically describes Melville as having 'delivered
himself up to Mahomed Akbar . . . having received some slight sword cuts in defend-
ing the colours of his regiment'.

[2] As Lady Sale later explains, Elphinstone and his companions had gone to parley with
Akbar Khan, who had prevented them from rejoining their troops. Elphinstone, whose
only wish by now was to die with the men he had led to destruction, had protested in vain.

Having brought our party safe to Jugdaluk, I now return to the proceedings of our unfortunate army; taking up the tale at the period when the ladies and their party took protection. On the 9th, a round Affghan tent was pitched for the ladies; and we felt the courtesy of the sirdars, who slept in the open air to give us shelter, even such as it was, for the wind blew in every direction.

Immediately after our departure the irregular horse, with the exception of about eighty men, went over in a body to the Sirdar; and as they were afterwards seen in company with a body of Affghan horse at about a mile distance, there was an attack from them apprehended: all was consternation. Several of our Sipahees absented themselves during the day, also a number of camp followers. A message was sent to Akbar Khan, and a hope expressed that he would not favour the desertion of the troops; and he promised that all going over to him should be shot, which was immediately made known to the men. One of the Mission chuprassies was caught in the act of going off, and shot.

Lieut. Mackay, assistant to Capt. Johnson, was sent in the afternoon to the Sirdar (to the fort where the ladies were), for the purpose of being the bearer of a letter to Gen. Sale at Jellalabad, to order him to evacuate his position. This letter was written by Major Pottinger.

All the dhooley bearers either deserted or were murdered the first day.

The whole of the camels and yaboos have been either taken by the enemy or plundered by our no less lawless camp followers and soldiers.

The greatest confusion prevailed all day; and anxiety and suspense for the ultimate fate of the army was intense; all expecting that if in a few hours they were not deprived of life by cold and hunger, they would fall by the knives of the Affghans; which, had they been then attacked, must indubitably have occurred; for on the return of the troops after their set-out in the morning, commanding officers had great difficulty in collecting sixty files a corps: but even of these many could scarcely hold a musket; many died of cold and misery that night. To add to their wretchedness, many were nearly, and some wholly, afflicted with snow blindness.

January 10th: No sooner was it light than the usual rush to the front was made by the mixed rabble of camp followers, Sipahees and Europeans in one huge mass. Hundreds of poor wretches, unable to seize any animals for themselves, or despoiled by stronger persons of those they had, were left on the road to die or be butchered.

After much exertion, the advance, consisting of the 44th, the only remaining six-pounder, and about fifty files of the 5th cavalry, managed to get ahead of the crowd. The Affghans were appearing on the hills early: on arriving at the Tunghee Tareekee, a narrow gorge about ten feet wide and two miles distant from their last ground, Capt. Johnson was sent with the advance: the heights were taken possession of by the enemy; who fired down incessantly on the road, from which they were inaccessible. The snow increased in depth as the army advanced. There is a gradual ascent all the way from Khoord Cabul to Kubber-i-Jubhar, a distance of five miles; the progress was necessarily slow, and many poor fellows were getting shot.

After getting through the pass, not above fifty yards in length, they proceeded to Kubber-i-Jubhar; where they halted for their comrades.

Latterly no Affghans had been seen, except at a distance; the horror of our people was therefore the greater when a few stragglers from the rear came up, and reported themselves as the remnant of the rear column, almost every man of which had either been killed or wounded: Capt. Hopkins had his arm broken by a musket ball. There was not not a single Sipahee left of the whole Cabul force.

A desperate attack had been made by a body of Affghans, sword in hand: our men made no resistance, but threw away their arms and accoutrements; and fell an easy prey to our barbarous and blood-thirsty foe.

The rear-guard was composed of the 54th regiment. On arriving at the narrow pass called Tunghee Tareekee, or 'the dark pass', a turn in the road shut out from their sight the enemy, who had followed close on their heels, but on whom they had received strict orders not to fire; although the Ghilzyes, from the heights and ravines, had kept up a sharp discharge, killing many Sipahees and camp followers, and cutting up all wounded and sick left behind. On arriving at the above-mentioned pass, the turn in the road allowed the Ghilzyes to close up, and a general attack was made on all sides: hundreds of Affghans rushing down from the rocks and hills cut to pieces their now reduced regiment.

Here Major Ewart, commanding 54th, had both his arms broken by bullets from the Juzails; Lieut. Morrieson, the adjutant, was wounded; and Lieut. Weaver, of the same corps, slightly. Lieut.

Melville, on observing the Jemadar, who carried the regiment's
colour, wounded and dropping his charge, seized it; and, after vainly
attempting to tear it off the staff, to which it was too firmly attached,
made his way on foot (his horse having been killed), with the colour
in his hand. This made him a mark for the enemy; and ere he got out
of the pass, being nearly, or quite, the last man of the column, or
rather rabble, he received a spear wound in his back, which threw
him on his face: ere well able to rise, a severe sword cut in the head
again laid him prostrate; but he contrived to crawl as far the the fast
retreating column; when again the knife of an Affghan wounding
him in the neck, and a spear in the chin, he gave all up for lost.[1] He
was now surrounded by a dozen Ghilzyes; and no man, save the dead
and dying, near him; when the enemy, observing a box of treasure
on the opposite side of the pass, left him, for the purpose of rifling the
money, either supposing they had already killed him, or intending to
return when they had secured the more valuable booty. This pause
gave Lieut. Melville an opportunity of escaping and regaining the
column; which, although weak from his wounds, he availed himself
of; and by going through the snow in the ravines, he contrived to
reach the column; where a pony without an owner, or saddle of any
description, presenting itself, he scrambled on to it; and, with the
assistance of a Mehter, gained the centre of the column, where the
44th and one gun still kept some order. Lieut. Melville was tied on
the gun, and was told by General Elphinstone, that he should be sent
over to the charge of the Sirdar, Akbar Khan, on reaching Tezeen, or
on any opportunity of going.

On a report of a large body of horse being observed in the rear,
the gun was ordered there; and Lieut. Melville was placed on a bank
on the road-side. The column passed on; and he was expecting the
fate of the other poor fellows who had fallen; when, providentially
for him, a horseman rode up, who had known him in cantonments
and strapped him on his horse, and took him over to the party of
horsemen, consisting of Akbar Khan and his followers; who received
him most kindly and, binding up his wounds, gave him a loonghee,
his regimental cap being cut to pieces.

The loonghee is the cloth worn as a turban commonly by the
Affghans, and is generally of blue check with a red border: those
worn by the Khyberries are much gayer, and have a large admixture
of yellow.

[1] cf. footnote to p. 111.

Melville gave to Omer Khan, the horseman who saved his life, seven rupees, being all the property he possessed.

Every particle of baggage was gone.

The small remnant of the army consisted of about seventy files of the 44th, fifty of the 5th cavalry, and one six pounder gun. Observing a body of cavalry in their rear, they determined to bring their solitary gun into position, and make a last effort for existence. Finding it was again Akbar Khan, Capt. Skinner (Assist.-Com.-Gen.) by direction of the General, went over, under escort, to him; to remonstrate on the attack made on our troops after a treaty had been entered into for our protection. He replied, he regretted it, he could not control the Ghilzyes (the inhabitants of this party of the country) with his small body of horse, about 300; but that as the remnant of our troops was merely a few Europeans, he would guarantee their safety, and that of all the European officers, to Jellalabad, if the General would conduct them all disarmed, whilst the Affghans were to have the use of their weapons. He said his motives for this were, that should they bring their arms with them, his own followers would be afraid of treachery. To this proposition the General would not assent.

Mackay returned with Skinner from the Sirdar, as the road to Jellalabad was said to be unsafe.

The troops continued their fearful march: the remnant of the camp followers, with several wounded officers, went ahead: for five miles they saw no enemy: all who could not walk were necessarily left behind.

They descended a long steep descent to the bed of the Tezeen Nullah. At this dip the scene was horrible; the ground was covered with dead and dying, amongst whom were several officers, they had been suddenly attacked and over-powered. The enemy here crowded from the tops of the hills in all directions down the bed of the Nullah, through which the route lay for three miles: and our men continued their progress through an incessant fire from the heights on both sides, until their arrival in the Tezeen valley, at about half-past four P.M.

The descent from the Huft Kohtul was about 2,000 feet; and here they lost the snow.

About 12,000 persons have perished!

A quarter of an hour after their arrival, the Sirdar, and a party came into the valley to a fort higher up belonging to his father-in-law, Mahommed Shah Khan. A signal was made to his horsemen to approach: two came, and Capt. Skinner, by the General's desire, accompanied them to Akbar Khan, to devise some means of saving the remnant—about 4,000 people of all descriptions.

Skinner returned at dusk, and brought back the same message as from Kubber-i-Jubhar, regarding disarming the Europeans: and again this was refused.

The General then decided, weak and famished as the troops were, and without any prospects of procuring provisions at Tezeen, to march at seven in the evening (they had left Khoord Cabul, fifteen miles from Tezeen, half-past six A.M.), and proceed, if possible, through the Jugdaluk pass by eight or nine the next morning. In this consisted their only chance of safety; for, should the enemy obtain intimation of their approach, the pass would be occupied, and the object defeated. Johnson pointed out to the General that Akbar Khan and his party could, by means of a short cut across the mountains, start long after them, and arrive before them, ready to oppose them.

Jugdaluk is about twenty-four miles from Tezeen; the pass about two miles long, very narrow, and commanded on both sides by high and precipitous hills.

At Tezeen General Elphinstone received a note in cypher from Capt. Conolly, warning him that Akbar Khan had quitted Cabul with the avowed intention of getting into his hands the person of the General, and all the married people and their families.

A message was sent to Akbar Khan that they were going to march to Seh Baba, seven miles from Tezeen (this place is sometimes called Tukeea-i-Fakeer): the road lies down the bed of a Nullah, with high hills on either side. The place is only remarkable from having a few trees and a grave or two under them; and from the latter I believe it takes its name.

The camp followers having been the bane of this unfortunate army, they hoped to move off quietly and leave them behind; but no sooner did they start, than they found that all who were able to stand were accompanying them. They left their remaining gun behind; and Dr. Cardew, who was mortally wounded at the dip into the Tezeen Nullah, was laid on the carriage to await death, which was rapidly approaching: he was found dead by Akbar's people the next morning.[1]

The night was fine and moonlit, and they reached Seh Baba about

[1] Cardew was on his way to meet his fiancee, who had just arrived in India from home. As George Lawrence wrote many years later, the poor girl's 'anticipations of happiness were thus for ever blighted by the stern vicissitudes of war'.

midnight; here a few shots were fired on them; and the rear being attacked, the whole remains of the 44th, with the exception of about nine files to form the advance, were ordered there; and thus the column remained until their arrival at Jugdaluk; their progress being again impeded by that evil which always attends Indian armies, the camp followers; who, if a shot is fired in advance, invariably fall back; and if in rear, rush to the front.

11th January: From Seh Baba the road turns off sharp to the right over the mountains to Jugdaluk; and across the Nullah is seen the short road to Cabul, but which cannot be travelled by guns or camels.

At Seh Baba, Dr. Duff (the Surgeon-General to the forces in Affghanistan), who had had his hand cut off with a penknife at Tezeen, in consequence of a severe wound, was from weakness obliged to lag behind, and was two days afterwards found murdered.

Bareekub is three miles from Seh Baba; there is a clear stream of water, and several caves cut in the rocks. Here our force observed a number of people in the caves; with whom they did not interfere, as they did not molest them. They eventually fired some volleys on the rear.

At day-break the advance arrived at Killa Sung, about seven miles from Seh Baba, where there are some streams of water: this is the general encamping ground, though very confined, and commanded by hills all round.

They proceeded about half a mile further on, and then halted, until the rear-guard should arrive; but they, having been much molested on the road, did not arrive for two hours. On their first arrival not an Affghan was to be seen; but shortly several made their appearance on the hills, and the number continued every moment to increase. Not a drop of water was procurable; nor would they get any until their arrival at Jugdaluk. They had marched for twenty-four hours consecutively, and had still ten miles to go before they could hope for rest. On being joined by the rear-guard they continued their march; the enemy in small numbers watching every opportunity to murder stragglers from the column.

At two miles from Jugdaluk the descent into the valley commences.

The hills on each side of the road were occupied by the enemy, who kept firing from their long juzails; and again the road was covered with dead and dying, as they were in such a mass that every shot told.

On arrival in the valley, a position was taken up on the first height near some ruined walls. As scarcely any Europeans of the advance now remained, and the enemy were increasing, the General called all the officers (about twenty) to form line and show a front: they had scarcely done so when Capt. Grant, Assistant-Adjutant General, received a ball through the cheek which broke his jaw.

On the arrival of the rear-guard, followed up by the enemy, the latter took possession of two heights close to our position: on which our force went for security within the ruined walls. The men were almost maddened with hunger and thirst: a stream of pure water ran within 150 yards of the position, but no man could go for it without being massacred.

For about half-an-hour they had a respite from the fire of the enemy, who now only watched their proceedings.

The General desired Johnson to see if there were any bullocks or camels procurable amongst the followers: he obtained three bullocks, which were killed, served out, and devoured instantly, although raw, by the Europeans.

A few horsemen coming in sight, they signed for one to approach: he did so, and on being questioned what chief was present, said Akbar Khan. A message was sent to the Sirdar by the General to know why they were again molested: the chief replied, he wished to converse with Skinner, who immediately accompanied the messenger. This was about half past three P.M. of the 11th.

After marching for thirty hours they lay down on the ground worn out by cold, hunger, thirst and fatigue: but scarcely had Skinner taken his departure, when volley after volley was poured into the enclosure where they were resting. All was instant confusion, and a general rush took place outside the walls; men and cattle all huddled together, each striving to hide himself from the murderous fire of the enemy.

At this time, twenty gallant men of the 44th made a simultaneous rush down the hill, to drive the enemy off the heights they occupied: in this they were successful; for, supposing they were followed by the rest, the foe took to flight ere our men could reach their position.

In about a quarter of a hour, as so small a party would not admit of any division, this party was recalled. They again entered within the broken walls; and instantly our inveterate foes were in their former position dealing death amongst them.

About 5 o'clock Skinner returned with a message that the Sirdar wished to see the General, Brigadier Shelton, and Johnson; and if they would go over to confer with him, he would engage to put a stop to any further massacre, and also to give food to our troops: and on condition of their remaining with him as hostages for General Sale's evacuation of Jellalabad, he would escort all the small remaining party in safety.

Mahommed Shah Khan, father-in-law to the Sirdar, and whose daughter is with the Dost at Loodianah, is one of the principal Ghilzye chiefs: he came at dusk with an escort to receive them; and they started in the confident hope that some arrangement would be entered into to save the lives of the remainder of the army. The General and the above-mentioned officers proceeded to the top of the valley for about two miles, and found the Sirdar and his party in bivouac; nothing could exceed the kind manner in which they were received. The chief, on hearing they had not tasted food for forty-eight hours, had a cloth spread on the ground; and a good pillau and other dishes, as also tea, were quickly brought; and they formed a circle round it, and all ate out of the same dish.

Their hunger, though great, was not to be compared to their thirst, which had not been quenched for two days.

The party consisted of the Sirdar, Akbar Khan, Mahommed Shah Khan, Abdool Ghyas Khan (son of Jubhar Khan), and a young lad called Abdool Hakeen Khan, nephew to the Sirdar. The attention of the Sirdar and his party was excessive; and after dinner they sat round a blazing fire, and conversed on various subjects. The General requested that Akbar Khan would early in the morning forward provisions to the troops, and make arrangements for supplying them with water: all of which he faithfully promised to do.

The General was anxious for permission to return to his troops; and offered to send Brig. Anquetil, should the Sirdar require an officer in his stead. Johnson, by the General's desire, pointed out to the Sirdar the stigma that would attach to him as commander of the force, were he to remain in a place of comparative security, whilst such danger impended over the troops. To this the Sirdar would not consent.[1] At about 11 p.m. the Sirdar promised he would early in the morning call the chiefs of the pass together, to make arrangements for a safe escort: he then showed them into a small tent, where, stretched on their cloaks, they found relief in sleep.

Our unfortunate force at Jugdaluk this day consisted of 150 men

[1] cf. footnote to p. 111.

of the 44th; 16 dismounted horse artillery men; 25 of the 5th cavalry. Not a single Sipahee with arms, no spare ammunition and the few rounds in pouch had been taken from the killed.

12th January: The English officers arose at sunrise, and found the Sirdar and his party were up. They showed them the same civility as over night; two confidential servants of the chief were appointed to wait on them; and they were warned not to attempt to leave the tent without one of these men, lest they should be maltreated or insulted by the Ghilzyes, who were flocking in to pay their respects to Akbar.

About 9 a.m., the chiefs of the pass and the country around Soorkhab arrived. Soorkhab is about thirteen miles from Jugdaluk, toward Jellalabad, and is the usual halting ground.

The chiefs sat down to discuss affairs. They were bitter in their hatred towards us; and declared that nothing would satisfy them and their men, but our extermination. Money they would not receive. The Sirdar, as far as words could prove his sincerity, did all in his power to conciliate them; and, when all other arguments failed, reminded them that his father and family were in the power of the British government at Loodianah; and that vengeance would be taken on the latter if mercy were not showed to the British in their power.

Mahommed Shah Khan offered them 60,000 rupees on condition of our force not being molested. After some time they took their departure to consult with their followers; and Mahommed Shah Khan mentioned to Johnson that he feared the chiefs would not, without some great inducement, resist the temptation of plunder and murder that now offered itself; and wound up the discourse by asking if we would give them two lakhs of rupees for a free passage. On this being explained to the General, he gave his consent; and it was made known to Mahommed Shah Khan, who went away and promised to return quickly.

The General again begged of the Sirdar to permit him to return to his troops; but without avail.

Johnson, by the General's desire, wrote early in the day to Skinner, to come to the Sirdar. This letter and two others, it is to be feared, he never received. A report was brought in that Skinner was wounded, but not dangerously; the Sirdar expressed much sorrow; poor Skinner died of his wound the same day.

Until 12 o'clock crowds of Ghilzyes with their respective chiefs continued to pour in from the surrounding country to make their salaams to Akbar Khan, to participate in the plunder of our unfortunate people, and to revel in the massacre of the Europeans. From their expressions of hatred towards our whole race, they appear to anticipate more delight in cutting our throats then in the expected booty. However, on a hint from the Sirdar, they changed the language, in which they conversed, from Persian to Pushtoo, which was not understood by our officers.

The Sirdar, to all appearance, whilst sitting with Johnson, endeavoured to conciliate them; but it very probably was only done as a blind to hide his real feelings.

In two instances, the reply of the chiefs was,—'When Burnes came into this country, was not your father entreated by us to kill him; or he would go back to Hindostan, and at some future day bring an army and take our country from us? He would not listen to our advice, and what is the consequence? Let us now, that we have the opportunity, take advantage of it; and kill those infidel dogs.'

At about 12, the Sirdar left them, and went on the top of a hill in rear of the British bivouac. He did not return till sunset; and in reply to the anxious inquiry when Mahommed Shah Khan would return they were always told immediately. Frequent assurances had been given that the troops had been supplied with food and water; but subsequently they learnt that neither had been given them in their dire necessity.

The Sirdar returned at dusk; and was soon followed by Mahommed Shah Khan, who brought intelligence that all was finally and amicably arranged for the safe conduct of the troops to Jellalabad. The Sirdar said he would accompany them in the morning early.

By the General's request, Johnson wrote to Brig. Anquetil to have the troops in readiness to march by 8 o'clock: he had also commenced a letter to General Sale to evacuate Jellalabad (this being part of the terms). Suddenly, and before the first note was sent off, much musketry was heard down the valley in the direction of the troops; and a report was brought in that the Europeans were moving off through the pass followed by the Ghilzyes. All was consternation. At first the Sirdar suggested that he and the officers should follow them: in this the General concurred. In a few minutes the Sirdar changed his mind; said he feared their doing so would injure the troops, by bringing after them the whole horde of Ghilzyes then assembled in the valley. He promised to send a confidential servant to the Meer Afzul Khan at Gundamuk (two miles beyond Soorkhab) to afford them protection; and agreed to start with them at midnight, as being mounted they would overtake the others before daybreak. When about to separate for the night, the Sirdar again altered the time of departure to the first hour of daylight. Remonstrances were of no avail; and our party were too completely in the power of the enemy to persist in what they had not the power to enforce.

Akbar Khan told Johnson, after Mahommed Shah Khan went out to consult with the chiefs of the pass, that the latter were dogs and no faith could be placed in them; and begged Johnson would send for three or four of his most intimate friends, that their lives might be saved in the event of treachery to the troops. Gladly as he would have saved his individual friends, he was under the necessity of explaining to the Sirdar that a sense of honour would prevent the officers deserting their men at a time of such imminent peril. The Sirdar also proposed that, in the event of the Ghilzyes not acceding to the terms, he would himself, at dusk, proceed with a party of horsemen to the foot of the hill where our troops were; and, previous orders being sent to the commanding officer for all to be ready, he would bring every European away in safety, by each of his horsemen taking up one behind him: the Ghilzyes would not then fire upon them, lest they should hit him or his men. But he would not allow a single Hindostanee to follow; as he could not protect 2,000 men, (the computed number). Johnson interpreted all this to the General: but it was deemed impracticable; as from past experience they knew how impossible it was even to separate the Sipahees from the camp followers. Four or five times during the day they heard the report of musketry in the direction of our troops; but they were always told that all fighting had ceased. This was subsequently proved to be a gross falsehood. Our troops were incessantly fired upon from the time that the General and the other officers quitted them to the time of their departure, and several hundreds of officers and men had been killed or wounded. The remainder, maddened with cold, hunger and thirst, the communication between them and the General cut off, and seeing no prospect but certain death before them by remaining in their present position, determined on making one desperate effort to leave Jugdaluk. Snow fell during the night.

My narrative now continues from information furnished by a friend remaining with the remnant of this ill-fated army. They halted this day at Jugdaluk, hoping to negotiate an arrangement with Akbar Khan and the Ghilzye chiefs, as before stated: but the continual firing, and frequent attempts made by the enemy to force them from their position during the day, but too well indicated that there was little or no chance of negotiations being effectual to quell hostilities, and admit of their resuming their march in safety: on the contrary, there appeared an evident determination still to harass their retreat to the very last.

Near the close of the day the enemy commenced a furious attack from all sides. The situation of our troops at this time was critical in the extreme: the loss they sustained in men and officers had been great during the day, and the survivors had only been able to obtain a scanty meal of camel's flesh: even water was not procurable without the parties proceeding for it being exposed to a heavy fire. The men, under all this suffering, perishing with cold at their post, bravely repelled the enemy; and would then have followed them from under the dilapidated walls had they been permitted to do so. During this conflict, Capt. Souter of the 44th, anxious to save the colours of his regiment, tore one of them from its staff, and folding it round his person, concealed it under the poshteen he wore: the other was in like manner appropriated by Lieut. Cumberland; but finding that he could not close his pea-coat over it, he reluctantly entrusted it to the care of the Acting Quartermaster-Sergeant of the 44th regiment.

Great anxiety prevailed amongst the troops, caused by the continued absence of General Elphinstone and Brigadier Shelton, the two seniors in command. It was resolved, as they did not return, to resume their march as soon as the night should shroud them from observation; and Brig. Anquetil, now in command, ordered the troops to fall in at eight o'clock: but before the men could take the places assigned to them, the camp followers, who were still numerous, crowded upon them as usual. At length between 8 and 9 o'clock they took their departure; which was rendered a very trying scene, from the entreaties of the wounded, amounting to seventy or eighty, for whom there was no conveyance; and therefore, however heartrending to all, they were necessarily abandoned, with the painful conviction that they would be massacred in cold blood, defenceless as they were, by the first party of Ghilzyes that arrived.

The enemy, who seem to have been aware of the intended removal, soon commenced an attack upon the straggling camp followers: and a number of Affghans, favoured by the darkness of the night, stole in amongst the followers that were in column, whom they quietly despatched, and proceeded to plunder. These daring men, however, were nearly all cut up or bayonetted by the enraged soldiery; who shortly after came upon an encampment of the enemy; in passing which they were saluted with a heavy fire, followed up by a sally upon the camp followers, as usual.

They proceeded on until they came to a gorge, with low steep hills on either side, between which the road passed, about two miles from Jugdaluk. Here two barriers had been thrown across the road, constructed of bushes and branches of trees.[1] The road, which had been flooded, was a mass of ice, and the snow on the hills very deep. The enemy, who had waited for them in great force at this spot, rushed upon the column, knife in hand. The camp followers and wounded men fell back upon the handful of troops for protection; thus rendering them powerless, and causing the greatest confusion; whilst the men, in small detached parties, were maintaining conflicts with fearful odds against them.

In this conflict, the Acting Quartermaster-Sergeant fell: and in the confusion, caused by an overwhelming enemy pressing on the rear in a night attack, it is not surprising that it was found impossible to extricate the colour from the body of the fallen man; and its loss was unavoidable. The disorder of the troops was increased by a part of them, the few remaining horsemen, galloping through and over the infantry in hopes of securing their own retreat to Jellalabad. The men, maddened at being ridden over, fired on them; and it is said that some officers were fired at; but that rests on doubtful testimony.[2] When the firing slackened, and the clashing of knives and bayonets had in some measure ceased, the men moved on slowly; and on arriving at the top of the gorge were able to ascertain the fearful extent of the loss they had sustained in men and officers. Of the latter, Brigadier Anquetil and above twenty others were missing. The troops now halted unmolested for an hour; during which time a few stragglers contrived to join them.

The country being now of a more open description, our small

[1] The barriers were of prickly holly-oak, 'well twisted together, about six feet high' (Colin Mackenzie).

[2] But the story still survives. As recently as 1963 an American Professor, Dr Dupree, was told by the local Afghans how 'many of the offices on horseback rode away from their men. And their men tried to shoot them down, but some escaped.'

force suffered less annoyance from the fire of the enemy: but the determination of the men to bring on their wounded comrades greatly retarded their marching; and from the troopers having proceeded onwards, the wounded could not be mounted behind them: thus their pace did not exceed two miles an hour. From time to time sudden attacks were made on the rear; particularly in spots where the road wound close under the foot of the hills, and there a sharp fire was sure to be met with. In this manner they went on till they reached the Soorkhab river, which they forded below the bridge at 1 a.m. on the 13th, being aware that the enemy would take possession of it, and dispute the passage. Whilst fording the river a galling fire was kept up from the bridge: here Lieut. Cadett of the 44th and several men were killed and wounded.

January 13th: From Soorkhab the remnant of the column moved towards Gundamuk: but as the day dawned the enemy's numbers increased; and unfortunately daylight soon exposed to them how very few fighting men the column contained. The force now consisted of twenty officers, of whom Major Griffiths was the senior, fifty men of the 44th, six of the horse artillery, and four or five Sipahees. Amongst the whole there were but twenty muskets; 300 camp followers still continued with them.

Being now assailed by an increased force, they were compelled to quit the road, and take up a position on a hill adjoining. Some Affghan horsemen being observed at a short distance were beckoned to. On their approach there was a cessation of firing: terms were proposed by Capt. Hay, to allow the force to proceed without further hostilities to Jellalabad. These persons not being sufficiently influential to negotiate, Major Griffiths proceeded with them to a neighbouring chief for that purpose: taking with him Mr. Blewitt, formerly a writer in Capt. Johnson's office, who understood Persian, that he might act as interpreter.

Many Affghans ascended the hill where our troops awaited the issue of the expected conference; and exchanges of friendly words passed between both parties. This lasted upwards of an hour; but hostilities were renewed by the Affghans,[1] who snatched at the

---

[1] Griffiths, when he later joined Lady Sale in captivity, told her that the British had opened negotiations by waving a white cloth. He subsequently learnt that the Afghans considered the waving of a loonghee to be an admission of unconditional surrender; they had therefore naturally resented the British refusal to hand over their weapons.

firearms of the men and officers. This they of course resisted; and drove them off the hill: but the majority of the enemy, who occupied the adjoining hills commanding our position, commenced a galling fire upon us. Several times they attempted to dislodge our men from the hill, and were repulsed; until, our ammunition being expended, and our fighting men reduced to about thirty, the enemy made a rush, which in our weak state we were unable to cope with. They bore our men down knife in hand; and slaughtered all the party except Capt. Souter and seven or eight men of the 44th and artillery. This officer thinks that this unusual act of forbearance towards him originated in the strange dress he wore: his poshteen having opened during the last struggle exposed to view the colour he had wrapped round his body; and they probably thought they had secured a valuable prize in some great bahadur, for whom a large ransom might be obtained.

Eighteen officers and about fifty men were killed at the final struggle at Gundamuk. Capt. Souter and the few remaining men (seven or eight) that were taken alive from the field were, after a detention of a month in the adjoining villages, made over to Akbar Khan and sent to the fort of Buddeeabad in the Lughman valley, where they arrived on the 15th of February.

III

The Captivity

On January 13th, the day that Major Griffiths's remnant of the 44th made its last stand at Gundamuk, Surgeon William Brydon rode alone into Jellalabad, the only British survivor of Elphinstone's army. But ahead of Lady Sale and her companions there still lay eight months of captivity in Afghan hands, and she devotes the remaining third of her book to this period of her adventures.

January 13th, 1842: We must now return to the General and his party. At 8 a.m. they mounted their horses; and with the Sirdar and his party rode down the pass, which bore fearful evidence to the last night's struggle. They passed some 200 dead bodies, many of them Europeans; the whole naked, covered with large gaping wounds. As the day advanced, several poor wretches of Hindostanees (camp followers, who had escaped the massacre of the night before) made their appearance from behind rocks and within caves, where they had taken shelter from the murderous knives of the Affghans and the inclemency of the climate. They had been stripped of all they possessed; and few could crawl more than a few yards, being frost-bitten in the feet. Here Johnson found two of his servants: the one had his hands and feet frost-bitten, and had a fearful sword cut across one hand, and a musket ball in his stomach; the other had his right arm completely cut through the bone; both were utterly destitute of covering, and had not tasted food for five days.

January 14th: We travelled over a dreadfully rough road: some of the ascents and descents were fearful to look at, and at first sight appeared to be impracticable.

At the commencement of the defile, and for some considerable distance, we passed 200 or 300 of our miserable Hindostanees, who had escaped up the unfrequented road from the massacre of the 12th. They were all naked and more or less frost-bitten: wounded and starving, they had set fire to the bushes and grass, and huddled all together to impart warmth to each other. Subsequently we heard that scarcely any of these poor wretches escaped from the defile: and that driven to the extreme of hunger they had sustained life by feeding on their dead comrades.

The wind blew bitterly cold at our bivouac; for the inhabitants of the fort refused to take us in; stating that we were Kaffirs. We therefore rolled ourselves up as warm as we could; and with our saddles for pillows braved the elements. General Elphinstone, Brig. Shelton, and Johnson considered themselves happy when one of the Affghans told them to accompany him into a wretched cow-shed, which was filled with dense smoke from a blazing fire in the centre of the hut. These officers and Mr. Melville were shortly after invited by Akbar Khan to dine with him and his party in the fort. The reception room was not much better than that they had left: they had, however, a capital dinner, some cups of tea, and luxurious rest at night; the room having been well heated by a blazing fire with plenty of smoke, with no outlet for either heat or smoke, except through the door and a small circular hole in the roof.

15th January: A bitterly cold wind blowing, we started at 7 A.M.; crossed two branches of the Punjshir river, which was not only deep but exceedingly rapid. The chiefs gave us every assistance: Akbar Khan carried Mrs. Waller over behind him on his own horse. One rode by me to keep my horse's head well up the stream. The Affghans made great exertions to save both men and animals struggling in the water; but in spite of all their endeavours five unfortunates lost their lives. We passed over many ascents and declivities; and at about 3 p.m. arrived at Tighree, a fortified town in the rich valley of Lughman.

The Sirdar desired the General, the Brigadier, and Johnson to take up their quarters with him, whilst the ladies and the other gentlemen were located in another fort.

A great number of Hindu Bunneahs reside at Tighree. We went to the fort of Gholab Moyenoodeen who took Mrs. Sturt and myself to the apartments of his mother and wife. Of course we could not understand much that they said; but they evidently made much of us, pitied our condition, told us to ask them for anything we required, and before parting they gave us a lump of goor filled with pistaches, a sweetmeat they are themselves fond of.

January 16th: Halted. They tell us we are here only thirty miles from Jellalabad. It being Sunday, we read prayers from a Bible and Prayer Book that were picked up on the field at Bhoodkhak.

January 17th: Early in the morning we were ordered to prepare to go higher up the valley. Thus all hopes (faint as they were) of going to Jellalabad were annihilated; and we plainly saw that, whatever might be said, we were virtually prisoners, until such time as Sale shall evacuate Jellalabad, or the Dost be permitted by our government to return to this country.

We had a little hail this morning; and shortly after, at about nine o'clock, we started, and travelled along the valley, which was a continuation of forts, until we arrived at Buddeeabad (about eight or nine miles): it is situated almost at the top of the valley, and close to the first range of hills towards Kaffristan.

Six rooms, forming two sides of an inner square or citadel, are appropriated to us; and a tykhana to the soldiers. This fort is the largest in the valley, and is quite new; it belongs to Mahommed Shah Khan: it has a deep ditch and a faussebraye all round. The walls of mud are not very thick, and are built up with planks in tiers on the inside. The buildings we occupy are those intended for the chief and his favourite wife; those for three other wives are in the outer court, and have not yet been roofed in. We number 9 ladies, 20 gentlemen, and 14 children. In the tykhana are 17 European soldiers, 2 European women, and 1 child: (Mrs. Wade, Mrs. Burnes, and little Stoker).

Akbar Khan, to our horror, has informed us that only one man of our force has succeeded in reaching Jellalabad (Dr. Brydon of the Shah's force: he was wounded in two places). Thus is verified what we were told before leaving Cabul; 'that Mahommed Akbar would annihilate the whole army, except one man, who should reach Jellalabad to tell the tale.'

Dost Mahommed Khan (the brother of Mahommed Shah Khan) is to have charge of us. Our parties were divided into the different rooms. Lady Macnaghten, Capt. and Mrs. Anderson and 2 children, Capt. and Mrs. Boyd and 2 children, Mrs. Mainwaring and 1 child, with Lieut. and Mrs. Eyre and 1 child, and a European girl, Hester Macdonald, were in one room; that adjoining was appropriated for their servants and baggage. Capt. Mackenzie and his Madras Christian servant Jacob, Mr. and Mrs. Ryley and 2 children, and Mr. Fallon, a writer in Capt. Johnson's office, occupied another. Mrs. Trevor and her 7 children and European servant, Mrs. Smith, Lieut. and Mrs. Waller and child, Mrs. Sturt, Mr. Mein, and I had another. In two others all the rest of the gentlemen were crammed.

It did not take us much time to arrange our property; consisting of one mattress and resai between us, and no clothes except those we had on, and in which we left Cabul.

Akbar Khan, Sultan Jan, and Ghoolam Moyen-oo-deen visited us. The Sirdar assured me we were none of us prisoners; requested that we would make ourselves as comfortable as circumstances would admit of; and told us that as soon as the roads were safe, we should be safely escorted to Jellalabad. He further informed me that I might write to Sale; and that any letters I sent to him he would forward. Of this permission I gladly took advantage to write a few guarded lines to say that we were well and safe.

January 19th: We luxuriated in dressing, although we had no clothes but those on our backs, but we enjoyed washing our faces very much, having had but one opportunity of doing so before, since we left Cabul. It was rather a painful process, as the cold and the glare of the sun on the snow had three times peeled my face, from which the skin came off in strips.

We had a grand breakfast, dhall and radishes; the latter large hot ones that had gone to seed, the former is a common pulse eaten by the natives; but any change was good, as we find our chupatties made of the coarse ottah anything but nice. Ottah is what in England is called pollard; and has to be twice sifted ere it becomes flour. The chupatties are cakes formed of this ottah mixed with water, and dried by standing by the fire set up on edge. Eating these cakes of dough is a capital recipe to obtain the heartburn. We parch rice and barley, and make them a substitute for coffee. Two sheep (alias lambs) are killed daily; and a regular portion of rice and ottah given for all. The Affghans cook; and well may we exclaim with Goldsmith: 'God sends meat, but the devil sends cooks'; for we only get some greasy skin and bones served out as they are cooked, boiled in the same pot as the rice, all in a lump. Capt. Lawrence divides it; and portions out our food as justly as he can. The chupatty is at once the plate and bread: few possess other dinner-table implements than their fingers. The rice even is rendered nauseous by having quantities of rancid ghee poured over it, such as in India we should have disdained to use for our lamps.

January 24th: A day or two ago the Sirdar sent some chintz to be divided amongst us. A second quantity was today given out; and we are working hard that we may enjoy the luxury of getting on a clean suit of clothes. There are very few of us that are not covered with crawlers, and, although my daughter and I have as yet escaped, we are in fear and trembling.

Dost Mahommed Khan took Mrs. Trevor's boys and some of the gentlemen out walking in the sugar-cane fields near the fort, which they enjoyed very much.

January 25th: The Sirdar sent eight pieces of long cloth to be divided amongst us. I fancy he is generous at little cost; and that it is all part of the plunder of our camp.

January 27th: A report that Sale has made another sally, and has taken a number of prisoners. I heard from him to-day: he has sent me my chest of drawers, with clothes, etc.: they were all permitted to come to me unexamined.

Far away in India, the first steps were being taken that would ultimately secure the release of Lady Sale and her companions. At the end of January news reached Lord Auckland of Brydon's arrival at Jellalabad and of the destruction of Elphinstone's army: he at once proclaimed that 'the most active measures have been adopted, and will be steadfastly prosecuted, for expediting powerful reinforcements to the Afghan frontier, and for assisting such operations as may be required in that quarter for the maintenance of the honour and interests of the British Government'. Regiments moved up to the frontier and on 5 February Major-General George Pollock arrived at Peshawar to take command of what was to become known as 'the Army of Retribution'.

February 9th: We hear that all our horses are to be taken away; as also our servants. Rain to-day, as if the clouds wept for our misfortunes.

February 10th: I received boxes from Sale, with many useful things;[1] and also books, which are a great treat to us. I wrote to him, but fear my letter will not reach him, as all notes that came for us were kept back by the Sirdar; who is very angry, having detected a private

[1] Lady Sale, it seems, was not very generous with her 'useful things'. Colin Mackenzie records how Mrs Eyre persuaded him to try to wheedle one or two needles out of Lady Sale, who had plenty. He said later that he had never exercised greater diplomacy in his life, but Lady Sale refused to part with a single needle. In contrast, says Mackenzie, young Mrs Mainwaring 'on receiving a box of useful articles from her husband at Jellalabad, most liberally distributed the contents among the other ladies, who were much in need'.

cossid between Capt. Macgregor and Major Pottinger; if we behave
ill again, the Sirdar says, woe will betide us. We had rain to-day.
Major Griffith arrived, with Mr. Blewitt.

February 11th: Rain. Today all arms have been taken from the officers,
on a promise that they shall be restored when we go away. I took poor
Sturt's sword myself and begged that the Sirdar would keep it himself; that we might be sure of its restoration, as being invaluable to his
widow. Dost Mahommed Khan, Abdool Guffoor Khan, etc. desired
me to keep it myself; acting in the handsomest manner, and evincing
much feeling on the occasion.

February 13th: A fine day. Not content with the arms given up, they
pretend our servants have others, and a general search took place to-
day; when all the poor wretches were fleeced of the few rupees they
had succeeded in securing on their persons.

February 14th: This is the day that Akbar Khan is to go over the river
towards Jellalabad to attack it. The 13th sent a quantity of clothes for
distribution amongst the gentlemen. I received a large packet of
letters, both from my family in the provinces, and also from England,
but no note from Sale; so the Sirdar is still angry about the private
correspondence. It was a very foolish attempt, for there was no news
of consequence to send; and rousing the Sirdar's suspicion is not the
way to make him kind to us.

February 15th: To-day we hear that our horses are not to be taken
away from us; and everything is to be done to make us comfortable.
There is an old adage, that 'Fair words butter no parsnips.'

February 19th: I heard from Sale. A friend writes me that there will
be no relief before April. At noon I was on top of the house; when an
awful earthquake took place. I had gone upstairs to see after my
clothes; for, servants being scarce, we get a sweeper, who also acts as
saces, to wash for us; and I hang them up to dry on the flat roof; we
dispense with starch and ironing and in our present situation we must
learn to do everything that is useful. But to return to the earthquake.
For some time I balanced myself as well as I could; till I felt the roof
was giving way. I fortunately succeeded in removing from my posi-

tion before the roof of our room fell in with a dreadful crash. The roof of the stairs fell in as I descended them; but did me no injury. All my anxiety was for Mrs. Sturt; but I could only see a heap of rubbish. I was nearly bewildered, when I heard the joyful sound, 'Lady Sale, come here, all are safe'; and I found the whole party uninjured in the courtyard. When the earthquake first commenced in the hills in the upper part of the valley, its progress was clearly defined, coming down the valley, and throwing up dust, like the action of exploding a mine. —I hope a soldier's wife may use a soldier's simile, for I know of nothing else to liken it to. Our walls, and gateways, and corner towers, are all much shaken, or actually thrown down. We had at least twenty-five shocks before dark; and about fifteen more during the night, which we spent in the courtyard. The end wall of the room Lady Macnaghten and party were in has sunk about two feet, and all the beams have started.

February 20th: I wrote to Sale, to tell him we were all safe. At 3 in the morning we had a pretty smart shock; and constant ones, some severe, and many very slight, on an average every half hour all day, and five or six slight ones at night. The gentlemen gave up their largest room to my party who were utterly roofless. Nearly all the others slept outside: but we had only one crack in the roof of our room, caused by part of the wall falling on it. The cold outside was intense; and the dew completely saturated the bed clothes last night; added to which, should the buildings come down, we were safer above, for the yard was so crammed that, in case of accident, half the people below must be crushed.

February 21st: At 1 in the morning a sharp shock made us run to the door. We had numerous light, and three or four pretty good shocks; they became more frequent in the evening. Part of our party made awnings in the court-yard to sleep under: but Mrs. Sturt and myself still preferred the house as safest.

Dost Mahommed Khan brought workmen to clear away the debris. He tells us our fort is the best of forty that have suffered in this valley —and that many are entirely thrown down. In one, a tower fell, and crushed five women and a man: others have not a wall remaining.

We have various reports regarding Jellalabad;—that it has been taken, that the walls and all the defences are thrown down, &c.

Dost Mahommed says that a man was sent as a spy to Jellalabad:

that Macgregor sent for him; and, with Sale, took the man round to show him the state of the place: that two bastions had sunk a little; but that they were not only able to withstand Akbar, but if he came against them they would meet him in the plain. It is said that Akbar intends sending Gen. Elphinstone away if he can get a palkee.[1] Lady Macnaghten has requested she may go with him; being, she says, differently circumstanced from the rest, who have most of them their husbands with them. Not even an animal's life was lost in our earthquake (I mean our fort). Lady M.'s cat was buried in the ruins, and dug out again.

February 22nd: My wounds are quite healed. We had earthquakes day and night; less severe, but equally frequent. A prop was put up in our room to support the broken roof. We experienced a curious shock in the evening like a heavy ball rolled over our heads. Some large pieces of hills have fallen, and immense masses of stone. I miss some large upright stones on the hills that divide us from Kaffristan, and looked in the distance like large obelisks.

February 23rd: This has been a very close and gloomy day; earthquakes frequent, and some very sharp ones. We hear that, at Charbagh, 120 Affghans and 20 Hindostanees were buried in the ruins.

Capt. Bygrave arrived, with one of his feet severely frost-bitten: we were all rejoiced to see him, having long supposed he had shared the fate of many. On the 12th January, perceiving that our army was utterly annihilated, he left the road at midnight, turned to the left, and took to the mountains: where he was out seven days and six nights. During a part of this time he was accompanied by Mr. Baness, the merchant from Delhi, who had with him a small bag containing coffee; on this they subsisted, taking each about six grains a day. When this was spent Baness proceeded on; and we afterwards heard that he got to Jellalabad, but so worn out with fatigue that he only arrived to die. Bygrave reached the Sirdar's camp in the afternoon of the 15th and remained there with him till the 21st, on which day he started for Buddeeabad; and has, as before remarked, this day joined the other prisoners.

February 24th: Very few shocks, and those gentle ones: but all last night and great part of today, particularly late in the evening, there

---

[1] *Elphinstone was by now very ill indeed with severe dysentery.*

was a tremulous motion as of a ship that has been heavily struck by a sea, generally feeling as if on the larboard quarter, and accompanied by a sound of water breaking against a vessel. At other times we have just the undulatory motion of a snake in the water: but the most uncommon sensation we have experienced has been that of a heavy ball rolling over our heads, as if on the roof of our individual room, accompanied by the sound of distant thunder.

General Pollock with 5,000 men is said to have arrived at Peshawer, as commander of the force in Affghanistan, and with full political power. The news came from a merchant, who has arrived from Peshawer.

February 25th: The earth is still unquiet, constantly trembling, with reports like explosions of gunpowder, but no severe shocks.

We hear that the camp followers we passed on the road are eating the bodies of those who die: eventually they must take their turn; for frost-bitten as they are, they never can leave the places we saw them at.

On 28 February, Lord Ellenborough arrived at Calcutta to take over from Lord Auckland as Governor-General.

March 3rd and 4th: Earthquakes as usual. To-day every servant that is frost-bitten or unable to work has been turned out of the fort: they were stripped first of all they possessed. I received two notes from Sale, dated the 11th and 16th.

March 9th: Several slight shocks at night; after which, great screaming and alarm. Husnoo, a sweeper, being a disappointed man, attempted to strangle Rookeria, a woman of the same cast. The gentlemen searched every corner; and the delinquent had to jump down the wall; in doing which he seriously hurt his back. There was no other mode of escape, as we are always locked in the square at night.

March 10th: The Affghans gave Mr. Husnoo a desperate flogging; and had it not been for the officers, would have hanged him afterwards; he was, however, stripped and turned out of the fort.

March 11th: The Mirza Bowadeen Khan is getting a paper signed by all of us, to say he has treated us well: from whence we suspect he thinks our party will eventually gain the ascendant.

March 14th: Earthquakes in plenty. Mrs. Boyd was confined early this morning; adding another to our list of female captives. In the evening Affghans came in with many reports; confirming the account that there have been three fights, in which the Affghans have been worsted; that after the last battle Akbar Khan in his retreat was fired at by an Affghan, and wounded in the body and arms.

The Affghans tell two tales: one, that Shah Shoojah had bribed a man with a lakh of rupees to assassinate Akbar; the other, that Capt. Macgregor gave Abdool Guffoor Khan (Akbar's cousin) the same sum to procure the like effect; and that Abdool and all his family have been put to death.

They say that Akbar Khan chafes like a lion taken in the toils, with his three wounds,—for he was previously wounded in the thigh. He allowed no one but Mahommed Shah Khan to enter his tent.

March 16th: I was made very anxious by a report that Jellalabad had been taken: it proved to be a piece of wit, to impose on those who were eager for news. The Mirza, as soon as he heard of it, left his tent to come and assure me that it was false, and to request I would not make myself unhappy about it.

Of authentic accounts the last are, that there was a burj between Sirdar's camp and Jellalabad, which Akbar wished to establish as an outpost, and intended taking possession of. 'Fighting Bob' (as Sale is called), having got intelligence of their intentions, sent a party of sappers and miners with supports during the night, who destroyed the work and returned; and on the Sirdar's party's arrival, they found their intended post annihilated.

Further accounts regarding the Sirdar's wound state, that it was purely accidental. A favourite Pesh Khedmut, who had accompanied Akbar Khan to Bokhara, and had been with him in all his changes of fortune, was assisting him to dismount from his horse, when some part of his dress catching upon his fire-arms, they went off, and the Sirdar was wounded through the arm and lungs. One account states, that the unfortunate man was instantly cut to pieces; another that he was burnt alive; and that to the last he took his oath on the Koran that the act was an accident. There is nothing too brutal or savage for Akbar to accomplish: he is known to have had a man flayed alive in his presence, commencing at the feet, and continuing upwards until the sufferer was relieved by death.

The Mirza has sent for nalbunds to shoe our horses; and there seems to be an idea that we shall not long remain here. We have lately made ourselves more comfortable: a temporary shed or two, composed of mats, have been erected since the great earthquake for the accommodation of those who were turned out of their rooms at that time, all of course at their own expense. We have also got stools to sit upon, and charpoys instead of lying on the ground; and a cujava, with boards nailed on it, serves me for a table—a decided luxury, there being but one other here. *Mirza,* in this man's case denominates a secretary. He is a kind of under-jailor (Dost Mahommed Khan being the principal one), who issues out all our allowance of good: to some he is civil, and has been so to me: to some very rude; and has even drawn his knife on one of the officers.

March 19th: No earthquake today. The Mirza is ordered off; and the Nazir of Mahommed Shah Khan is come in his place.

The Nazir begins well: says the Mirza cheated us of our allowance; that two sheep and twenty fowls are to be distributed daily, one seer of ottah, and one of rice to each room, with ghee in proportion; and that we are to have keshmish, sugar and tea, monthly.

March 21st: The no-roz, or vernal equinox. Mr. Melville brought us a bouquet of narcissuses, which we highly prized, for it is long since we have seen even a blade of grass.

The report of today is, that troops have at length arrived at Jellalabad; having lost 1,000 out of 3,000 men in forcing the Khyber pass.[1]

All the forts about this place are filling fast with wounded men of Akbar's army; and skirmishes are said to take place daily at Jellalabad, in which we never hear of the Sirdar being victorious.

A nalbund is come to this fort and is shoeing all our horses, we paying for the same. This looks like preparation for a move; but we trust it will not be precipitate flight to Khoolloom with Akbar Khan, as we have heard it hinted.

March 26th: Letters from Jellalabad. The 31st, and 9th Queens, a regiment of Dragoons, two of Native Cavalry, eight of infantry, three eighteen-pounders, three nine-pounders, and six six-pounders,

[1] The report was untrue. Pollock's army did not begin its advance through the Khyber until 5 April; Jellalabad was relieved a few days later. Pollock's casualties were nothing like as heavy as Lady Sale had been told.

are expected there on the 1st of April. Gerard has been wounded. Abbott hit by a spent ball: all well, thank God!

This news is very different from what we heard this morning, which was that those left at Cabul and Ghuznee have been sent to Bokhara to be sold as slaves; and that our turn would come next.

The thermometer of our spirits has risen greatly. We hear from Jellalabad that all at Cabul are well, and that Ghuznee has been obliged to surrender; but that the officers are all well, safe and taken care of, as we are here.

Earthquakes in the usual number.

March 31st: The weather has cleared up again. Today's report is that we go on Monday to Tagow or Kaffiristan. The people are becoming very civil; ask if we will spare their lives, and are sending their women away. We tell them that all who behave well to us will have their property respected, and be well treated.

They say that Sultan Jan is really gone with 3,000 men to the Cholah Khyber; that our force coming up gives no quarter; that the Affghans sent spies in the guise of country people, with things to sell, to see what loot the Feringhees had. They report that not only the soldiers, but also the officers, are packed close in small palls, without beds, chairs, tables or anything but the clothes on their backs.

April 1st: A famous hoax went round, that a letter had come from Macgregor, that government were going to ransom us from Mahommed Shah Khan for three lakhs of rupees, and that we were to leave Buddeeabad on Wednesday, that Sultan Jan had been defeated in the Khyber, and that Akbar Khan had fled to Cabul.

April 6th: Further reports assure us that Shah Shoojah left Cabul to proceed to Begramee, where his tents were pitched; but he had not got further than Musjed, where John Hicks's tomb is, in front of the Bala Hissar gate, when he was cut down in his palkee by the son of Zeman Khan and was immediately cut to pieces.[1]

April 10th: We were hurried from daybreak to get ready. Mahommed Shah Khan has taken away all Lady Macnaghten's jewels, to the value

[1] The report of the murder of Shoojah and of the assassin's identity was true. John Hicks was an artillery officer who had died at Kabul in the service of the Mogul Emperor Aurangzeb as early as 1666. His tomb is mentioned by many of those who wrote eyewitness accounts of the First Afghan War.

of above a lakh of rupees; and her shawls, valued at between 30,000 and 40,000 rupees.

The Mirza has returned; he, and the Nazir promise to send a box, which I have no means of carrying, as also our servants, who are unable to go with us to Jellalabad to Sale: however, as they crammed the box into their own godown, I strongly suspect they mean to keep it to themselves. My chest of drawers they took possession of with great glee—I left some rubbish in them and some small bottles, that were useless to me. I hope the Affghans will try their contents as medicine, and find them efficacious: one bottle contained nitric acid, another a strong solution of lunar caustic!

April 11th: We got an early breakfast; and soon after started again; leaving the soldiers, two European women (Mrs. Wade and Mrs. Burnes), and the child, Seymour Stoker, with all the maimed servants and those that would not go with us. The women and child certainly ought to have accompanied us.

We went to Ali Kund, a rather long march, and found the Sirdar there, seated in his nalkee, and looking very ill. He was particular in bowing to us all, making every demonstration of civility.

Three tents were pitched for us on a pretty and green spot. The valley was beautiful under cultivation; and to us doubly so, from our not having seen a blade of grass for so long a time. The field pea was in blossom; several sorts of cranesbill, gentian, forget-me-not, campions etc.

Having taken the precaution to have some fowls roasted over night, we got a good meal; and we design, whenever we march, and can procure them, to do the same.

April 12th: Set out at eight A.M., and arrived at our ground at five P.M. A very long march over a sterile country. We only twice met with water, which was very shallow, and so sandy that our horses would not drink it. We did not see a vestige of a habitation, nor any cultivation.

April 13th: Made a march of about twelve miles: the country sterile and rocky; the road rather better than yesterday; only one very awkward ascent, when all the ladies got out of their kujavas. I always ride; and have my own saddle: but some of the ladies are obliged to ride gentleman fashion, sitting on their beddings instead of saddles.

April 14th: We were detained a long time at the Cabul river; which we crossed on a jhala (or raft) supported on inflated skins; and encamped close to the bank, but further down the stream, as the current was very rapid: the river is said to be twenty feet deep at some places. Here we found Akbar Khan. Our baggage came up at dusk, as also the tents; but a great deal did not get over, and has to wait for daylight. Several horses swam over; and their efforts and those of their riders, were a source of great interest to us.

On 16 April General Pollock's force reached Jellalabad, sardonically played in by the garrison's band to the old Jacobite tune, 'Oh, but ye've been long o'coming'.

April 17th: This day I was attacked with fever.

April 18th: Halted. I was worse today; a pleasant prospect, as we daily expect to march.

April 19th: A miserable day, and we marched through heavy rains to Tezeen.

The Sirdar could only get two camels with kujavas; but gave up his own palkee to Lady Macnaghten and me. I was utterly incapable of sitting on horseback: however, as I had to sit backwards, with very little room, nothing to lean against, and keep a balance against Lady M. and Mrs. Boyd's baby, I benefited but little, except in the grandeur of a royal equipage. My turban and habit were complately saturated by the rain; and I shivered as I went. On arrival at the fort I was told to go into the room where Mahommed Shah's and other chief's ladies were. They received us with great kindness; and kept heaping up three large fires for us to dry our clothes by. The court-yard was a deep mass of mud; and in the evening Affghans carried us on their backs across it to another apartment, which was nicely covered with *numdas:* our beddings were all regularly sopped through. The whole of the baggage was sent on to the camp with our servants. A dinner was cooked for us—a huge dish of rice, with dhye (sour curds) in the centre and ghee poured over all! This is a favourite Affghan dish, and therefore my bad taste must be arraigned for thinking it not eatable. Fortunately I had a little tea and sugar in a bag, suspended from the crupper of my saddle: they gave us some milk and I found tea the most refreshing repast. We stretched ourselves on the numdas (coarse felt carpets) in our still wet clothes. In the night I began shivering again; and Capt. Anderson, my nearest bed-mate, covered me with a bed cloak, which, strange to say, soon imparted warmth to me. We slept, large and small, thirty-four in a room 15 feet by 12; and we lay on the floor, literally packed together, with a wood fire in the centre, and using pine torches for candles.

April 20th: The Sirdar fears if he is taken by us, we shall either hang him or blow him from a gun. Mahommed Shah Khan is in a great fright also. Sultan Jan appears to be our bitterest enemy. The Sirdar says *he alone* could take us through the country: or, if he wished it, he could assemble 5,000 men at any point to attack us.

It is said that Mackenzie is to go to Jellalabad on a secret mission. He will not be allowed to take any letters for individuals.

We had rain all day; and our wet chogahs, etc. hanging up, increased the damp. I wrote a few lines in pencil to Sale by a trooper who expected to go with Mackenzie, recommending both this trooper himself (Oomar Khan), and the Rajah Ali Bahadur to him: both have been very useful to us. We had rain all day, and three earthquakes.

Mackenzie did not go after all.

Mrs. Waller increased the community, giving birth to a daughter:[1] she, Mrs. Waller, and Mr. and Mrs. Eyre, got a room to themselves and their children, diminishing our number to twenty-nine. A slight earthquake, and a fine night.

April 21st: A fine sunshiny day: we went out to camp; getting on the first horses we could find: mine was a half-starved beast that could scarcely put one foot before the other. We had scarcely a mile to go. We hear that we are to halt here one day; and then go on to Zenganah, where the snow is four feet deep, and to stay there for four months. Rain in the evening; and very heavy rain at night. The General, who is said to be dying, Pottinger, Mackenzie, Dr. Magrath, the Eyres and Wallers are left at the fort.

Major Pottinger expostulated with Akbar; and told him that surely he did not make war on women and children, and that it was great cruelty to drive us about the country in the way they are doing; that when the Dost [*i.e. Dost Mahommed, Akbar's father*] and the ladies of the family (amongst them Akbar's wife, the daughter of Mahommed Shah Khan) went to Hindostan, they travelled with every comfort

[1] Akbar's jovial comment to George Lawrence was, 'the more of us the better for him'.

procurable, and probably many more than they would have experienced in their own country. To this he replied, I will do whatever you wish: but Mahommed Shah Khan is gone to Cabul; the very bread I eat I get from him; and until he returns I cannot do anything.

April 22nd: We were roused before daylight with orders to march immediately; and as we had fully expected to halt for another day or two, all was confusion.

I was still too weak to ride; and Mrs. Boyd kindly gave me her place in the kujava, I carrying her baby. It was my first attempt, and the conveyance was a particularly small one of the kind; for when the resai was put in to sit on, there was not one foot and a half square; and I found (being rather a tall person) the greatest difficulty in doubling up my long legs into the prescribed compass.

On first starting, we passed on our right a large mountain-slip, caused by the earthquake near to a cave, where there are a great number of bodies. The hills were very precipitous on our left, and high on both sides. We also passed a cave at some small distance, in front of which were some dead bodies and many bones strewed about: and from the blood close to its entrance, there is every reason to believe that the inhabitants were supporting nature by devouring each other.[1] I saw three poor wretches crawling on hands and knees just within the cave: but all we had to bestow upon them was pity, not unmingled with horror at the evidence of cannibalism but too apparent. These miserable creatures called to us for that relief which we had it not in our power to afford; and we can only hope that their sufferings were speedily terminated by death.

April 23rd: Being still very weak, I am glad to hear we are likely to halt here eight days.

April 24th: The General (Elphinstone) died last night, and his remains are to be sent to Jellalabad. Mackenzie was sent there on a secret mission just afterwards.[2]

Mahommed Shah Khan says he will not give us any thing besides ottah. I supposes he keeps all the good things for the Affghan ladies;

[1] As other accounts make clear, these were an unhappy remnant of camp-followers who had taken part in the retreat.

[2] Mackenzie was sent by Akbar on parole to Jellalabad to see if terms could be negotiated with General Pollock. Mackenzie reached Jellalabad on 25 April.

some of whom inhabit two mud huts on the hill, and the others are lodged in black tents more fragile than our own. Mahommed Rufeek, our present keeper and purveyor, has purchased twelve sheep on his own account for us; and Akbar Khan has sent twelve camels to Cabul to bring rice and ghee. We are also busy making chebootras: we hang up our resais and blankets for roof and walls, and find they make very comfortable places to sit in all day.

April 27th: The Sirdar and Major Pottinger paid us a visit. The former tells us we are not to be angry; that nothing is procurable here; that he has sent to Cabul for every thing for us. He brought some native shoes and cloth for distribution. Miller and Moore, the two soldiers who attended on the General, have been liberated: but Akbar says that it is not prudent to let them go at present, as the roads are unsafe!

April 28th: We have converted our chebootras into arbours made of juniper. We were driven from ours today before dinner by a shower of rain. At night we had thunder, hail, and showers of rain, that came on in gusts.

We have just heard that Miller was disguised as an Affghan to lead the camel that conveyed the General's body. Moore looked too English to attempt it. Near Jugdaluk, the party of ten horsemen were attacked, and the box, which was supposed to contain treasure, broken open. We at first heard that they had mutilated the poor old man's body; but only a few stones were thrown, one of which struck the head.

Miller was beaten a good deal, and wounded with a knife; but saved his life by saying he was a Mussulman: he had to return. The body was sent on; but I believe there is as yet no authentic account of its arrival at Jellalabad.[1]

It is reported that the Dost has written to Akbar Khan to say, that, if there is any chance of regaining the throne, he was to fight for it; but if not, not to drive us women and children about the country; as it was against his interest that we should be ill treated. Perhaps he pities the wives of all these Ghilzye chiefs, who go wherever we do: they however have the best and largest kujavas, and plenty of them;

[1] Akbar had chivalrously ordered that Elphinstone's body should be taken to Jellalabad, where it eventually arrived and was buried with full military honours. Elphinstone lies there today, in an unmarked grave, in what is now a fortress of the Afghan army.

whilst with us, many ladies unfit to ride, are forced to do so, and even without side or any saddles; for myself, I would rather walk than be again packed into a kujava.

May 2nd: In a conference with Pottinger, Troup and many other English and Affghans—amongst the latter Mahommed Shah Khan—Akbar Khan became greatly excited. He said, that on the religious cry being raised, he killed the Envoy, he destroyed our army; and now that he has drawn down the vengeance of the British upon him, the rest are deserting him: that he has kept his feelings pent up within his own breast, until they have preyed upon his vitals; and that, were he in power now, he would exterminate every one of the recreant Mussulmans who have deserted him and left him to obloquy.

May 4th: 200 horsemen have been sent from Cabul to the Sirdar, (Akbar Khan): Zeman Shah Khan invites him to assume the throne. He was sleeping when they arrived; but the prospect of a crown soon chased his slumbers; and he was quickly back on horseback with Pottinger, leaving orders for Troup, on his arrival, to follow. Mackenzie was not to go to Jellalabad; but to wait half way for further orders from the Sirdar.

The Sirdar has been urgent (but ineffectually of course) with Mr. Eyre to go to Cabul to lay his guns for him. We hear that the hostages are all again with Zeman Shah Khan.

May 7th: I have before adverted to Mackenzie's secret mission to Jellalabad. It was first, to ascertain what terms our party would propose: the reply was an offer of two lakhs of rupees for all the prisoners, and that the sooner we were given up to our own people the greater would be the friendship of our government; but that the grand question of peace or war, and the settlement of the country, must depend upon replies to be received from the Governor-General. The Sirdar has sent in his rejoinder by Mackenzie; saying, he does not want money;[1] nothing but the friendship of our nation; and that if the ladies and children go, he cannot part with the gentlemen yet.

---

[1] But according to Kaye, Akbar was demanding eight lakhs of rupees, plus an annual pension of two lakhs. J. A. Norris, in his admirable account of *The First Afghan War*, surmises that Akbar may have been too proud to tell his prisoners that he was trying to sell his support to the British.

May 8th: Serjt. Deane's wife, a Persian woman, has been taken by force and married to a younger brother of Mahommed Shah Khan. Whenever this man enters her presence, she salutes him with her slipper. It is only within a few days that she has been told of Deane's death: she appears to have been sincerely attached to him; and is represented as a very pretty young woman.

The man who took the General's body to Jellalabad has returned. He seems highly pleased with the present he has received of 200 rupees: and it appears to have had a good effect; for he reports in glowing terms on the grand turn-out for the funeral, the salvoes fired, etc. on the occasion; and the magnificent appearance of our troops.

May 10th: Capt. Anderson's little girl was restored, to the great joy of her parents.[1]

By now, as Lady Sale says, 'parties ran high at Cabul'. The various factions, led by Akbar Khan, Futteh Jung (heir-apparent of the deceased Shoojah), Zeman Shah Khan, who had been temporarily King during the insurrection, Amenoolah and others were all at loggerheads.

Now is the time to strike the blow, but I much dread dilly-dallying just because a handful of us are in Akbar's power. What are *our* lives when compared with the honour of our country? Not that I am at all inclined to have my throat cut: on the contrary, I hope that I shall live to see the British flag once more triumphant in Affghanistan; and then I have no objection to the Ameer Dost Mahommed Khan being reinstated: only let us first show them that we can conquer them, and humble their treacherous chiefs in the dust.

May 11th: Major Pottinger writes that there is no present chance of our liberation.

Akbar Khan professes that he does not want money from us; but he laughs at our offer of two lakhs for the whole party; and has sent back to say he wishes for eight. It has been recommended that we shoulder offer him five; but the general opinion is that we shall remain in captivity till all is settled.

---

[1] Mary Anderson, aged four, had been treated 'with the greatest possible kindness', according to Eyre, by Zeman Shah Khan and his family. When restored to her parents she could still understand English, but could speak only Persian, particularly the phrase, 'My father and mother are infidels, but I am a Mussulman'.

May 16th: I kept the anniversary of my marriage by dining with the ladies of Mahommed Shah Khan's family. It was an extremely stupid visit. They were, generally speaking, inclined to *embonpoint,* largely formed and coarsely featured; their dress inelegant, and of the coarsest materials. The dress, which covers the whole person, nearly resembles a common night-dress; and has tacked on to it coins, or other pieces of silver or gold, such as crescents, etc., all over the sleeves, the front and the sides, from the shoulders to the feet. They wear their hair in innumerable small plaits hanging down: these are arranged once a week after taking the bath; and the tresses are then well stiffened with gum. The Cabul women are much addicted to the use of both white and red paint; and they colour not only the nails, as in Hindostan, but the whole hand up to the wrist, which looks as though it had been plunged in blood, and to our ideas is very disgusting. A chuddah is thrown over the head and shoulders in the house, as in Hindostan; and when they go out they wear the bourka, ru-i-bund, and legwraps: high-heeled iron-shod slippers complete the costume. After a time an extremely dirty cloth was spread over the numdas in front of us, and dishes of pillau, dhye or sour curd, and fernez or sweet curd, were placed before us. Those who had not taken a spoon with them ate with their fingers, Affghan fashion;—an accomplishment in which I am by no means *au fait*. We drank water out of a tea-pot.

May 17th: I heard this morning that part of my letters regarding the siege had arrived in England, and been laid before the Court of Directors.

May 21st: I received two notes from Sale dated the 15th; informing me that he had received a highly gratifying letter from Lord Ellenborough, and another from Sir Jasper Nicholls, regarding the holding of Jellalabad, the chupao on Akbar's camp, etc.; and stating that the 35th were to be made light infantry; the Company's troops to have medals, and to bear 'Jellalabad' and a mural crown on their colours: also that Lord Ellenborough would request Her Majesty's permission that the 13th should be similarly honoured.[1]

Chintz, sugar candy, tea, and cheese, distributed amongst the ladies; they were sent to us by our friends at Jellalabad: also Shalu

[1] And so they were.

(Turkey red cotton cloth) and jean, with boots and shoes for the gentlemen. We also received the March overland mail.

The captives were now moved by Akbar up to Kabul, passing en route *many signs of the massacre in January. At the Huft Kotul, for example, 'we came upon a sad scene of decaying bodies, amongst which poor Major Ewart's was still recognisable'. The road was in places 'dreadful to go through: both to the sight and smell equally offensive'. On 25 May they arrived at Kabul, where party fighting was still in progress, and were placed in a fort behind the Siah Sung hills. Here Akbar joined them.*

May 25th: The Sirdar says he will not remain here when our force comes up, but retire to the Kohistan, and allow the English to take Cabul: after which he will come forward with an offer to go to Hindostan, and take his father's place, if they will permit the Ameer Dost Mahommed Khan to return and rule in this country.

Pollock was still stationary at Jellalabad, as was General Nott at Kandahar. Both had received orders originating from the new Governor-General, Lord Ellenborough, ordering a withdrawal from Afghanistan: but both had procrastinated. There were constant rumours among the Afghans that the British were about to march on Kabul. Akbar, to raise the sinews of war, kidnapped Amenoolah Khan in the hopes of extracting money from him.

June 7th: If Akbar procures even one lakh of ready cash, he can do much mischief; by raising troops even for a few weeks to annoy our force. The celerity with which troops are raised is quite astonishing to us; who are accustomed to see recruits drilled for a length of time. Here, every man is born a soldier; every child has his knife,—that weapon which has proved so destructive in the hands of a hostile peasantry, incited against us by the moollahs, who threaten eternal perdition to all who do not join in the cause of the Ghazeeas; whilst heaven filled with Houris, is the recompence for every man who falls in a religious war. With them, the only expense attending the soldier consists in his pay, which is scanty; his horse, if he have one, is his own; and every Affghan is armed completely with some three or four of these knives, of different sizes—from that as long as a sword to a small dagger—pistols, and a juzail; which latter predominates over the matchlock: they carry much further than our muskets; so that when our men are beyond range to hit them, they pour a destroying fire on us.

June 26th: Fearing a chupao on Budeeabad, all the prisoners there were brought away: they were fed on bread and water only after we left. The day after our departure, Mrs. Wade (wife of a sergeant) changed her attire, threw off the European dress, and adopted the costume of the Mussulmans; and, professing to have changed her creed also, consorted with the Nazir of our inveterate enemy, Mahommed Shah Khan, and gave information of some plans laid by the men for their escape; which nearly caused them all to have their throats cut. Having reported to her Affghan paramour the manner in which her husband had secreted some gold mohurs in his jorabs, he was of course plundered of them. The Hindostanees were stripped of every article of clothing they possessed; and had even the rags taken off their sores, to ascertain there was no money concealed: they were then turned out. Some got to Jellalabad; through the kindness of a Hindu Bunneah, who sent them down on a jhala; others have been made slaves. Of the unfortunate servants Mrs. Sturt and I left behind us, we have no tidings.

When Lady Sale and the officer prisoners, with their wives and children, had been moved to the Kabul neighbourhood, the other ranks had been left at Budeeabad.

Of so incorrect a personage as Mrs. Wade[1] I shall only further say, that she is at Mahommed Shah Khan's fort with her Affghan lover; and has taken with her young Stoker. As he is the son of a man in Sale's regiment, I am doing all I can to get the Sirdar (through Capt. Troup's entreaty) to have him brought here; and again placed under Mrs. Burnes's care.

July 1st: The Sirdar has promised that Stoker shall be sent back to us; but he has not yet arrived.[2]

July 8th: Mishdeen belongs to Sultan Khan. This is the place we are likely to go to, if we are removed from hence. When little Tootsey (Capt. Anderson's child) was carried off in the Khoord Cabul pass,

---

[1] The enraged Sergeant Wade declared that when General Pollock reached Kabul he would petition to have his wife hanged. They were both among those finally rescued, but it is not known whether Wade carried out this threat.

[2] This is Lady Sale's last mention of little Seymour Stoker, not yet three years old. But we know from Mackenzie's memoirs that he died just before the prisoners were rescued. He had been cruelly ill-treated by the abominable Mrs Wade.

she was taken direct to Cabul; and the Khan rode up and down the streets with her; offering her for sale for 4,000 rupees. After some negotiation regarding the price, Conolly purchased the child. . . . Nothing could exceed the kindness of Zeman Shah Khan, both to the hostages and the little girl; who became much attached to her new friends. Taj Mahommed Khan and many others did all they could, consistently with the safety of both parties, to make them comfortable.

July 14th: Mrs. Trevor gave birth to another girl, to add to the list of captives.[1]

Two earthquakes to-day.

July 24th: At two p.m. Mrs. Sturt presented me with a granddaughter;—another female captive.

July 27th: Troup arrived from Jellalabad. Nothing has been decided on which tends towards our release.

July 28th: Troup, who purchased a quantity of things of all kinds for us at Jellalabad, *opened his shop:* and I procured arrow root, cotton gloves, reels of cotton, tape, soap, jalap, and cream of tartar.

Troup left us in the evening, and went to the Wuzeer. He expects to be sent to Jellalabad; and so I gave him more of my Journal, to take to Sale.

July 31st: Had Skinner lived, he would have thrown more light than any other person upon the late events; as he was the bearer of the messages, more especially of the one sent on the night before the Envoy's death. It is as nearly certain as such an event can be, that poor Skinner, who was evidently a dupe to Akbar Khan, was put to death by his orders. At Jugdaluk, after the General, the Brigadier, and Johnson were in the Sirdar's power, Major Thain went to the other officers and said, 'I fear there is treachery: poor Skinner has been shot; and had the object of the Affghan only been to kill a Feringhee, he would not have passed *me* to shoot *him*.' There can be little doubt, that the Sirdar was anxious to put out of the way one who could give such fearful evidence against him. Trevor was also much in the

[1] This posthumous child (it will be remembered that Trevor had been killed with Macnaghten) brought Mrs Trevor's brood up to *eight*.

Envoy's confidence; and he also became a victim. I have, however, heard that Skinner was not in reality the dupe he appeared to be: and that he had expressed to the Envoy his conviction that the Sirdar was not trustworthy. Yet, if so, it is strange he should have placed the faith he did in him during the retreat; and have advised our going over to him;—unless indeed he saw further into Akbar's policy than others; and believed that we should be treated with honour and kept by him as a *dernier ressort*. What will now be our fate seems very uncertain: but I still think he will not cut our throats;—not out of love to us, but because the other chiefs would resent it; as, having possession of us, they could at least obtain a handsome sum as our ransom.

Lord Ellenborough had given General Nott the option of retiring from Kandahar to India by way of Kabul. Nott elected to do so, and on 7 August he began his march from Kandahar to the capital. Pollock, from Jellalabad, marched on Kabul a fortnight later.

August 9th: We hear that the Kandahar force is coming up; and it is expected that the one from Jellalabad will do the same. . . . The servants have a report that we are forthwith to be taken away, to, or towards, Bokhara. For two days there have been eight camels here, with their surwans ready; which looks as if the Wuzeer meditated our removal, in case of the force coming up.

August 13th: There is now an idea,—whether only the fertile emanations of prisoners' brains or not, time must unfold,—but an opinion prevails, that Akbar is so ungallant as to be heartily tired of dragging the women and children about the country at his heels; and that, if any flight is designed, it will be that of himself and four hostages; Pottinger, Lawrence, and Troup, to be decidedly three of them: we are not so certain of the fourth; but at present we have selected either Gen. Shelton or Capt. Johnson.

The news that Nott had marched from Kandahar reached the captives at Kabul on 15 August. Akbar told them that Pollock, at Jellalabad, had not yet moved, but that if he did the prisoners would be moved out of his reach at half an hour's notice 'to a fine climate, with plenty of ice', which they correctly guessed to be Bameean. Pollock marched on the 20th.

August 21st: The late newspapers have not a little amused me. They show that the editors catch at every expression, used in any letters they have read; or on any comments they hear on news from Affghanistan. A regular controversy has arisen between one, who asserts that Lady Sale in her letters evinces a strong prepossession in favour of Akbar Khan, and another, who thinks Lady Sale wrote as she did, because she was a prisoner; to which the first rejoins, that he does not think Lady S. would under any circumstances write that which was false. *There* he is right; but I would not have written on the subject at all, unless I wrote as I thought: if people misunderstand, it is their fault and not mine. Again, they say it were better I had never written at all. Perhaps so: but it seems that details were wanting; my letters to Sale gave those; and he thought them of sufficient consequence to send them to the Governor-General and the Commander-in-Chief. They were afterwards sent to England by the former; and, if the papers tell truth, excited some attention in the highest circles. As to my "great prepossession" in favour of Akbar, my greatest wish is that Gen. Nott's force should march up to Ghuznee; release the prisoners there; and then that a simultaneous movement should take place of Nott's and Pollock's forces upon Cabul. Once again in power here, I would place Akbar, Mahommed Shah and Sultan Jan *hors de combat*: befriend those who have befriended us, and let the Affghans have the Ameer Dost Mahommed Khan back, if they like. He and his family are only an expense to us in India; we can restore them, and make friends with him. Let us first show the Affghans that we can both conquer them, and revenge the foul murder of our troops; but do not let us dishonour the British name by sneaking out of the country like whipped Pariah dogs. Affghanistan will become a by-word among the nations. Had we retreated, as poor Sturt proposed, without baggage, with celerity (forced marches to get through the snow), and had the men stood by us (a doubtful point,—they were so worn out and dispirited), we might have figured in history; and have cut out Xenophon's account of the retreat of the 10,000.

As to the justice of dethroning the Ameer Dost Mahommed, and setting up Shah Shoojah, I have nothing to say regarding it; nor regarding our policy in attempting to keep possession of a country of uncivilized people, so far from our own; whence all supplies of ammunition, money etc., must be obtained. Let our Governors-General and Commanders-in-chief look to that; whilst I knit socks for my grand-children: but I have been a soldier's wife too long to sit down tamely, whilst our honour is tarnished in the sight and opinion of savages. Had our army been cut to pieces by an avowed enemy, whether in the field or the passes—let them have used what stratagems they pleased,—all had been fair. Akbar had shone as another William Tell; he had been the deliverer of his country from a hateful yoke imposed on them by Kaffirs; but here he stands, by his own avowal freely made, the assassin of the Envoy;—not by proxy, but by his own hand. I do believe, he only meant to make him prisoner; for the purpose of obtaining better terms and more money: but he is a man of ungovernable passions; and his temper when thwarted is ferocious. He afterwards professed to be our friend;—we treated with him;—great was the credulity of those who placed confidence in him: still they blindly did so;—even after the letter was received from Conolly, at Bhoodkhak, confirming the previous warnings of his intentions towards us. He followed us, with his blood-thirsty Ghilzyes. Mahommed Shah Khan, his principal adviser, I might almost say his master, is the most inveterate of our enemies.[1] Akbar is a jovial smooth-tongued man: full of compliments and good fellowship; and has the knack of talking over both kaffirs and true believers.

To our cost, he did talk our chiefs over; and persuaded them of his friendship; but said that those sugs (dogs) of Ghilzyes were intent on murder and plunder; and totally unmanageable. In this way he hovered on our flank and rear: and when our people were massacred and his bloodhounds in human shape were tolerably glutted with their blood, the scene was changed; although it was constantly reacted. In the distance, a group of horsemen invariably appeared: they were beckoned to; questioned as to what chief was present,—it was invariably Akbar, who always pretended good faith, said his 300 horsemen were too few to protect us from the Ghilzyes, etc.,—and then, the following day witnessed a repetition of the slaughter, and pretended friendship; for that this friendship was a mere pretence, was acknowledged by him when he said, 'I was the man who killed your Envoy with my own hand; I destroyed your army; I threw aside all ties of family, deserted every thing, for the faith of Islam; and now I

---

[1] In 1963 an Afghan who claimed to be a grandson of Mahomed Shah Khan (but more probably his great-grandson) boasted to Dr Louis Dupree, of Pennsylvania State University, that 'my grandfather was a great man in the war against the British; it was he who was guardian of the British prisoners. They were not very brave, but my grandfather did all he could to make them comfortable . . . my grandfather always was a gentleman'. But most of the British, in particular George Lawrence, agreed with Lady Sale's assessment of the Khan.

am left to bear the opprobrium heaped on me by the Feringhees, whilst no one supports me: but were I in power, I would make the chiefs remember it!' and he then uttered maledictions on their heads. He has kept his word; has been a bitter enemy to all who have shown the slightest kindness to us; and grinds their money out of them by threats and torture.

A woman's vengeance is said to be fearful; but nothing can satisfy mine against Akbar, Sultan Jan and Mahomed Shah Khan. Still I say that Akbar, having for his own political purposes done as he said he would do—that is, destroyed our army,—letting only one man escape to tell the tale, as Dr. Brydon did,—and having got the families into possession;—I say, having done this, he has ever since we have been in his hands, treated us well:—that is, honour has been respected. It is true that we have not common comforts; but what we denominate such are unknown to Affghan females: they always sleep on the floor, sit on the floor, etc.—hardships to us. We have bought common charpoys at two rupees each; that is, a bed formed by four poles and ropes tied across and across them. Had we tables and chairs, we have not space for them; so many inhabit the same apartment. Individually I have no right to complain on this subject; as Lady Macnaghten, Mrs. Mainwaring, Mrs. Boyd, Mrs. Sturt, and I, occupy the same apartment. Capt. Boyd makes his bed on the landing-place of the stairs, or on the roof of the house; so that we have no *man*-kind amongst us, except the Boyds' two little boys, and Mrs. Mainwaring's baby. This little fellow was born just before the insurrection broke out in Cabul (in October): his father had gone with Sale's brigade; and we always call him Jung-i-Bahadur.[1]

After so long enduring the misery of having gentlemen night and day associated with us, we have found this a great relief.

The Wuzeer gives us rations of meat, rice, ottah, ghee, and oil; and lately fruit. At first our food was dressed for us; but it was so greasy and disgusting, that we asked leave to cook for ourselves. That again was a matter of taste: one person likes what another does not. By us a strong cup of coffee is considered a luxury; whilst an Affghan the

---

[1] Years after Lady Sale's death the Jung-i-Bahadur married one of her granddaughters. He returned to Kabul, an officer in the Indian Army, in the Second Afghan War, where he was greeted by an aged Afghan who had taken the news of his birth—in the old Commissariat Fort—to his father, who had already left Kabul with Sale's brigade. He died, Lieut.-Colonel E. P. Mainwaring, in 1922 and two of his children are alive today (1968).

other day, who had some given to him (he had never tasted any before), pronounced it bitter and detestable.

It is true, we have been taken about the country; exposed to heat, cold, rain, etc.; but so were their own women. It was, and is, very disagreeable: but we still are, *de facto,* prisoners; notwithstanding Akbar still persists in calling us—honoured guests: and, as captives, I say we are well treated. . . . We suffered more from uncleanliness than anything else. It was above ten days after our departure from Cabul, before I had the opportunity to change my clothes, or even to take them off and put them on again, and wash myself: and fortunate were those who did not possess much livestock. It was not until our arrival here (near Cabul) that we completely got rid of *lice,* which we denominated infantry: the fleas, for which Affghanistan is famed (and particularly Cabul), we call light cavalry.

The servants, of course, were worse off than ourselves; and, not having as good wardrobes as we had, communicated their pests, of the insect tribe, to the children they carried about; and thus the mothers obtained a double share. Bugs have lately made their appearance; but not in great numbers: the flies torment us; and the mosquitoes drive us half mad. But these annoyances, great as they are, are the results of circumstances which cannot be controlled; and when I say this, I suppose I shall again be accused of prepossession in favour of the Wuzeer. We ought, however, to bear in mind, that the Affghans are not addicted to general ablution: they wash their hands before and after their meals, which is but *comme il faut,* as they eat with their fingers; and they constantly wear the same clothes a month. This is not economy. The Wuzeer will take his bath perhaps once a week; and change his clothes: and the women never think of doing so oftener; and only open their hair at such times; which is kept smooth for that period by the application of gum to its innumerable plaits. Here again is a difference between their tastes and ours, who so enjoy bathing twice a day. . . .

Nothing can exceed the folly I have seen in the papers regarding my wonderful self;—how I headed the troops, etc. etc. It puts me in mind of Goldsmith's verses on Mrs. Blaze; in which he remarks, that 'the king himself has followed her, when she has gone before': and certainly I have thus headed the troops; for the chiefs told me to come on with them for safety's sake: and thus I certainly did go far in advance of the column; but it was no proof of valour, though one of prudence. . . . The only thing that has given me pleasure in the

Indian papers, is a subscription set on foot by the civilians, to purchase a sword, to be presented to Sale; because it shows that they appreciate his conduct; and I know that he will value it most highly.

As the armies of Pollock and Nott converged upon the capital, Akbar ordered his captives to be moved from the Kabul neighbourhood. They were on the road from 25 August until 3 September, when they arrived at their destination, Bameean, some hundred miles west of Kabul. Some, including Lady Sale, rode on ponies, others, with their children, travelled in camel litters. Two officers (Dr Berwick and Lieutenant Evans) with thirty-five British soldiers who had been left behind, sick, at Kabul on the original evacuation by the British, had joined the party. Their Afghan escort was under the command of one Saleh Mahommed, who had deserted the Shah's service eighteen months before and now, as news of the victories of Pollock and Nott filtered through, soon showed himself ready to change sides once more. Eldred Pottinger, the senior political officer of the prisoners' party, quickly took advantage of Saleh Mahommed's amenability and local chieftains began to come over to the British side. On 6 September Nott recaptured Ghuznee and on the 13th Pollock routed Akbar and his army at Tezeen.

September 14th: Zulficar Khan, Salamid Khan, and other chiefs joined us.

It would be a great injustice to Major Pottinger not to mention the active part he took in affairs. From his perfect knowledge of the Persian language, and his acquaintance with the manners and customs of the people, he well knew how to manage them, and take advantage of the slightest opening on their part in our favour. His coolness and decision were only equalled by the promptness with which he met the wishes of the chiefs; giving them *barats* on the neighbouring lands, empowering them to receive the government rents, etc.; all which documents, though he executed them with an air of great condescension and with the gravity of a judge, he well knew were mere pieces of waste paper: yet they had a magic charm for the time, which was all we required.

Saleh Mahommed, on the promise by Pottinger of a large reward, had now come over completely to the British side. He feared, however, that Akbar might make a desperate attempt to recapture the prisoners, and it was therefore decided to marched eastwards in the direction of the British forces. The party set out on 16 September. On the same day Pollock reached Kabul (Nott's force joined him there two days later) and immediately sent his military secretary, Sir Richmond Shakespear, with 600 Kuzzilbash cavalry, to rescue the prisoners.

September 16th: Saleh Mahommed Khan came up to us; and speaking in Persian to Capt. Lawrence, told him that he had succeeded in getting a few muskets; which, together with ammunition, he had brought with him on a camel: and requested that he would ask the men, which of them would take them; it being his wish to form a small advance guard of Europeans, as a *show*. Capt. Lawrence then said, 'Now, my lads, here's Saleh Mahommed Khan has brought arms and ammunition for some of you: who volunteers to take muskets?'

I blush to record that a dead silence ensued. Thinking the men might be shamed into doing their duty, I said to Lawrence, 'You had better give *me* one, and I will lead the party'; but there was still no offer: and he told our General, that it was useless; and he had better take them on. It is sad to think the men were so lost to all right feeling. . . .

September 17th: At two in the morning we were roused by the arrival of a horseman with a letter from Sir Richmond Shakespear; who is coming with 600 Kuzzilbash horsemen to our aid.

We marched eleven miles to the forts at the foot of the Kaloo pass. We arrived at our ground at mid-day, and were sitting under the walls of one of the forts, sheltering ourselves from the sun until the arrival of our tents; when, at three o'clock, Sir Richmond arrived; and was received, with *one* exception, with heartfelt pleasure. That one, Gen. Shelton, could not forget the honour due to his rank as the senior military man; and was much offended at Sir R. not having called on him first, and reported his arrival in due form. Even were this a military duty, Sir Richmond was perfectly exonerated in its omission; for the greater part of us ladies and some gentlemen had seated ourselves where he must pass, anxious to offer our acknowledgements to him for his prompt assistance.

Lady Sale and her companions continued their eastward march under Shakespear's escort, but even now they did not consider themselves out of the wood, for Akbar's cousin, Sultan Jan, was rumoured to be hovering near, with a large body of Afghans. But a more substantial rescue force was now well on its way.

September 19th: We had proceeded but a short way on our journey, when a horseman arrived with a note informing us, that Sale was close at hand with a brigade. I had had fever hanging about me for some days; and, being scarce able to sit on my horse, had taken my place in a kujava; the horrid motion of which had made me feel ten times worse than before I entered it. But this news renovated my strength. I shook off fever and all ills; and anxiously awaited his arrival, of which a cloud of dust was the forerunner. Gen. Nott was near Urghundee, and consequently close to us; and Gen. Pollock requested he would send a brigade to our assistance. This he refused, much to the disgust of his officers, alleging that his troops were fatigued. On this, Gen. Pollock sent Sale with a brigade, at a few hour's notice. He left Siah Sung two miles east of Cabul; and made a forced march on the 19th (his sixtieth birthday) to Urghundee: he halted there that night; and on the following morning left his camp standing, and marched to meet us. At the pass near Kote Ashruffee he left his infantry to hold the position, and proceeded at the head of the 3rd dragoons. A party of Sultan Jan's men were in this neighbourhood; and some Kokhes in the immediate vicinity were driven off by the Juzailchees. Had we not received assistance, our recapture was certain: but as it was, they dared not attack the force they saw. It is impossible to express our feelings on Sale's approach. To my daughter and myself happiness so long delayed as to be almost unexpected was actually painful, and accompanied by a choking sensation, which could not obtain the relief of tears.[1] When we arrived where the infantry were posted, they cheered all the captives as they passed them; and the men of the 13th pressed forward to welcome us individually. Most of the men had a little word of hearty congratulation to offer, each in his own style, on the restoration of his colonel's wife and daughter: and then my highly-wrought feelings found the desired relief; and I could scarcely speak to thank the soldiers for their sympathy, whilst the long withheld tears now found their course. On arriving at the camp, Capt. Backhouse fired a royal salute from his mountain train guns: and not only our old friends, but all the officers in the party, came to offer congratulations, and welcome our return from captivity.

[1] Sale, too, was overcome by emotion. Colin Mackenzie, another of the released prisoners, rode beside him for a quarter of an an hour before bringing himself to congratulate the General. 'The gallant old man turned towards me and tried to answer, but his feelings were too strong; he made a hideous series of grimaces, dug his spurs into his horse and galloped off as hard as he could.'

September 21st: At three o'clock we resumed our march to Cabul; and passed through the great bazaar; where the shops were shut, and all looked very desolate, and unlike the busy city it was when we were here last year, and the inhabitants found their trade prosper under our rule. We were greeted, on our arrival at the camp at Siah Sung, with a salute of twenty-one guns.

And now my Notes may end. Any further journals of mine can only be interesting to those nearly connected to me.

The Sales returned from Afghanistan with Pollock's 'Army of Retribution' and reached India in late December 1842, to find that the new Governor-General, Ellenborough, had determined to make General Sale and his 'Illustrious Garrison' from Jellalabad the heroes of the war. Then came home leave and a triumphal welcome in England. The Times *of 26 July 1844 reported the arrival at Lyme Regis (landed by pilot-boat from a becalmed East Indiaman) of 'Major-General Sir Robert Sale, the equally heroic Lady Sale and their widowed daughter, Mrs. Sturt and child'. As soon as their presence in the town was known the inhabitants 'vied with each other in offering their congratulations, while the church bells poured forth their merriest strains of harmony to welcome the gallant veteran and his truly courageous lady to their native land after so many actions and "hair-breadth" scapes by flood and field'. The Sales were royally entertained in Londonderry, Liverpool and Southampton and were received by the Queen at Windsor. Astley's Circus made the Afghan war the basic of a spectacular pièce de résistance which culminated in the return of the British captives. 'The meeting between Lady Sale and her husband, for the first time after her imprisonment,' reported* Punch *'took place in the prompter's box, through the exertions of the call-boy. . . . The heroic manner in which she fought the double sword combat with six Afghans, whom she put to flight, drew down the loudest praise.'*

At the end of 1844 Florentia returned to India with her husband, who had been appointed Quartermaster-General of the Queen's troops in the East Indies. A year later the first Sikh War broke out and 'Fighting Bob' was mortally wounded at the battle of Moodki on 18 December 1845. He died three days later. The Pictorial Times, *in February 1846, celebrated the event with a tremendous leader headed 'HONOUR TO THE BRAVE' and beginning, 'Another poean of glory—another deep-toned voice of victory is thundered to us from the shores of Indian rivers, and the battle-fields of British might!' More sadly, with emotion getting the better of syntax, 'the strength of England's love for such surviving sons as Gough and*

Hardinge is not more enduring for her living than her lost: and truly and beautifully does she blend with their honourable prowess a sacred and affectionate sorrow for the death of Sale!'

Florentia, who was granted a special pension of £500 a year by the Queen, spent her widowhood on a small estate in the hills near Simla. Her daughter, Alexandrina Sturt, remarried and, with her second husband, Major Holmes, was one of the first victims of the Mutiny. As they drove out together on 24 July 1857 four mutineers of the 12th Irregular Native Cavalry rode up and beheaded them both as they sat in their carriage.

By then, however, Florentia herself was dead. In 1853 she decided to visit South Africa for reasons of health, and died at Cape Town on 6 July, a few days after her arrival. She lies buried in the Church of England Cemetery at Cape Town, with a simple granite obelisk to mark her tomb. The inscription reads:

'Underneath this stone reposes all that could die of Lady Sale.'

Appendix I

Doctor Brydon's Ride

William Brydon's Account from memory and memoranda made on arrival of the retreat from Cabool in 1842

William Brydon was born in 1811. He entered the Company's Army Medical Service, and had been seconded to Shah Soojah's service in Afghanistan. Later, in the Mutiny, he served with considerable gallantry at the siege of Lucknow, for which he was awarded the C.B. He retired in 1859 and died in his native Scotland in 1873.

It was given out to the troops in Cabool on the 5th of January that arrangements had been completed for a retreat to Hindostan. Such of the sick and wounded as were unable to march were left under medical charge of Drs. Berwick and Campbell, and Lieutenant Evans, H.M. 44th, in command. Captains Drummond and Walsh, and Lts. J. Conolly, Webb, Warburton, and Airey were placed as hostages in the hands of Mahomet Zeman Khan. The sick were lodged in Timour Shah's fort, the hostages with the new king, Shah Soojah.

Jan. 6th: The retreat commenced this day about 9 a.m. a temporary bridge having been thrown across the Cabool river for the passage of the infantry; the guns, cavalry, baggage, etc. fording the river, which was about 2 feet deep. The 5th N.I. formed the advance guard, with a hundred sappers and the guns of the mountain train, under Brigadier Anguetil [*sic*].

Next came the main body, under Brigadier Shelton, followed by the baggage, in rear of which came the 6th Regiment, Shah Soojah's force, to which I belonged. We did not leave cantonments till nearly dusk, immediately followed by the rear guard, composed of the 5th Lt. Cy. 54th N.I., 2 H.A. guns, and part of H.M. 44th. All the guns, excepting those of the H.A. and M.T., were left in the cantonments, together with a large quantity of magazine stores. I saw Lt. Hardyman, 5th Lt. Cy., killed by a shot from the enemy, who had entered the cantonments and fired upon us from the walls immediately the troops left the gates, and in a short time set fire to all the buildings. Each officer carried away what little baggage he could on his own animals. I, having six ponies, reserved a favourite chestnut for myself, and mounted all my servants. But before I left cantonments, I saw my best horse, which was carrying my boxes of clothing, in charge of my groom, seized by the enemy, who dashed in among the baggage and carried off a great amount of public and private property without resistance, between cantonments and the Siah Sung Hill, at which place the two guns with the rearguard were abandoned. We moved so slowly that it was near midnight before we reached our encamping ground across the Loghur river, a distance of only about five miles. But even this short march, with the darkness and deep snow, was too much for the poor native women and children. Many lay down and perished, and the cries of others who had lost their way were truly heartrending. On arriving at our ground the scene was sad indeed: the snow several inches deep. Only one small tent, saved from the general pillage, was pitched, and occupied by the General and as many more as could find room in it, and the troops lying in the snow, or sitting round fires mostly fed by portions of their own clothing. I rolled myself in my sheepskin cloak, and taking my pony's bridle in my hand, lay down among the men of my regiment and slept.

Jan. 7th: When I awoke in the morning I found the troops preparing to march, so I called to the natives who had been lying near me to get up, which only a very few were able to do. Some of them actually laughed at me for urging them, and pointed to their feet, which looked like charred logs of wood; poor fellows, they were frostbitten, and had to be left behind. This day—advance guard 54th, M.T., rear guard H.M. 44th and M.T.[1]—our march was to Boothak, a distance again of about five miles; and the whole road from Cabool was at this time a dense mass of people. In this march, as in the former, the loss of property was immense, and towards the end of it there was some sharp fighting, in which Lt. Shaw, 54th N.I., had his thigh fractured by a shot. The guns of the M.T. were carried off by the enemy, and either two of the H.A. guns were spiked and abandoned. I saw a gallant but fruitless charge made by Lt. Macartney, to try and recover a horse of his own that was being carried off, he with difficulty regaining his troops. Few had anything to eat, except those who, like

[1] 'Mountain Train' of artillery; it consisted, pathetically, of three mule guns.

myself, followed the Afghan custom of carrying a bag of parched grain and raisins at their saddle-bow. There was rather less snow than on our former encamping ground, and the night was passed like the former, the pony only getting a few bites of grass from the ground and having the saddle-girths slackened. Up to this time I had seen nothing more of my servants or of their ponies.

We were tricked into encamping here, instead of at once pushing on through the Pass, by Akbar Khan, who sent to say he must make arrangements with the chiefs to let us through; but in truth that he might have time to get the hills well manned before we entered the Pass; and some of his horsemen who accompanied me are said to have called to the enemy in Persian to 'spare', and in Pushtoo, which the hillmen speak and few Europeans understand, they exhorted them 'to slay the Kaffirs'.

Jan. 8th: This morning we moved through the Khoord Cabool Pass with great loss of life and property; the heights were in possession of the enemy, who poured down an incessant fire on our column. Great numbers were killed, among them Captain Paton, and Lt. Sturt of the Engineers, by a shot in the groin; many more were wounded, of whom were Lady Sale and Captain Troup; and when we arrived at our ground at Khoord Cabool, Captain Anderson's eldest child was missing. All the stragglers in the rear were cut up by the enemy, who descended as soon as the main body had passed. The Pass is about three-and-a-half miles long, with a small stream running through it, which had to be crossed about thirteen times in transit; it was covered with ice, but not strong enough to bear a man, and I had an awkward accident about the middle. I suppose I had forgotten to tighten the girths, and my saddle turned, tumbling me into the water at a place where the enemy's fire was particularly sharp. I managed to get close under a rock to right the saddle, and both I and my horse escaped untouched.

Jan. 9th: We halted at Khoord Cabool this day, scarcely annoyed by the enemy at all; and I was glad to find three of my servants out of the five that had been with me in Cabool, the Bheestie (water-carrier), Khidmutgar (table attendant) and sweeper; those missing being the syce (groom), carried off with the horse the first march, and a tailor. To the Bheestie I had given a bag of barley to carry on his pony, and he had filled his mussuck or water-skin with pistachio nuts, so the animals got a feed of corn and myself and my servants made a hearty meal on the nuts. At this place, by treacherous promises, Akbar Khan induced the General to make over to his care all the married officers and their families and some wounded officers.

Jan. 10th: Resumed our march about 10 a.m., and were immediately attacked, and numbers fell in a small rocky gorge, Tarakie Tungie, just outside the camp, before we ascended the Huft Kotul (Seven Hills). At the moment of starting the sergeant-major of our regiment brought some eggs and a bottle of wine, which he got from a box left by some of the ladies, and gave them to Captain Hopkins, who divided them with Captain Marshall, Lt. Bird and myself. The eggs were not boiled but frozen quite hard, and the wine, also, to the consistency of honey, a little only in the centre being fluid. This was a terrible march, —the fire of the enemy incessant, and numbers of officers and men, not knowing where they were going from snow-blindness, were cut up. I led Mr. Baness, a Greek merchant, a great part of the way over the high ground, and often felt so blind myself that from time to time I applied a handful of snow to my eyes, and recommended others to do so, as it gave great relief. Descending towards Tazeen, the whiteness was not so intense, and as the sun got low the blindness went off; but the fire of the enemy increased, and as they were able to get very close to us in the Pass, which we now again entered, it was very destructive. So terrible had been the effects of the cold and exposure upon the native troops that they were unable to resist the attacks of the enemy, who all the way pressed hard on our flanks and rear and, on arriving at the valley of Tazeen towards evening, a mere handful remained of the native regiments which had left Cabool. Among those wounded I saw Drs. Duff and Cardew, placed on a gun carriage, but they did not long survive. Dr. Bryce, just on entering the Pass, was shot through the chest and when dying handed over his will to Captain Marshall.

At Tazeen, when we halted, we found there were killed or missing, besides those named, five officers of the 5th N.I.,—Swayne, Miles, Deas, Alexander and Warren, one of the 37th, Ewart of the 54th, and Dr. Magrath. After a short rest, when it was quite dark, our diminished party moved on, setting fire to the carriage, and leaving the last of the H.A. guns on the ground, and a great number of the remaining camp followers who would not, or many could not, move further. We passed pretty quietly through the Tazeen valley, but were again fired upon when we entered the hills, especially near a small river where Brigadier Shelton unfortunately halted his men to return their fire, thereby losing heavily.

Jan. 11th: We marched all night, the cavalry the advanced guard, and arrived at Kutta Sung this morning, having sustained more loss from the enemy firing on us from the heights all the way. We halted a short time here. Captain Dodgin. H.M. 44th, gave me a biscuit and a sardine; very acceptable indeed they were, as I had eaten nothing since the frozen eggs the morning before. As we pushed on to Jugdulluk we found wild liquorice, chewing the roots of which refreshed me much. We reached it about noon, still hard pressed by the enemy from the hills; and close to the camp ground Lt. Fortige,[1] H.M. 44th, was killed. Shortly after our arrival the General, Brigadier Shelton and Captain Johnson went to Akbar Khan, and were retained as hostages for the march of the troops from Jellalabad, and safe conduct for us. We were encamped in an old enclosure, which, however, gave us very little shelter from the enemy, who had possession of the surrounding hills—from which they never ceased firing. Captain Skinner of the Commissariat was killed, and many officers and men wounded; among the latter—whose wounds I dressed—were Captains W. Grant and Marshall, the former had his jaw shattered, and M. a shot through the chest. Poor Marshall, Bird and I had dined on a portion of a fat Arab charger that had been shot, slices of which we grilled over a fire of brushwood, during which operation M. lost the only bit of rock-salt we had, and looked on it as a very bad omen. I suppose it fell in the snow and melted. Shortly afterwards he volunteered to lead a party to try and drive the enemy from a hill from which they specially annoyed us, and he was wounded before he had gone many yards.

We did not move from Jugdulluk till about an hour after dark on the 12th, when an order was given to march, owing (I believe) to a note being received from General Elphinstone telling us to push on at all hazards, as treachery was suspected. Owing to this unexpected move on our part we found the abattis and other impediments which had been thrown across the Jugdulluk Pass undefended by the enemy who nevertheless pressed on our rear and cut up great numbers. The confusion now was terrible; all discipline was at an end. I started leading poor Marshall's horse, who was unable to guide it; and Blair,

[1] Eyre spells the name 'Fortye'.

Bott, and another wounded officer, all of the 5th Lt. Cy., were on a camel close to me. We had not gone far in the dark before I found myself surrounded, and at this moment my khidmutgar rushed up to me, saying he was wounded, had lost his pony, and begged me to take him up. I had not time to do so before I was pulled off my horse and knocked down by a blow on the head from an Afghan knife, which must have killed me had I not had a portion of a Blackwood's magazine in my forage cap. As it was, a piece of bone about the size of a wafer was cut from my skull, and I was nearly stunned, but managed to rise on my knees, and seeing that a second blow was coming, I met it with the edge of my sword, and I suppose cut off some of my assailant's fingers, as the knife fell to the ground; he bolted one way, and I the other, minus my horse, cap, and one of my shoes,—the khidmutgar was dead; those who had been with me I never saw again.

I regained our troops, scrambled over a barricade of trees made across the Pass where the confusion was awful, and I got a severe blow on the shoulder from a fellow who rushed down the hill and across the road, and here I picked up with Captain Hopkins, and alongside his horse I walked for some distance, holding on to the stirrup; in this way I overtook a Hindostanee mochee (saddler) of the Shah's Cavalry, who told me he was wounded and dying, and begged me to take his pony or someone else would. I tried to encourage him but he fell off, carrying away one of the stirrups, and I found the poor fellow shot through the chest and dead. I then mounted his pony, and riding towards the front, I met Brigadier Anguetil, who asked me how they were getting on in the rear, and when I told him, he rode back and was never seen again. The men were running up the hills on the sides of the road and on in front, throwing away their arms to lighten themselves, and could not be kept together or controlled; so Captain Bellew, the Quartermaster-General of the force, assembled all he could find mounted, and formed us into an advanced guard (about forty). We moved steadily on, fired at from the hills as we passed along, which were blazing with watch fires, only once losing our way in the darkness, but regaining it again after a short detour. During this night we all suffered from most intense thirst, and my shoeless foot, which was unfortunately in my only stirrup, felt as if it were being burnt, so I was glad to find, in a bag with other things at my saddle-bow, a piece of list which I wound round the Iron.

Jan. 13th: At daybreak we found ourselves at Gundumuck, and had lost all traces of those in our rear. Here a dispute arose as to the road, there being two,—one over the hills and the other through the Neemlah valley, in which was a large village. I having been encamped for about three months in quiet times in this neighbourhood and knowing both roads, recommended the former, while Mr. Bailiss, a clerk in one of the public offices, said the other was safest and best; so our small party split, half going each way. Those by the valley were attacked and killed by the villagers, except Mr. Bailiss, who was taken prisoner (and afterwards, I heard, taken to Peshawur, where he died of fever). We proceeded over the hills without seeing a single individual. Shortly after entering on the plain we rested a little while in a small grassy glen, and let our horses have a bit of grass, such as it was. My saddle a wooden one, of a kind then common in the Punjaub, with a high peak in front. And from it I now removed the bags which were very heavy, containing saddler's tools, bullets, a pistol (which none of the bullets would fit), a chain and spikes for picketing a horse, etc. All these I threw away, except the pistol, which I put in my pocket. On starting, after a quarter of an hour's rest, our party consisting of Captains Bellew, Hopkins, and Collyer, Lts. Bird, Steer, and Gray, Dr. Harper, Sergeant Freil, and five or six other European soldiers. We shortly came in sight of the village of Futtehabad on the plain, and about fifteen miles from Jellalabad; all here seemed quiet, and Captain Bellew said he would go and enquire into the state of the country. In a short time he came back and told us that all was quiet, and that if we would wait he would bring us some bread, promised by the headman of the village; in about a quarter of an hour he returned again and said he was afraid he had ruined us, as from the village, which was on a mound, he could see the cavalry coming up on all sides; and he had no doubt that some signal had been given to gather them while we were kept waiting (probably a red flag we saw ourselves). He begged us to keep together and move slowly on, the armed villagers following and called to him to come back, as they were friends. Captain Bellew did so and was immediately killed. At the same time the villagers fired on us and the cavalry charged among us; one fellow cut at me, which I guarded, and then he cut down poor Bird, and it became a case of utter rout, out of which all that got clear were Captains Hopkins and Collyer, Dr. Harper, Lt. Steer and myself. The three former being well mounted left Lt. Steer and me behind, telling us they would soon send us help; after riding on a short distance, Lt. Steer said he could go no further, as both he and his horse were done (the latter was bleeding from the mouth and nostrils)—he would hide in one of the many caves we knew were in the hills about half a mile to the right of the road. I tried hard to persuade him to push on, as the plain was sprinkled with people tending sheep and cattle, who must see him. But he would not, so I proceeded alone, for a short distance unmolested, then I saw a party of about twenty men drawn up in my road, who, when I came near, began picking up large stones, with which the plain abounded, so I with difficulty put my pony into a gallop, and, taking the bridle in my teeth, cut right and left with my sword as I went through them. They could not reach me with their knives, and I was only hit by one or two stones. A little farther on I was met by another similar party who I tried to pass as I did the former, but was obliged to prick my poor pony with the point of my sword, before I could get him into a gallop. Of this party, one man on a mound over the road had a gun, which he fired close down upon me, and broke my sword, leaving about six inches in the handle. But I got clear of them, and then found that the shot had hit the poor pony, wounding him in the loins, and he could now hardly carry me. But I moved on very slowly, and saw some five horsemen draped in red, and supposing they were some of our irregular cavalry, I made towards them, but getting near found they were Afghans, and that they were leading off Captain Collyer's horse; so I tried to get away, but my pony could hardly move, and they sent one of their party after me, who made a cut at me, which I guarding with the bit of my sword, it fell from the hilt. He passed me, but turned and rode at me again. This time just as he was striking, I threw the handle of the sword at his head, in swerving to avoid which, he only cut me over the back of the left hand. Feeling it disabled, I stretched down the right to pick up the bridle. I suppose my foe thought it was for a pistol, for he turned at once and made off as quick as he could. I then felt for the pistol I had put in my pocket, but it was gone, and I was quite unarmed, and on a poor animal I feared could not carry me to Jellalabad, though it was not in sight. Suddenly all energy seemed to forsake me, I became nervous and frightened at shadows, and I really think would have fallen from my saddle, but for the peak of it and some of the people from the fort coming to my assistance, among the first of whom was Captain Sinclair, H.M. 13th, whose servant gave me one of his own shoes to cover my foot. I was taken to the Sappers' mess, my wounds dressed by Dr. Forsyth, and after a good dinner, with great thankfulness, enjoyed the luxury of a sound sleep, most hospitably lodged by Captain Francis Cunningham, whose quarters I shared during the whole siege. On examination, I found that I had a light sword wound on the left knee, besides my head and left hand, and that a ball had gone through my trousers a little higher up, slightly grazing the skin, but how, and when, these happened I know not.

The poor pony, directly it was put in a stable, lay down and never rose again. Immediately on my telling how things were, General Sale dispatched a party to scour the plain in the hopes of picking up any stragglers, but they only found the bodies of Captains Hopkins and Collyer and Dr. Harper. The second night after my arrival, poor Mr. Baness was brought in by a Fakir from near Futtiabad, to whom he had done a kindness on a former occasion: in marching up to Cabool he saved the Fakir's mulberry grove from being destroyed by some Sikh soldiers. Mr. Baness only lived one day, being perfectly exhausted by his sufferings from cold and hunger.

Appendix II

Lady Sale's

VOCABULARY

of Persian, Hindostani and other
Oriental words employed in
this volume

Akukzye. The name of one of the great Afghan tribes.

Aloo–baloo. The wild sour cherry.

Aman. The cry for mercy—quarter.

Ameer. Commander or chief.

Ana. A small coin; sixteen of which make a rupee. Its value is about three-halfpence.

Ashurpee. A mohur—a gold coin. Its value is about thirty shillings English.

Ayah. A female attendant—a nurse.

Bahadur. A bravo—a boaster or braggadocio; also a brave man—a hero.

Bahadur (verb). To boast or brag.

Bala hissar. Upper citadel—royal palace.

Barats. Legal documents—assignments—promissory notes.

Barukzye. The name of one of the five great Douranee tribes.

Bash or bosh. Nothing—humbug.

Bashee. A head-man.

Bedanas. A sort of mulberry.

Behmaru. The name of a village near Cabul. The word signifies 'the husbandless'.

Bhanghys. Baggage—boxes. They are boxes hung at each end of a pole and carried on a man's shoulder.

Bheestees. Water-carriers.

Bhoosa or boussa. Chopped straw—chaff. Hindostani.

Bhoodkhees. Presents.

Bildars. Excavators—sappers.

Bourj or burj. A fortified hill or tower.

Bukshees. Gifts—presents—douceurs.

Bukhraeed. A Mohammedan feast. The festival of the goat; held to commemorate the history of Abraham and Ishmael (Isaac).

Bunneah. A trader—a corn-merchant or dealer in grain, flour, etc.

Cafila. A caravan—a convoy.

Cass. A kind of furze.

Caupoochees. Porters.

Chaoney. An encampment—cantonments.

Charpoys. A bed on four poles, with ropes crossed over them.

Chattak. A measure for grain, etc. The sixteenth part of a seer, or about 2 oz English.

Chebootras. Small thick mats, on which slaves usually sit or squat.

Chillum. The part of the hookah, or pipe, containing the lighted tobacco—hence used for the pipe itself.

Chillumchee. A wash-hand basin.

Chiragh. A lamp.

Chogah. A sort of cloak.

Chokey. A police station.

Chouk. A bazaar—a street. Also the portion of the taxes excused to the native chiefs for keeping the passes open, and for keeping the tribes in check.

Chowdry. The chief man or head of a bazaar.

Chuddah. A sheet or veil.

Chupao. A night attack—a surprise —a foray.

Chupao (verb). To attack by night— to surprise by stealth.

Chupatties. Unleavened cakes, made of ottah.

Chuprassy. A messenger—a servant bearing a badge or brass plate.

Chuttah or chatta. An umbrella or parasol.

Compound. An enclosed space—the ground round a house.

Cossid. A courier—an express—a foot messenger.

Crore. Ten lakhs of rupees, or one million pounds sterling.

Dak. Letter post.

Dallies. Baskets for fruit, etc.— panniers.

Dewan. A steward.

Dhal. A kind of split pea—pulse.

Dhooley. A palanquin for the sick.

Dhye. Sour curds.

Dooranee. The general name of the five great tribes; the Populzye, Barukzye, Nurzye, Barmizye and Akhuzye.

Durbar. Levee.

Duffodar. A non-commissioned officer of cavalry.

Elchee. An ambassador—an agent.

Eusofzyes. An Afghan tribe north of Peshawer.

Fakirs. Devotees—mendicants.

Fatcha. The prayer for the reigning monarch—a part of the Mohammedan service; the reading of which is equivalent to doing homage.

Feringhees. Europeans—Franks—foreigners.

Fernez. Sweet curds.

Fouj. An army.

Ghee. Clarified butter.

Ghuzee or ghazeea. A champion of religion—a fanatic.

Gilzye. The name of a great Afghan tribe.

Gobrowed. Dumbfounded—at a nonplus.

Godowns. Storehouses—granaries.

Golees. Balls—bullets.

Golundaz. Artillerymen—literally, throwers of balls.

Goor. Coarse brown sugar or molasses.

Goorkha. A native of Nepaul; literally 'cowherd'.

Gulas. Cherries.

Hamaum. A hot bath—baths; commonly written *hummums*.

Haut. A measure equal to half a yard—a cubit.

Havildar. A serjeant in the native troops.

Hazir-bashes. The king's bodyguard. The words imply 'Ever ready'.

Hookm. An order—permission—the word of command.

Hoosseinee-angoor. A peculiarly fine sort of grape, of immense size, called the 'bull's eye'.

Huft Kohtul. The seven passes.

Hurkaru. A messenger.

Janbaz. The Afghan cavalry.

Jee. Life—spirit—'with right goodwill'.

Jeerga. An assembly or council—a diet.

Jemadar. A native officer, holding the rank of lieutenant.

Jhala. A raft.

Jingals. Wall pieces, carrying a ball of about a quarter of a pound.

Jorabs. Boots.

Jung. The fight or battle.

Juwans. Young men.

Juzail. The long rifle of the Afghans.

Juzailchees. Riflemen.

Kaffirs. Infidels.

Kaloss. Safe—free. Finished.

Kazanchez. A treasurer—a treasury.

Keshmish. Raisins—grapes.

Khan. A nobleman. In Cabul the title is assumed by every one.

Khelluts. Dresses of honour.

Khootba. The prayer for the king.

Kirkee. A wicket or window.

Kos. A measure of distance, equal to about two English miles.

Kote. A fort.

Kotilla Taj-i. The name of a pass, literally, 'the crown of the mountains'.

Kotilla Murdee. The dead men's pass.

Kujavas. Camel-panniers.

Kulassy. A tent pitcher—a baggage servant.

Kulma. The Mohammedan creed.

Kuneh. A private dwelling.

Kurtoot. The name of a village—literally, 'the donkey's mulberry'.

Kurwar or khurwah. A measure; equal to 700 lb English.

Kuzzilbashes. Persians; or persons of Persian descent, residing in Cabul.

Kyde. Prison. The root of the vulgar English 'quod'—to put in quod.

Kysee. The white apricot.

Lakh. One hundred thousand.

Lakh of rupees. Ten thousand pounds sterling.

Larye. A battle—an engagement.

Lascar. An attendant on guns, magazines, etc.

Loonghee. The cloth of a turban.

Loot. Plunder.

Loot (verb). To sack—to plunder.

Mast. Curds.

Maund. A measure of grain; about 80 lb English.

Maush. A sort of grain.

Meerza. A secretary—a Mohammedan writer.

Meer wyse. A teacher—the high priest.

Mehmandar. A cicerone—a man of all work—a factotum.

Mehter. A class of camp-followers—a sweeper.

Mohur. A coin, generally gold; its value is about thirty shillings English.

Moolah. A priest.

Moong. Pulse.

Moonshee. A secretary or interpreter.

Muezzin. The call of the *Faithful* to prayers.

Mushk. A leathern bag for holding water—a goat's skin.

Musjid. A temple or place of worship.

Nagura. A set of drums which the natives beat to announce the presence of the King or any great chief.

Naib. A deputy or lieutenant.

Naich. A corporal in the native troops.

Nal. A horse-shoe.

Nalbunds. Farriers.

Nalkee. A palanquin.

Nans. Cakes of bread. (? Latin, *Annona*).

Nawaub. A prince. Nabob.

Nazir. A master of the household.

Neemchees. A kind of spencer made of sheepskins.

Neencha. A coat.

No-roz. The Vernal Equinox. The Mohammedan New Year's Day.

Nullah. The bed of a river; also used for a river.

Numdas. Coarse felt carpets.

Ooloos. The tribes or clans. To summon the Ooloos answers to our 'calling out the militia'.

Oorsees. Open-work lattices.

Ottah or attah. Ground wheat—flour, or rather what is called pollard.

Palkee. A palanquin.

Pall. A kind of tent.

Pesh khedmuts. Attendants.

Pillau. A dish of meat and rice.

Posha khana. An armoury.

Poshteen. A sheepskin; also a fur-pelisse.

Pushtoo. The language of the natives of Afghanistan.

Pyjania. Loose trousers.

Raj. A government—a province.

Rajah. A prince.

Ressalah. A troop of horse.

Rezai or resaiz. A counterpane—a quilt.

Rui-band. A veil.

Rupee. A silver coin; its value is about two shillings English.

Saces. A groom.

Sahib. Sir—master.

Salaam. Salutation. To make salaam—to pay one's respects.

Seer. A measure; about equal to 2 lb English.

Shah bagh. The king's garden.

Shah guzees or shahghasses. The household troops—the 'yeomen of the guard'. Officers of the court.

Shah-zada. A king's son—a prince.

Shalu. Red cotton cloth from Turkey.

Shikar. Field sports.

Shikagurs. Hunting grounds—preserves.

Shoke. A hobby—a mania.

Shroffs. Native bankers—money changers.

Shubkoon. A surprise at night.

Shytan. The devil.

Siah Sung. The black rock.

Siahs. A large sect of the Mohammedans; opposed to the Soonees.

Sipahees. The native Hindostanee troops. Sepoys.

Sir-i-chusm. The name of a village—the words signify 'the head of the spring'.

Sirdar. A general. The title assumed by Akbar Khan.

Sirdar-i-Sirdan. The chief of the generals. Generalissimo.

Soonees. A large sect of the Mohammedans.

Subadar. A native officer, holding the rank of captain.

Sugs. Dogs. *A term of contempt.*

Sungah. Breastwork. Fortifications.

Surda. A species of melon. The *cold* melon.

Surwans or surwons. Camel drivers—grooms.

Setringees. A kind of small carpet.

Suwars. Horsemen—troopers.

Syud. The title of a chief of the Ooloos.

Syud. A holy man—a saint.

Syuds. A sect of the Mohammedans; claiming to be the descendants of the prophet; and who therefore wear the green turban.

Tattoes. Ponies.

Topes. Tombs—mounds—barrows. There are several in Afghanistan, built in the time of Alexander.

Topshee bashee. The commander of the artillery. 'The master-general of the ordnance.'

Turnasook. The red plum.

Tykhana. A cellar.

Usufzyes. An Afghan tribe north of Peshawer.

Vakeel. A deputy—a commissioner —one who acts or negotiates for another.

Wuzeer. Vizier.

Wuzeerat. The office of vizier.

Xummuls. Coarse blankets.

Yaboos. Afghan ponies.

Yaghi. Rebellious—in a state of rebellion—or of independence.

Zenana. A harem.

Zerdaloos. Apricots.

Zilzilla. An earthquake.

Zubberdust. Overbearing—'with the strong arm'.

Zuna. A dwelling.

Appendix III

List of Civil and Military Officers killed during the Rebellion, at and near Cabul[1]

Between 12 October 1841 and 6 January 1842, the day of leaving Cabul

POLITICAL

Sir W. H. Macnaghten, Bart	Murdered at a conference on 23 Dec.
Sir Alexander Burnes	Murdered in his own house in the city on 2 Nov.
Capt. Broadfoot, 1st Eng. Regt.	Murdered in Sir A.B.'s house in the city on 2 Nov.
Lieut. Burnes, Bombay Inf.	Murdered in Sir A.B.'s house in the city on 2 Nov.
Lieut. Rattray	Murdered at a conference at Lughmanee in Kohistan on 3 Nov.

H.M. 44TH

Lieut.-Col. Mackrell	Killed in action at Cabul on	10 Nov.
Capt. Swayne	Killed in action at Cabul on	4 Nov.
Capt. M'Crea	Killed in action at Cabul on	10 Nov.
Capt. Robinson	Killed in action at Cabul on	4 Nov.
Lieut. Raban	Killed in action at Cabul on	6 Nov.

5TH N.I.

Lieut.-Col. Oliver	Killed in action at Cabul on	23 Nov.
Capt. Mackintosh	Killed in action at Cabul on	23 Nov.

37TH N.I.

Capt. Westmacott	Killed in action at Cabul on	10 Nov.
Ensign Gordon	Killed in action at Cabul on	4 Nov.

35TH N.I.

Lieut. Jenkins	Killed in action at Khoord-Cabul on	12 Oct.
Capt. Wyndham	Killed in action at Jugdulluk	12 Nov.

[1] Taken from *The Military Operations at Cabul* (alternatively entitled *Journal of an Affghanistan Prisoner*) by Lieut. Vincent Eyre, Bengal Artillery (John Murray, 1843).

APPENDIX III

H.M. 13TH LIGHT INFANTRY

Lieut. King	Killed at Tezeen on	12 Oct.

LOCAL HORSE

Capt. Walker, 1st N.I.	Killed at Cabul on	23 Nov.

27TH N.I.

Lieut. Laing	Killed at Cabul on	23 Nov.

SHAH'S SERVICE

Capt. Woodburn, 44th N.I.	Killed at Cabul on	23 Nov.
Capt. Codrington, 49th N.I.	Killed at Chareekar	23 Nov.
Ensign Salisbury, 1st V. Regt.	Killed at Chareekar	23 Nov.
Ensign Rose, 54th N.I.	Killed at Chareekar	23 Nov.
Dr Grant, Bombay Est.	Killed at Chareekar	23 Nov.
Lieut. Maule, Artillery	Killed in his camp at Kahdarrah	3 Nov.
Capt. Trevor, 3rd Light Cav.	Killed at a conference	23 Dec.
Local Lieut. Wheeler	Killed in his camp at Kahdarrah	3 Nov.

From 6 January up to 12 January 1842 inclusive on the retreat

STAFF

Dr Duff, Supt-Surgeon	Killed between Tezeen and Seh Baba	10 Jan.
Capt. Skinner, 61st N.I.	Killed at Jugdulluk	12 Jan.
Capt. Paton, 58th N.I.	Killed at Khoord-Cabul pass	8 Jan.
Lieut. Sturt, Engineers	Killed at Khoord-Cabul Pass	8 Jan.

HORSE ARTILLERY

Dr Bryce	Killed on march to Tezeen	10 Jan.

5TH LIGHT CAVALRY

Lieut. Hardyman	Killed outside the cantonment	6 Jan.

H.M. 44TH

Maj. Scott	Killed on march to Tezeen	10 Jan.
Capt. Leighton	Killed on march to Tezeen	10 Jan.
Lieut. White	Killed at Junga Fareekee	10 Jan.
Lieut. Fortye	Killed at Jugdulluk	10 Jan.

5TH N.I.

Maj. Swayne	Killed at Junga Fareekee	10 Jan.
Capt. Miles	Killed at Junga Fareekee	10 Jan.
Lieut. Deas	Killed at Junga Fareekee	10 Jan.
Lieut. Alexander	Killed at Junga Fareekee	10 Jan.
Lieut. Warren	Killed at Junga Fareekee	10 Jan.

54TH N.I.

Maj. Ewart	Killed on march to Tezeen	10 Jan.
Capt. Shaw	Killed on march to Tezeen	10 Jan.
Lieut. Kirby	Killed on march to Tezeen	10 Jan.

37TH N.I.

Lieut. St George	Killed at Khoord-Cabul Pass	8 Jan.

H.M. 44TH

Lieut. Wade	Killed at Jugdulluk	12 Jan.

27TH N.I.

Dr Cardew	Killed at Tezeen	10 Jan.

After leaving Jugdulluk on the 12th to the final massacre

STAFF

Maj. Thain, H.M. 21st Ft A.D.C.	Jugdulluk Pass	12 Jan.
Capt. Bellew, 56th N.I.	Futtehabad	13 Jan.
Capt. Grant, 27th N.I.	Gundamuk	13 Jan.

HORSE ARTILLERY

Capt. Nicholl	Jugdulluk Pass	12 Jan.
Lieut. Stewart	Gundamuk	13 Jan.

5TH LIGHT CAVALRY

Lieut.-Col. Chambers	Jugdulluk Pass	12 Jan.
Capt. Blair	Jugdulluk Pass	12 Jan.
Capt. Bott	Jugdulluk Pass	12 Jan.
Capt. Hamilton	Gundamuk	13 Jan.
Capt. Collyer	Near Jellalabad	14 Jan.
Lieut. Bazett	Jugdulluk Pass	12 Jan.
Dr Harpur	Near Jellalabad	14 Jan.
Veterinary Surgeon Willis	Doubtful	

H.M. 44TH

Capt. Dodgin	Jugdulluk Pass	12 Jan.
Capt. Collins	Gundamuk	13 Jan.
Lieut. Hogg	Gundamuk	13 Jan.
Lieut. Cumberland	Gundamuk	13 Jan.
Lieut. Cadett	Soorkab	12 Jan.
Lieut. Swinton	Gundamuk	13 Jan.
Ensign Gray	Doubtful	
Paymaster Bourke	Jugdulluk	12 Jan.
Q.M. Halahan	Jugdulluk Pass	12 Jan.
Surgeon Harcourt	Jugdulluk Pass	12 Jan.
Asst Surgeon Balfour	Doubtful	
Asst Surgeon Primrose	Gundamuk	13 Jan.

5TH N.I.

Capt. Haig	Doubtful	
Lieut. Horsbrough	Gundamuk	13 Jan.
Lieut. Tombs	Doubtful	
Ensign Potenger	Doubtful	
Lieut. Burkinyoung	Doubtful	
Dr Metcalfe	Gundamuk	13 Jan.

37TH N.I.

Capt. Rind	Gundamuk	13 Jan.
Lieut. Steer	Jugdulluk Pass	12 Jan.[1]
Lieut. Vanrenen	Near Soorkab	13 Jan.
Lieut. Hawtrey	Gundamuk	13 Jan.
Lieut. Carlyon	Doubtful	

54TH N.I.

Capt. Anstruther	Doubtful	
Capt. Corrie	Doubtful	
Capt. Palmer	Doubtful	
Lieut. Weaver	Gundamuk	13 Jan.
Lieut. Cunningham	Gundamuk	13 Jan.
Lieut. Pottinger[2]	Neemla	13 Jan.
Lieut. Morrison	Gundamuk	13 Jan.

[1] This seems to be an error. Dr Brydon (who presumably knew) says that Steer was the last officer he parted from on 13 January. See Appendix I.

[2] Lieutenant Thomas Pottinger was the younger (half-) brother of Major Eldred Pottinger.

H.M. 13TH LIGHT INFANTRY

Maj. Kershaw	Doubtful	
Lieut. Hobhouse	Gundamuk	13 Jan.

SHAH'S SERVICE

Brig. Anquetil	Jugdulluk Pass	12 Jan.
Capt. Hay, 35th N.I.	Gundamuk	13 Jan.
Capt. Hopkins, 27th N.I.	Near Jellalabad	13 Jan.
Capt. Marshall, 61st N.I.	Jugdulluk Pass	12 Jan.
Lieut. Le Geyt, Bombay Cav.	Neemla	13 Jan.
Lieut. Green, Artillery	Gundamuk	13 Jan.
Lieut. Bird, Madras Est.	Futtehabad	13 Jan.
Lieut. Macartney	Gundamuk	13 Jan.

List of Officers saved of the Cabul Force

In imprisonment in Afghanistan

POLITICAL

Maj. Pottinger, C.B.	Wounded at Chareekar on	6 Nov.
Capt. Lawrence	Wounded in action at Cabul on	23 Nov.
Capt. Mackenzie, Madras Est.	Wounded in action at Cabul on	23 Nov.

STAFF

Maj.-Gen. Elphinstone, C.B.	Wounded on retreat at Jugdulluk (Died at Tezeen on 23 April)	12 Jan.
Brig. Shelton		
Capt. Boyd, Asst. Comm.-General		
Lieut. Eyre, Arty D.C.O.	Wounded in action at Cabul	22 Nov.

HORSE ARTILLERY

Lieut. Waller	Wounded in action at Cabul	22 Nov.

H.M. 44TH

Capt. Souter	Wounded on retreat at Gundamuk	13 Jan.

H.M. 13TH

Lieut. Mein	Wounded in action under Gen. Sale at Khoord-Cabul Pass	Oct.

37TH N.I.

Maj. Griffiths	Wounded on retreat in Khoord-Cabul Pass	8 Jan.
Dr. Magrath		

SHAH'S SERVICE

Capt. Troup	Wounded on retreat in Khoord-Cabul Pass	8 Jan.
Capt. Johnson		
Capt. Anderson		

PAYMASTER

Capt. Bygrave	The toes of one foot nipped off by frost on retreat
Mr Ryley, Conductor of Ordnance	

54TH N.I.

Lieut. Melville	The toes of one foot nipped off by frost on retreat near Huft Kotul	10 Jan.

SHAH'S SERVICE

Dr Brydon	Escaped to Jellalabad

Ladies

Lady Macnaghten
Lady Sale
Mrs Trevor, eight children
Mrs Anderson, three children
Mrs Sturt, one child
Mrs Mainwaring, one child
Mrs Boyd, three children
Mrs Eyre, one child
Mrs Waller, two children
Conductor Ryley's wife, Mrs Ryley, three children
Private Bourne's (13th Light Infantry) wife, Mrs Bourne
Mrs Wade, wife of Sergeant Wade.[1]
Mr Fallon clerk }
Mr Blewitt, do. } Not in the service

[1] Sergeant Wade, who is described as 'baggage-sergeant to the Cabul mission', also survived the captivity in Afghanistan. But Private Bourne's name does not appear in the list of survivors.

Select Bibliography

EYRE, VINCENT. *The Military Operations at Cabul.* 1843.

GLEIG, REV. G. R. *With Sale's Brigade in Afghanistan.* 1846.

KAYE, SIR JOHN. *History of the War in Afghanistan.* 1851.

—— *Lives of the Indian Officers.* 1880.

LAWRENCE, SIR GEORGE. *Forty-three Years in India.* 1874.

MACKENZIE, LIEUT.-GEN. COLIN. *Storms and Sunshine of a Soldier's Life.* 1886.

MARSHMAN, J. C. *Memoirs of Major-General Sir Henry Havelock.* 1860.

STOCQUELER, J. H. *Memoirs and Correspondence of Major-General Sir William Nott.* 1854.

Index

Place names are printed in italics

Foreign Devils on the Silk Road:
The Search for the Lost Treasures of Central Asia

Peter Hopkirk

'highly readable and elegant'
Times Literary Supplement

'difficult to put down. . . irresistible'
Daily Telegraph

The Silk Road, which linked imperial Rome and distant China, was once the greatest thoroughfare on earth. Along it travelled precious cargoes of silk, gold, and ivory, as well as revolutionary new ideas. Its oasis towns blossomed into thriving centres of Buddhist art and learning.

In time it began to decline. The traffic slowed, the merchants left, and finally its towns vanished beneath the desert sands to be forgotten for a thousand years. But legends grew up of lost cities filled with treasures and guarded by demons. In the early years of this century, foreign explorers began to investigate these legends, and very soon an international race began for the art treasures of the Silk Road. Huge wall paintings, sculptures, and priceless manuscripts were carried away, literally by the ton, and are today scattered through the museums of a dozen countries.

Peter Hopkirk tells the story of the intrepid men who, at great personal risk, led these long-range archaeological raids, incurring the undying wrath of the Chinese.

'Recounted with great skill . . . opens a window onto a fascinating world'
Financial Times

The Great Game:
On Secret Service in High Asia

Peter Hopkirk

'Nobody else alive could handle this terrific subject with such a combination of skill, knowledge, enthusiasm and insight. Peter Hopkirk is truly the Laureate of the Great Game.'
Jan Morris

'There can be few more fascinating subjects, or few authors better qualified to write about it'
Sir Fitzroy Maclean, *Independent*

For nearly a century the two most powerful nations on earth—Victorian Britain and Tsarist Russia—fought a secret war in the lonely passes and deserts of Central Asia. Those engaged in this shadowy struggle called it 'The Great Game', a phrase immortalized in Kipling's *Kim*. When play first began the two rival empires lay nearly 2,000 miles apart. By the end, some Russian outposts were within 20 miles of India.

This book tells the story of the Great Game through the exploits of the young officers, both British and Russian, who risked their lives playing it. Disguised as holy men or native horsetraders, they mapped secret passes, gathered intelligence, and sought the allegiance of powerful khans. Some never returned. The violent repercussions of the Great Game are still being felt throughout Central Asia today.

'An immensely readable and magisterially detached work. One gripping chapter follows another. As a narrative of adventure and war it is impressive.'
Financial Times

'brilliant . . .'
Patrick Leigh Fermor, Book of the Year Choice, *Telegraph*

Quest for Kim:
In Search of Kipling's Great Game

Peter Hopkirk

'a fascinating, brilliantly written book'
Times Literary Supplement

'a unapologetic homage to the book that changed
Hopkirk's life'
William Dalrymple, *Sunday Times*

This book is for all those who love *Kim*, that masterpiece of Indian life
in which Kipling immortalized the Great Game. Fascinated since childhood by this strange tale of an orphan boy's recruitment into the
Indian secret service, Peter Hopkirk here retraces Kim's footsteps
across Kipling's India to see how much of it remains.

To attempt this with a fictional hero would normally be pointless. But
Kim is different. For much of this Great Game classic was inspired by
actual people and places, thus blurring the line between the real and
the imaginary. Less a travel book than a literary detective story, this is
the intriguing story of Peter Hopkirk's quest for Kim—and a host of
other shadowy figures.

'vital for someone like me who reads *Kim* every two years:
a brilliant jigsaw with few pieces missing'
Patrick Leigh Fermor *Spectator, Books of the Year*

'This beautifully written and beguiling travel book will
fascinate even those who have never read *Kim*'
Robert Carver, *Scotsman*

On Secret Service East of Constantinople:
The Plot to Bring Down the British Empire

Peter Hopkirk

'Hopkirk has made the extraordinary field of Central Asian espionage his own . . . an enthralling story.'
Observer

'He recreates, with much verve and brilliance, the clandestine attempts by Britain's imperial rivals to subvert the British Empire in India.'
Guardian

Under the banner of a Holy War, masterminded in Berlin and unleashed from Constantinople, the Germans and the Turks set out in 1914 to foment violent revolutionary uprisings against the British in India and the Russians in Central Asia. It was a new and more sinister version of the old Great Game, with world domination as its ultimate aim.

Here, told in epic detail and for the first time, is the true story behind John Buchan's classic wartime novel, *Greenmantle*, recounted through the adventures and misadventures of the secret agents and others who took part in it. It is an ominously topical tale today in view of the continuing turmoil in this volatile region where the Great Game has never really ceased.

'told with great fluency, authority and narrative skill . . . a story which no single book has told before'
Sunday Telegraph

Setting the East Ablaze
On Secret Service in Bolshevik Asia

Peter Hopkirk

'Hopkirk's narrative is irresistible, his style lucid and as events in Afghanistan show, his theme is ominously topical.'
E. C. Hodgkin, former Foreign Editor of *The Times*

'the stuff of a dozen adventure movies . . . everything a ripping good yarn should be'
New York Times

'Let us turn our faces towards Asia', exhorted Lenin when the long-awaited revolution in Europe failed to materialize. 'The East will help us conquer the West.'

Peter Hopkirk's book tells for the first time the story of the Bolshevik attempt between the wars to set the East ablaze with the new gospel of Marxism. Lenin's dream was to liberate the whole of Asia, but his starting point was British India. A shadowy, undeclared war followed.

Among the players in this new Great Game were British Indian intelligence officers and the professional revolutionaries of the Communist International. There were also Muslim visionaries and Chinese warlords — as well as a White Russian baron who roasted his Bolshevik captives alive.

Here is an extraordinary tale of intrigue and treachery, barbarism and civil war, whose violent repercussions continue to be felt in Central Asia today.

'This was by no means the last round in the Great Game, but the way Hopkirk tells it, it was one of the most exciting.'
Far East Economic Review

'a classic example of truth outpacing fiction'
Times Literary Supplement

Trespassers on the Roof of the World:
The Race for Lhasa

Peter Hopkirk

'as vivid and gripping as a John Buchan novel'
Evening Standard

'A marvellous book, well researched and beautifully written—a treat for armchair explorers everywhere.'
New Statesman

No other land has captured man's imagination quite like Tibet. Hidden away behind the highest mountains on earth, and ruled over by a mysterious God-king, it was for centuries a land forbidden to all outsiders.

In his remarkable, and ultimately tragic narrative, Peter Hopkirk tells of the forcible opening up of this secretive Buddhist kingdom by inquisitive Western travellers during the 19th and 20th centuries, and the race to reach Lhasa, Tibet's sacred capital.

This epic, often harrowing tale, which ends with the Chinese invasion of 1950, draws on a colourful cast of gatecrashers from nine different countries. Among them were adventurous young officers on Great Game missions, explorers, and mountaineers, mystics, and missionaries. All took their lives in their hands, including three intrepid women. Some were never to return.

'a rich harvest of harrowing adventures, which Mr Hopkirk recounts in fascinating detail'
Daily Telegraph